ROAD TO NOWHERE
mishaps of an indie musician

Simon Parker

Invocations Press

ROAD TO NOWHERE
mishaps of an indie musician

Simon Parker

First published 2014
© Simon Parker 2014
All uncredited photos: Simon Parker
Cover & design: Simon Parker & John Shire

978-0-9568021-6-3

Download FREE **Road To Nowhere** related music at

www.villareal1.bandcamp.com

For Shirley

contents

chapter | page

intro

In conversation, I have a nasty habit of staring vacantly into the middle distance, usually somewhere just over the shoulder of the other person. This instantly creates the false impression that something incredibly interesting is happening just out of view of my acquaintance. Of course, when the unsuspecting individual swivels round to find nothing there, these debates tend to end rather abruptly, or, more often than not, with me having to apologise for the destruction of a perfectly decent piece of human interaction. Such anti-social lapses in concentration can only be the by-product of suffering more than two decades of an extended pop star apprenticeship where virtually nobody listened to anybody else's advice. Ever. We were all far too interested to see who *else* had just walked into the room to take much notice of the person standing in front of us. Shallow doesn't begin to cover it.

Music is beguiling. It beckons you in with golden promises of wealth and immortality. Those seemingly innocent twelve notes have the ability to transfix both the listener *and* the player. This means that over the years a vast army of unsigned musicians have all fallen hypnotized into a world where time appears to stand still as dreams are vigorously pursued. When consumed by such an overwhelming obsession, day-to-day problems are counterbalanced with an uncanny ability to remain utterly convinced that rock star status is hiding at the end of the very next rhyming couplet or poorly attended gig. It is only very much later, when those 'not-as-young-as-you'd-like-to-be' blues come-a-calling that the mist finally starts to lift; almost imperceptibly at first but slowly clearing to reveal the devastating question... "So why have you gambled the best years of your life in pursuit of something as ridiculous as a record deal?"

That's the moment every musician fears and my own soul searching has led to this wordy salute to those of us willing to wreck both our nervous systems *and* bank balances in the heady pursuit of an unsustainable dream. And it doesn't end there, as my musical shortcomings have continued to haunt me like an angry wasp circling the very last can of Cresta on this planet. I mean, it's tough enough recalling one's own glorious failures let alone having to then sit down and write about them for a bunch of strangers' *schadenfreude*.

Being involved with bands for such a long time, I watched as the life of an unsigned musician grew to resemble an awkward and gangly kid hanging around at the edge of the pitch, secretly hoping to be picked from a dwindling bunch of no-hopers. Ever since Brit Pop's last hurrah of wanton cash-splurging on a bunch of the great unwashed back in the mid-90s, one by one the lights have gone out all over the music industry until we reach today's dimly lit scenario where kids study hard but only dabble in bands as a distraction from their coursework. And you can't blame them when they are constantly told that the record business is dead on its feet; totally kaput.   But   I came from a place where pop stars were sacrosanct, and those aliens beaming down to perform on Top of the Pops every week were deities built only for extreme idolization purposes. I still remember marvelling at the heroic hairstyles of mid-80s Echo and the Bunnymen pomp, or smirking at Robert Smith's 'bad-on-purpose' lip-synching technique on those fleeting Thursday evenings. These were statements that said 'Ok, we're taking part in the game, but we're doing it *our* way'. Back then you had to dedicate yourself to the cause if you wanted to become one of the untouchables. So I did. And this is what I got in return.

This being *my* book, I have obviously decided to eschew the usual glorification of Rock's fabled inner circle for a more selective but equally distinctive plethora of eighties and nineties artists who currently reside somewhere in deep space, light years from the musical radar. My record collection is full of such artists and outside of a handful of weirdly successful oddities like The Cure, I'm determined to revisit a bunch of obscure gems throughout this cautionary tale of taking one's ambitions to illogical extremes.

All hail St. Jude, the patron saint of lost causes.

And come revel in my story...

Now then, where was I?

Oh yes, busy staring somewhere just over your shoulder, if I remember rightly...

REMOVE THE RECORD FROM THE SLEEVE AND PLACE ONTO YOUR TURNTABLE.

HERE WE GO TWO, THREE, FOUR...

► **chapter one**

ERASE/REWIND

To our left, the Palace Pier - all funfair rides and sugar highs. To our right we have the burnt-out spectacle that was once the West Pier. It's now derelict and broken, like a giant insect that's been trampled underfoot.

Welcome to August gone mad in my adopted hometown of Brighton. The promenade is swarming with the young and the old, all busily turning themselves unhealthy shades of pink before the clouds roll over and drive them back indoors again. In amongst this human barbecue, I'm looking for somewhere to sit down and catch up with myself following a lifetime spent running a race that didn't appear to have a finishing line. As I venture forwards through the frying bodies, I am acutely aware that the jukebox in my head is subverting a favourite song to fit the situation.

Standing on a beach with a bun in my hand
Staring at the sea, staring at the tans...

(Adapted from The Cure's *Killing an Arab*. With apologies.)

I love The Cure. Have done since I first saw a picture of Robert Smith in 'Flexi Pop' circa 1982. Still, I wouldn't actually start buying any of their records for a while yet, but following this crucial first encounter I always knew that The Cure were going to be there for me. As I sat in the back of my parent's car, struggling to see through those plumes of exhaled Embassy low tar, the rain beat hard against the windscreen on yet another doomed family holiday. But music was going to save me, and bands like The Cure were my new religion.

Over the years, The Cure have gone on to become Crawley's most successful Goth-pop exports. More importantly, they have even occasionally ghosted across my own exploits as a jobbing musician. And that is why you and I are gathered here on the beach today, pebbles probing our nether regions as pterodactyl-sized seagulls dive-bomb our sandwiches.

See, I really need to offload the story of my time in music. And you seem a likely candidate, with ears worth bending. I desire a few moments of your time and in the absence of a psychiatrist it's all coming down on your shoulders.

So, if you're sitting comfortably, we'll begin…

My name is Simon Parker and I was born a little after 11am on the 29th of March 1967, just a few weeks prior to Robert Smith celebrating his eighth birthday. Now, due to the fact that I am petrified of confined spaces, I found myself vacating the womb somewhat prematurely that particular morning. But should I have managed to stay put for just a short while longer, I could quite feasibly have been born on the very same day as the singer of The Cure. To someone as deluded as me, this, of course, was evidence that I was born to have a career in indie pop.

Since the mid-1970s, I have been completely besotted by the desire to play in a band. From any number of dimly-lit backrooms I have painstakingly alerted the world to my musical 'talents'. Indeed, I have tried just about every cul-de-sac known to man and beast in the pursuit of making music for a living. But in truth I never really got much further than performing through a long line of faltering sound systems that crackled and farted like an old man holding a damp sparkler.

It is very possible that I was one of those headstrong fools who truly believed they were going to sell a lot of records and while away their golden years viewing the world from a tinted tour-bus window. Secretly, I used to fantasize about the trappings of imminent fame and fortune. But worse still, I even had my own downfall and retirement all planned out. After releasing a raft of woefully

5

self-indulgent solo albums I would have finally given it all up in a fit of 'they don't understand me' pique to lock myself away in a leafy country retreat, never to be troubled by day jobs or daylight again. So before I had even sold one record I was already contemplating my inevitable slide into obscurity. That about sums me up.

But of course, in reality none of this ever happened. To the best of my knowledge, those terrible names that I saddled my groups with were never actually etched onto any school kid's pencil case. Sure, I did get to that hallowed status of being a member of a signed band on more than one occasion, but confusingly, this only led to a plethora of even more debilitating circumstances and outcomes.

ADVENTURES WITH THE CURE

Before we go any further, it should be legally clarified that, despite a number of close shaves, I've never actually met a member of The Cure whilst they were on active service with the band. And the closest I ever got to lead singer Robert was way back in 1992, not long after I unlawfully clambered over an eight-foot wall onto his back lawn, drunk, stupid and brandishing a second generation cassette of my band 'The Violet Trade'. Now, how's that for a bad name? Don't worry. There will be others. Plenty of others.

Ah, the foolishness of youth. Actually, I was already twenty four years old and should have known better than to throw myself into the garden of one of my all-time heroes. But a lethal mixture of lunchtime cider and the fact that Robert's house was no more than a mere five-minute stagger from my girlfriend's abode on the sleepy south coast of England (look, another coincidence!), left me with the ridiculous notion that Sir Bob might enjoy that somewhat muffled copy of *Sold To The Man With No Ears*, not to mention a quick kick about in his back garden (should he have a ball).

So I lumbered towards my destination with the sole intention of alerting the world to the greatness of my band, positive that Robert would be glad to make my acquaintance and then go off and do his bit by getting us signed to Fiction records.

Luckily for me, nobody was at home that day and miraculously I wasn't set upon by any bloodthirsty security Goths. But as I wobbled delusionary across Bob's back garden, pathetically waving my TDK offering above my head like a tattered white flag... tell me, just what the fuck was I thinking?

Not enough Cure talk for you? Ok, try this one for size. On another Violet Trade-related occasion (Spring 1990), my band had just enlisted the services of a good-looking guy called Marc Gallup. Marc just so happens to be the nephew of Cure bass player Simon Gallup, and with the lure of drink and drugs (not to mention a go in my hand-knitted oversized cardigan) we had somehow managed to bribe the poor fool into playing bass on a few VT numbers at a musty old shack in our decrepit hometown of Chichester. Actually, the Lavant Village Hall was a good couple of miles outside the city perimeter, but the indie musician knows no bounds when put to the test - especially if there's nowhere else to play for miles around. So, despite the strict no alcohol policy, my band arranged to hire the venue and stage its own gig. Of course, boys being boys, The Violet Trade dismally failed to adhere to this 'no booze' promise within seconds of being granted access to the hall. Various friends dutifully turned up and removed large consignments of supermarket beer from the boots of their cars before carefully dumping them all in our makeshift bar next to the stage. Come show time the band and audience (approximately one hundred friends and family) were as drunk as Terry Wogan on Eurovision night and ploughing through the cheap booze. Lavant Village Hall was quickly awash with spilt beer from discarded cans, which lent the dance floor a somewhat treacherous edge, as moshing friends found to their cost as they sailed into the front of the stage.

Fast-forward a couple of hours. Picture the innocent caretaker returning to lock up amid chaotic scenes of sexual debauchery not usually witnessed on a village cricket pitch. There followed the issuing of an instant lifetime ban to a slightly-worse-for-wear Violet Trade, which only compounded the crushing realisation that our Cure-related bass player had carelessly neglected to inform his Uncle Simon we were playing a gig in a town where nothing remotely exciting was ever likely to happen unless we organized it.

History will recall that Simon Gallup, along with the rest of The Cure, was probably thousands of miles away on a world tour at the time. But it is moments such as this that lull gullible unsigned musicians like myself into believing their own imminent rise to stardom might just be somewhere around the next u-bend.

Looking back now, it does seem pretty weird that The Violet Trade had so effortlessly ended up with a blood relative of The Cure in its ranks. After all, we had only been rehearsing for a couple of months, yet there we were, already perilously close to my long time musical mentors. Surely, if I needed a sign from the heavens that I was on the right track, then this was it.

Wasn't it?

TALK TALK

Aside from The Cure, mystical 80s chameleons Talk Talk have always been my other favourite band on the planet. Thanks to this unswerving yet unhealthy devotion, Talk Talk will later play a part in helping to prove my musical existence to the world.

But I'm already jumping way ahead and need to give you more background into just why I spent over twenty years languishing in the muddy ditches of the record industry.

ME, MYSELF AND I

It won't surprise you to learn that I was born the same night 'Top of the Pops' used to air. The snappily-named Englebert Humperdinck was the nation's number one on the week I first burst into this world, and it was his *Please Release Me* single that was conquering ladies of a certain age all over our fair isles in 1967. Of course, the relevance of said song title in relation to my premature birth has never been lost on this here fool. Surely, this was merely the very first in a long line of pop-informed co-incidences pointing to impending greatness?

My long-suffering parents, Shirley and David, had found love at R. J. Acford's Bookbindery in Chichester, and were later hitched within the leafy confines of mid-60s West Sussex. Impressively, they have now been married for over forty years and are still patiently waiting for me to write my first hit single so that they can finally afford to split up. Just joking, Mum.

Chichester is an ornate and quiet Cathedral hamlet, notable for very little outside of its ancient architecture and the town's peculiar ability to bore local citizens into secret drinking sessions on the nearest allotments. After a bohemian spell spent living in converted railway carriages, Mum and Dad were afforded a council house on the Parklands estate. When my sister Nicola joined us in November 1970, the Parkers settled at a modest three-bedroom semi on Barton Road. It was from the cramped confines of a tiny bedroom at number 25 that my unshakeable love of music first reared its ugly little head.

When discussing children's television, it's common knowledge that the 1970s was the Mack Daddy of wonky and experimental programming. Young imaginations were irrevocably bent out of shape thanks to the vast array of science fiction presented to kids during this era. You can trace the effect it had on humanoids of a certain age via modern day greats such as 'The League of Gentlemen' and 'Look Around You'.

Make no mistake. The era of tin foil jump suits, souped-up golf buggies and men sporting more make up than their female counterparts, would soon open up unlimited new possibilities for the generation destined to follow punk rockers to the front of the dole queue.

MY TOP TEN SCI-FI & SUPERNATURAL T.V. PROGRAMMES OF THE 70s

1. Children of the Stones
2. U.F.O.
3. The Tomorrow People
4. Dr Who (Tom Baker era)
5. Space 1999
6. Ace of Wands
7. Star Trek/Thunderbirds/Stingray (1960's throwbacks - so included here as a three-for-one package to fob you off)
8. Shadows
9. Tales of the Unexpected
10. Blake's 7

(Note: Most of these programmes were enjoyed from my vantage point behind the sofa in the lounge).

I AM A ROCK

Before poop scooping was introduced, playing football at your local park was a risky affair that usually involved returning home with a particularly ferocious dog turd mercilessly decorating the sole of one's shoes. If this wasn't bad enough, the boy racer had just been invented and he whiled away his days by belting up and down the main road behind the goalposts in his new Ford Capri, mercilessly squashing the living daylights out of Auntie Ann's birthday football.

I was schooled at Parklands County Primary and by September of 1976, my classmates and I were in the hands of a bearded beatnik called Nick Phillips. This corduroy clad hipster (complete with scholarly elbow patches) encouraged my first forays into short stories and clumsy poetry. But far more importantly, Mr Phillips was also responsible for delivering the first of my life-changing musical experiences. You know what I'm talking about here, right? That unique and peculiar sensation derived from hearing a pivotal piece of music for the very first time. Whereupon, within seconds of the song starting, the mind and the heart join together in cartwheeling altitude loss as the magical piece of music penetrates deep into your skull. The world spins around you at a thousand miles per hour and you start to feel sea-sick, but in a good way.

Thanks to Mr Phillips, I experienced my inaugural 'eureka' moment just as the drums kicked in on Simon and Garfunkel's *I Am a Rock*. It was here, at precisely 0:18 seconds into the track, that my tiny world suddenly went all three-dimensional for the first time. Huge bursts of bright colour exploded before my eyes in a sub-psychedelic blast. My mind was being irrevocably blown by music at just ten years old. Of course, it's wholly possible that I may have also downed too much orange squash at lunchtime, but I like to think it was the music that caused those vivid aural hallucinations on that most memorable day.

And that's all it took. From this point on I fell helplessly in love with pop music and completely distracted myself from any semblance of a normal academic future.

THE DARK SIDE OF THE LOUNGE

I began searching beyond the television set into the previously unchartered waters of my parent's record collection. Happily for me, mum owned the very same Simon and Garfunkel greatest hits collection that Mr Phillips had just shared with us. I've often wondered why our teacher had decided to ply us with pop music that day. Maybe he had argued with his wife that morning and just needed to hear the song for his own sanity. I don't recall that we ever listened to music in the same manner again. But whatever the reason, I was totally hooked and feel I should thank Mr Philips for his introduction to the thing that would both wreck and nourish my life from here on in.

I spent more than a few afternoons absorbing other S&G tracks before rifling through the first few records in my parents stash. It turned out to be a treasure trove of goodies and I instantly adored the Beach Boys. It was like listening to liquid sunshine. Within days, I was pulling out decent mid-70s fayre by acts such as The Carpenters, Neil Diamond and The Stylistics. All was good in my new middle of the road listening experience. But as my investigation ventured further into the sideboard, I started to notice a bunch of grizzled looking freaks, resplendent in aviator shades and cheesecloth shirts. This was obviously my Dad's part of the collection where the likes of Status Quo, Canned Heat, Rolling Stones and The Eagles all stood scowling at me on those first innocent meanderings down the slightly hairier side of life. It should be noted that this unshaven approach didn't really apply to the Stones who, amazingly, managed to remain relatively clean-shaven throughout this particularly razor-shy period. Anyway, these new musical acquaintances made me feel slightly uneasy and got me thinking that there was something I wasn't being told about real life at primary school. Up until this point, the closest I had ever come to a drug crazed lunatic was that time when granddad had gotten a bit carried away at the works' party, only to be put to bed very early on Christmas Eve. Now I was being compelled by a fast-developing musical gene into devouring an entire collection of demonic entities from the dark side of the lounge.

God bless the 1970s.

OUT OF THE BLUE

Within a few months my musical preferences were becoming slightly more refined. Or maybe they were just becoming more like Dad's. Whatever the truth of the matter, it was enough for my parents to buy me my very own copy of The Electric Light Orchestra's mighty *Out of the Blue* album. Friends would be invited over just to marvel at those marvellous slabs of luminous blue vinyl. For a while I was as popular as the Fonz (even though I looked more like Richie Cunningham). But when I started pointing out Bill Wyman's somewhat less than photogenic features on the back of those old Stones albums, a lot of my more sensitive playmates ran for the hills and refused to come round for tea anymore.

It felt great to be agreeing with my father on a topic as weighty as music. Saturday mornings were often spent enthusiastically prancing around the front-room with a tennis racket, miming to the symphonic strains of *Sweet Talkin' Woman* and *Turn to Stone*. Just me that is. Dad never actually took part in this wholly enjoyable exercise; although he would always have been welcome should he have wanted to join in. But only as back-up guitarist. The solos were strictly my territory.

Around this time, toothy weird-beards were populating the stages at Top of the Pops. In the days before corrective dental surgery and links to other people's record collections, outer space oddballs all made a living by keeping us glued to the box every Thursday night. Like most Dads of the era, my own moaned about each and every new band with classic seventies put downs such as "Pooftah's!" and "They're bloody miming". Thinking about it now, he only really came alive when Pan's People got their bits out.

My sister's unhealthy infatuation with Showaddywaddy led to many heated musical debates between the pair of us, and our war of words continues to this day, especially after a few drinks at Christmas. In the eyes of an esteemed Electric Light Orchestra fan like me, Showaddywaddy existed solely to be sneered at. If I'm not mistaken, my first forays into musical snobbery had started before my eleventh birthday even happened.

Radio was God-like at this time. Sunday evening's Top 40 broadcasts were the place to go to discover the new chart positions of top acts such as The Motors and Hot Chocolate. Actually, I have a bit of a story about Hot Chocolate. Back in the day, I would paper my bedroom walls with posters of any bands I had ever vaguely heard

13

of, and one such portrait showed the boys from Hot Choc dressed only in bathrobes. It was obviously 'one for the ladies' but my sister took this as a sign that I was gay and would regularly show her friends around my room when I was out; desperately trying to gauge opinion about her 'troubled' brothers sexuality. In the end I discovered Kate Bush and the rumours subsided, but this infatuation bought with it a whole set of new problems as Kate was often photographed in a leotard in her early career.

Technology was slow back then. Computer games knew no greater graphic than two white lines at opposing edges of the television screen, endlessly batting a square white dot (can dots be square?) back and forth. For a time this was the way to spend your school holidays but constant gaming left your parents' television sets with ghostly white lines etched into either side. Evenings were often spent convincing my folks to let me use the telephone and 'Dial-A-Disc'. This was achieved by excitedly punching in the numbers '1' and '6' and then being connected to a pathetic monotone recording of some random chart tune after six o'clock when the rates were cheaper. Heady days indeed...

In the summer of 1979, my faithful Slazenger tennis racket and I shared a final lap of honour around the front room when ELO hit pay dirt with their *Discovery* album. But the times they were a-changing and when the Boomtown Rats unleashed *The Fine Art of Surfacing* in November 1979, my allegiances were abruptly diverted. At that cloudy moment where the 70s started to look and sound a little more like the 80s, I became aware of strange and exotic new sounds, courtesy of a raft of recorded-off-of-the-radio artists such as The Jam, The Police, Blondie and The Gibson Brothers.

'Smash Hits' was the hip new magazine for those of us with a passing interest in reciting the lyrics to our favourite songs, and I quickly became a New Wave kid. Debbie Harry and Joanna Lumley fought for their own piece of wall space in my bedroom, consigning ELO and Hot Chocolate to the dumper, or at least to the very back of my record collection. I also binned that offending

14

'bathrobe' picture and started spending all of my pocket money on the mighty 7" single.

SPEAK AND SPELL

That very same year I embraced secondary education for the first time. Chichester High School for Boys was a forbidding experience but it was here that my musical development increased at a fair rate of knots. I'm not quite sure this was the point of school, but it's definitely the main gift education bequeathed to me. Suddenly, The Undertones, The Jam and Gary Numan became the crucial names to bandy about with those clever and brutish types loitering in the corridors.

Chichester High School for Boys did exactly what it said on the tin - it didn't teach the female of the species. This was because they were all located twenty yards away at next door's Chichester High School for Girls. God, some days the fog of sexual tension was so thick that the air around the place resembled a Dickensian pea-souper. The only way to communicate with girls (don't worry, I wasn't about to do this for a good few years yet) was to stray into a fabled 'no-man's-land' at the bottom of the playing fields where the two schools abutted. But this was something only the very foolish Teddy boy attempted to do.

Consequently, lunchtimes were often rather exciting affairs with reddened, leather-faced teachers puffing and wheezing as they chased randy Elvis-a-likes around the school perimeter.

TWO TONE vs. THE MELTING POT

The Two-Tone movement arrived not a moment too soon and played a huge part in saving me from disappearing into musical blandness with Randy Vanwarmer and his brethren of turgid AOR cronies. Thursday evenings lit up like a firecracker whenever The Specials and Madness lurched about on TOTP in their tonic suits and pork-pie hats. As a result, Two-Tone bands quickly became heroes to 11 and 12 year olds everywhere. Dr Marten must have been a very happy man. I can still remember the day when The Specials *Too Much Too Young* made it all the way to Number 1 in early 1980. It felt like a real victory, only I couldn't quite put my finger on what we had just won. After all, most of us were still too dumb to fathom the politics behind Two-Tone's sentiments, but the ensuing seventeen years would certainly teach my generation about the evils of voting for the Conservative Party. Anyway, at the time it was cool just to stand around and watch the Two-Tone suedeheads celebrate by volleying random school bags out onto the bypass, or by chalking the letters 'VD' onto the backs of unsuspecting blazers.

Musically speaking, other parties were always vying for our teenage vote. Heavy rock attracted greasy-haired lads in sawn-off denim and a face full of volcanic acne. This period gave rise to a new batch of future stadium fillers such as Iron Maiden, Def Leppard and Judas Priest. But metal never got my vote. There just wasn't enough melody. Other clans hung about in different areas of the school canteen. Soul boys and disco freaks went all squishy at the sight of a furry die and chased after girls who had been christened 'Sharon' or 'Tracy', of which there were many at the time. The afore-mentioned Teddy boy tried hard to distance himself from ageing novelty bands like Matchbox and Darts with a series of quotes from James Dean movies and some impressively bryl-creemed hairstyles, whilst the occasional out-of-date glam rocker flounced about in his sister's fake-fur coat, reeking of a heady mixture of Patchouli oil and 'Football Crazy' crisps. Meanwhile, in the corner of the school library, your average day-to-day Beatle obsessive fervently expounded suspect conspiracy theories about how the CIA were out to get John Lennon. Mainstream pop was still reeling from the Bee Gees going disco whilst Prog Rock was safe in the hands of Pink Floyd and those legions of boys with slightly introverted older brothers. 'Ant Warriors' were the style gurus for about ten minutes, before most jumped ship to re-invent themselves as 'New Romantics' a few days later.

Self-confessed 'Futurists' proclaimed undying love for anything with a synthesizer on it, but then had to suffer constant threats of violence and ridicule out on the playground for choosing to wear their blazers inside out.

Only Mod made any real impact on me, and this was more to do with the fact that I quite liked the trousers. In the early 80s, Modernist subculture had begun (stay) pressing for new recruits thanks to the chart success of The Jam, not to mention another successful re-run of 'Quadrophenia' on the TV. Mod quickly became the lifestyle most lads aspired to when puberty hit and hormones rattled like a set of wind-up dentures. The wealthier boys zipped around the car park on motorbikes that sounded like your sister's hairdryer jammed on full blast, whilst pretty Modettes successfully hair-sprayed their eyelids shut whenever the wind unexpectedly changed direction.

Even though I loved music, I didn't actually pledge allegiance to any particular style during my first year at secondary school. This led to me being viewed suspiciously by some, but my record collection remained eclectic and grew with purchases by Narada Michael Walden one week, Blondie and Ultravox the next. It was a funny old time.

FRIENDS

My closest friends during this illuminating period were two football-loving vandals by the names of Andrew Howick and Robbie Wheeler. Rob was a hulking presence who lived across the road from Andy on the Little Breach estate and became more like our personal minder as time wore on. Both were a little younger than me and, despite severe protestations from my lofty position of having seen it all the previous year, Andy and Rob willingly signed up to become apprentice Mods when they started at Chichester High School in September of 1980.

Within weeks of their arrival, my best friends were struggling to afford nasty-looking boating blazers and over-priced Dobie Gray imports. From the safety of my cheap

Clark's copies, I laughed whenever their flimsy moccasins let in water and relentlessly heckled the pair about their tiny button-down collars whilst all the while my own snapped in the breeze like a pair of demented scissors.

The early 1980s would prove to be a fantastically fertile and popular period in the life of the 7". Chichester High School for Boys was a huge melting pot of influences and cultural demigods. All fashions and creeds appeared to be catered for. I knew that I had to be seen to be flying the flag for something. Peer pressure and my own burning desire to have a band to hero worship meant that the time had finally come to set out my own exciting musical stall and show the world just what I was made of.

Of course, being an obtuse child, I ended up choosing a band that weren't your average teen idols.

XTC

Being a fan of XTC was (and still is) like joining a secret cult. For some, it's an obsession that gets taken a little too seriously, with obsessives rifling through lead singer Andy Partridge's bins for discarded socks or old demos, whilst the more 'normal' amongst us are happy to spend a lot of money tracking down those hard to find vinyl platters.

It's likely that my introduction to the band came with 1979's *Making Plans for Nigel*, but it wasn't until my fourteenth birthday in 1981 that I finally bought one of their releases. *Black Sea* was, and still is, an amazing record. As we all know, good albums don't age; they just mature like a decent wine. And *Black Sea* is a great vintage made by a well-oiled gigging machine at the height of its powers.

It has never been a particularly fashionable thing to admit to liking the Swindon wonder boys: for most they were always the odd taste, the Marmite of the new wave scene. But once smitten there's no turning back in XTC world, and even though I might now go a few weeks between blasts of their music, the moment one of their tunes pops up I'm back there reliving the group's former glories and the peculiar way in which they struggled to penetrate the hearts (and ears) of our nation.

You see, XTC records had a nasty habit of stalling just outside of the charts, and as a kid, this used to infuriate me no end. Constantly banished to the side-lines by those fans of more successful artists, XTC and I were rewarded with just one top 10 position in the UK charts, when *Senses Working Overtime* lurched all the way to number 10 in early 1982.

Nowadays, XTC are a shining example of the good old times when record companies used to invest more than just money into the longevity of its artists. A little faith and patience could go a long way back then, but sadly this is something that has long-since vanished in an industry now constantly searching for a quick return on its investment. XTC records rarely recouped, but over the course of ten albums for Virgin, the band steadily developed a unique body of English pop music. Of course, I'm painting a pretty Utopian picture here and the reality of the situation was that XTC were tied into a deal so miserly and draconian that they eventually had to down tools and stop recording for over five years before Virgin finally got the message and dumped them. Band and paymaster fell out so badly that the ill feeling over royalties rumbles on until this day. So come on Virgin (or should I say Universal?), how about making amends? We the fans urgently need to replace our obliterated greatest hits videos with a decent quality DVD.

Despite their sustained lack of commercial success, XTC's influence on subsequent generations has filtered down through the years, peaking around 2004 when Kaiser Chiefs and The Futureheads (amongst others) appropriated their jerky new wave sound. At the time I was sharing an office with Mark Nicholson, the manager of (then) fleetingly famous four-piece 'The Ordinary Boys'. One day, future Celebrity Big Brother star-turn Preston phoned up and innocently asked his mentor for a list of artists he should be investigating. Mark turned to me for my thoughts and I proffered XTC's *Drums and Wires*, whereupon a cold, stony silence descended upon the room, catapulting me back to those far off days when I used to receive exactly the same reaction from friends at school.

Looking back, I'm proud that I chose to plant my flag in XTC soil, as I'm probably owed a lot more musical kudos than if I had plumbed for Jo Boxers or Roman Holiday. The only negative was the group's complete lack of image. At best, XTC resembled a freak accident at a jumble sale. And so did I, thanks to the fact that I would spend the early 80s imitating the bands 'look' and waste a lot of my life hunting for striped granddad shirts and dickie-bow ties, herringbone jackets and black turtleneck sweaters.

And believe me, that was the good stuff.

MY TOP 10 XTC ALBUMS (POSSIBLY IN ORDER)

1. Skylarking
2. Black Sea
3. Drums and Wires
4. Mummer
5. Wasp Star
6. The Big Express
7. Nonsuch
8. Apple Venus
9. English Settlement
10. Oranges and Lemons

EVERYBODY'S GONE TOP OF THE POPS

Around the time of my fifteenth birthday, I became the unelected chairman of a strange gang of rabid chart enthusiasts. Without fail, every Tuesday lunchtime we would congregate at the end of the school playing fields with a smuggled-in radio, just so that we could be the first to witness that week's official Top 40 countdown. It was an elite club (meaning that membership never strayed into double-figures) but we earned a modicum of respect from fellow school kids who all presumed we were off to the far-reaches of the school for cigarettes and clandestine meetings with girls from the neighbouring buildings. Of course, we were doing nothing of the sort, but as a member of this secret society each and every one of us felt just that little bit more important to know the movers and shakers of the new chart, two whole days before Top of the Pops finally spilled the beans to the other fifteen million or so music enthusiasts in the UK.

Due to XTC's frequent misfiring in the hit singles department, it wasn't long before I was creating my own 'fantasy' run-downs, where I would religiously re-draw the week's chart titles using screwed up bits of paper from a velvet bag, thus instantly creating my own biased (and massively rigged) edition of the hit parade. This quickly became a vehicle for outpourings from my own leaking brain of imaginary bands and made-up song titles, which was the reason 'Simon Parker' (the sensitive solo artist) started enjoying his own big hits in the UK Top 40 in 1981/2. And I hadn't even had to learn to play an instrument. It would be all downhill from here.

What started as an innocent-sounding song title soon morphed into a wince-inducing rhyming couplet. Eventually, three full-blown verses and rousing chorus of glorious teen-angst would be filling the back pages of my notebook. Somehow, I had become a lyricist.

MY TOP 5 REALLY BAD SONG IDEAS OF 1982

1. *If I Could Reach The Sky* - slow, anthemic weepie that Westlife would have killed for. Possibly.
2. *The Ghost* - turgid spooky nonsense where the song's narrator is revealed as being dead in the very last line. More predictable than the flimsiest 'Tales of the Unexpected' storyline.
3. *Burning Heart Stop* - upbeat dance floor filler. I invented rave. But I kept it in my head.
4. *So Lost In Love* - another anthem. Probably cribbed from Air Supply or REO Speedwagon who were busy filling the charts with a lot of windswept proto-mullets around this time.
5. *White China* - nope. I have no excuses or explanations. It was just very BAD.

The time has come for us both to meet my first musical co-conspirator. Suddenly, the possibilities of playing in a real band and writing proper songs were going to offer me even more distractions from the daily rigors of schoolwork.

The Young Pretender attempting that tricky 'C' chord

▶ chapter two

THE FIRST CHORD IS THE DEEPEST

Phillip Bennett was the motor-mouthed kid of class 2M. He was always shouting about something, and thinking about it now, he probably had a mild case of Tourette's syndrome. Things like that went largely unnoticed back then. Besides, there was nothing that a quick clip around the ear couldn't sort out.

Now, as we all know, most decent front-men in bands suffer from some form of anti-social quirk, and I'm sure Phil's attention-seeking wouldn't have been lost on me during that first awkward afternoon spent cheating at the cross-country race together. Also along for the ride/walk/run on this momentous day was a quiet kid called Jake Tully, already famed for his impressive pipe-smoking antics. A pipe? At fourteen years old? No wonder he was so short.

Our first conversation would have gone along these lines:

ME: (Out of breath and running like a girl to catch up with them) "So what are you two tossers up to then?"
THEM: (in unison) "Nothing. You bender."
ME: "Can I join in?"
THEM: "If you must"
ME: (wasting no time in getting to the point) "Do you like music?"
THEM: "Yeah..."
ME: (interrupting) "So do I! Aren't Dépêche Mode and OMD ammmaazzzing...?"

Back then people still had musical opinions and preferences. Ask anyone today and it's all so ironic and infuriating. 'Oh I like everything, you know, The Beatles,

Zep, Beyonce. And isn't Dubstep great? I totally understand where it's coming from..."

Utter bollocks. But back in 1982 we still had prejudice and admiration in equal quantity. It was just a little bit awkward that both Phil and Jake objected to OMD and Depeche Mode so vehemently. Worse still, neither had heard of XTC. But, believe me I would soon change all that.

MY TOP 5 DEPECHE MODE SINGLES.

1. Enjoy the Silence
2. Blasphemous Rumours
3. Dreaming of Me
4. Never Let Me Down Again
5. I Feel You

MY TOP 5 O.M.D. SINGLES.

1. Souvenir
2. Joan of Arc
3. Electricity
4. Talking Loud and Clear
5. Enola Gay

A few days after this encounter, Phil and I first dared set foot in Jake's bedroom. Well, I say 'bedroom', but more accurately it was a guitar workshop and electrical power hazard. Jake was already building guitars and amplification, and so his room was a mass of discarded parts and bare wires. It's no surprise that in later life Jake would become an electrician for the National Grid. He remains a lord of the overcrowded wall socket.

Despite the threat of frequent electric shocks, we formed our first band that day. Jake was a proficient guitarist, happiest when endlessly soloing along to a Jimi Hendrix or Cream album. Phil thwacked away on an acoustic guitar that had been lent up against a radiator for too much of its life whilst impressively spitting his Tourette's into one of Jake's homemade microphones. Of course, this was made from some unreliable Russian kit parts that interfered with the reception on his parents' television set, so we were forced to abandon vocals early on, which was probably a good thing really. Phil's potty-mouth was in danger of going into hyper drive now that he had a way to be heard all over the house. As for myself, I just stood around posing in an old grey waistcoat (gee, thanks for the fashion tip Andy Partridge), occasionally jabbing at the odd key on a Casio VL-Tone keyboard. This was the one made famous by novelty German band Trio on their *Da Da Da* single, although the only thing I really did was to mess about with the tempo on the 'bossa nova' rhythm preset and look busy. Like Chris Lowe from Pet Shop boys, only a little bit earlier.

We sounded truly dreadful, like some sort of horrendous musical experiment to harness three decades of unrelated music into one long jam, but Phil and I came away realizing that we quite liked the idea of writing songs together. We also came away with mild burns after one of Jake's contraptions unexpectedly burst into flames mid-'song'. But it had been worth it. The Wasps were born.

I was buzzing. We were off to a flying start.

Sorry.

Phil Bennett

Simon Parker

THE WASPS

Most of our earliest tracks were written at Phil's parents' impressive penthouse flat which overlooked the Chichester Cathedral and city centre precinct. For a simple boy from the council houses this was a very cool place to be invited to, and when we weren't busy messing around with the Minns Music home organ we could be found out on the patio, lobbing dried up dog turds down onto the unsuspecting pedestrians below. It was heaven.

Phil always wrote the music whilst I took care of the lyrics. We were like a juvenile Elton John and Bernie Taupin, minus the talent and stupid sunglasses. Our first attempts at melody culminated in the songs *Getting On My Nerves* and *Thursday Afternoon*. The latter was a 'protest' song written after one of our friends got caught buying pot in the changing rooms next to the football pitches. The whole thing was a set up by the rugby boys (the "hash' in question was actually half an Oxo cube wrapped in silver foil). Like most skinny kids, the rugby contingent was our sworn enemy at the time, and so, via a cheap personal stereo that did the rounds during the lunch break, I played brief bursts of *Thursday Afternoon* to anyone who showed the slightest interest. And to an even larger number who showed absolutely no interest at all. Phil and I were so incensed about our friend's plight that we declared ourselves an autonomous state, even though we didn't actually know what one of those was. It felt as if we had become the outsiders, good guys living outside of the school's old-fashioned rules. Therefore, it became my God-given duty to continue writing desperately terrible songs. So that's exactly what I did. When our mate Joey was subsequently pardoned and allowed to return to studies, he listened to the track and cast me a horrified look that told me all I needed to know about The Wasps' song writing abilities in 1982.

Slowly I fathomed out that I would need to learn how to play an instrument if I really wanted to become a musician. I was clever like that. I then spent the next three months saving up about £50 whilst Phil just shouted obscenities at his parents until they gave in and bought him a guitar and amplifier. Another lesson learned in the subtle differences between working and middle class children, folks...

SATELLITE OF LOVE

A few months later, whilst pulling out my fillings on a lethal 'Texan' bar, I noticed a small faded card in the window of my local newsagents:

FOR SALE - SATELLITE GUITAR AND AMPLIFIER.
VERY LOUD. £50 o.n.o.

Knowing very little about musical equipment, but understanding the general meaning of the word 'loud', I cycled round to the posh part of the estate to investigate this just-within-my-price-range combo. Greeted by a heavy metal cave dweller, I was thrust into a bedroom dripping with the fragrance of dead pets and fresh poo. But it was worth the scorched nostrils, for over in the corner of that dank hovel lay the key to another world - a battered and scratched electric guitar. And to make things even better it was black.

At this point in time I knew precisely two first-position chords. And it usually took me five minutes to reset my fingers before I could move between them. Naturally, my demonstration of virtuosity left a lot to be desired. So I clung to my 'G' Major for all I was worth, thrumming like a boy possessed by the spirit of just one ill-fretted chord. Mr Metal flicked a switch and the amp hissed into life and immediately picked up the frequency of any taxicabs cruising the local vicinity. The strings were so far from the fret board you could have slid a book in the gap and the tuning heads creaked ominously every time I pretended to give the instrument a quick tweak. I actually made the guitar sound even worse by fiddling around with it, and as I began to panic, I smashed the strings as hard as I could, which instantly caused next door's dog to howl its disapproval at my untutored cluster of notes that hung in the air like an unwanted fart at the dinner table.

Embarrassment very quickly got the better of me. Resplendent in a natty leather jerkin, this heavy metal salesman surveyed me with suspicious eyes that silently accused me of being a new romantic come to bum him in his bedroom. Fumbling for words (and music) I simply handed over the £50 and got the hell out of Dodge.

Dragging my new toys behind me, I struggled out into the street and loaded up my protesting Halfords Racer for some intensive learning sessions in the sanctity of my own (marginally) better smelling bedroom.

Fame and stardom were surely little more than a bike ride away.

THE WALNUT AVENUE DISASTER

As evening fell, electric lights spluttered into life to illuminate living rooms and kitchens. I zigzagged through the estate like a drunken tortoise, absentmindedly gazing into scenes of centrally-heated domesticity until, somewhat unexpectedly, I happened upon a brightly lit lounge with a young couple vigorously shagging in full view of the neighbourhood (well, in front of me and my new guitar/amp combo at least). Travelling at such a ridiculously slow speed I copped a decent eyeful of the partially clothed lovers piggy-backing away on the settee just before the bicycle's momentum carried me out of view. Like any other inquisitive teenager with vitally important things such as guitars and sex on his mind, it was at this point that I foolishly attempted a one-hundred-and-eighty-degree turn to go back and have another look. After all, this was by far the closest I would come to having intercourse for a good few years yet. Sadly, as I attempted the sudden change of direction, my new guitar wedged itself in the spokes of the front tyre. This catapulted me over the handlebars in comical slow motion, with both the amplifier and bicycle landing on top of my prostrate body with a dull thud. Things like this just weren't supposed to happen on Walnut Avenue.

The commotion must have alerted that fornicating couple to my crumpled presence, because when I finally succeeded in throwing the bike and amp off my objecting bones, the show was well and truly over. Never has such a hasty exit been made, even though I was now cut, bruised and in possession of a bike no longer capable of travelling in a straight line anymore.

Once safely back home, my parents gave me a look of helpless pity as I tried to tune my new prized possession. Dad phoned the local taxi rank just to piss me off, whilst Mum politely enquired as to why I was bleeding. But both parents sat patiently through a beyond jazz version of *Little Donkey*, partially misinterpreted from Bert Weedon's helpfully unhelpful 'Play in a Day' tutorial.

High times at Barton Road, huh?

For a while I gamely persevered with a set of baffling instructions decoded from a grinning fifties heartthrob, but I already knew that I was fighting a losing battle. The Satellite guitar refused to stay in tune for longer than ten seconds at a time and pressing down on the strings was like squeezing on barbed wire.

Back at school, I casually informed Phil that what The Wasps really needed was a somewhat more sophisticated approach and that I was totally prepared to invest in a brand new keyboard. So, just a short while after the last scab from the Walnut Avenue disaster had finally healed over, I successfully begged my father into signing as the guarantor on a nifty little Casio MT400V. This budget synthesiser came with single touch chord playability for hopeless sods like me.

It would be a fair while before I even looked at another guitar, and I was always careful to take the long way home should I find myself heading in the direction of that sex house on Walnut Avenue.

OUR FAVOURITE SHOP

The glorious path to rock'n'roll Valhalla beckoned my gang with its alluring tales of drink, drugs and black magic women. Yet instead of setting off on a colourful voyage of discovery, we choose mainly to gather on Phil's top floor balcony retreat and kick bits of sun dried dog plops at one another. I consoled myself by buying as much music as pocket money would allow. During school holidays, my friends and I started visiting nearby Portsmouth in search of a better class of record shop. At this point Chichester's best option was W H Smith. Enough said.

Despite various disparaging remarks from the Farah-clad Pompey casuals, Rob, Andy and I stumbled upon the ailing Tricorn shopping centre, once dubbed 'the market in the sky', but now little more than a gigantic concrete dinosaur sulking in the shadows of the busier high street. Outside of the occasional tramp pissing in a boarded-up doorway, the centre was deserted, save for a couple of struggling businesses. One of these just so happened to be the best record shop I have ever had the pleasure to spend money in.

Domino Records (no relation to the fabled record label) was a chart return shop that boasted every conceivable format going. Its racks were bulging with coloured vinyl, poster packs and general pop junk that, to a fifteen-year old, was manna from the heavens. But its most appealing feature was an extensive marked-down section where ex-chart flops could be purchased for 29p each. This is where my 7" single collection started in earnest. Songs that I had heard only once or twice on the radio (thank you Janice Long, Richard Skinner, Kid Jensen and Radio Luxembourg) were plucked from the shelves, or more often than not the bargain bin and worshipped back at Barton Road.

Here, I could forget all about the woes of schoolwork and Simon Bates' strangely Shane McGowanesque gnashers.

TOP 5 RECORDS RESCUED FROM DOMINO'S SALE RACKS

1. The Cure – Hanging Garden (double single)
2. Psychedelic Furs – Dumb Waiters (playable sleeve version)
3. Pete Shelley – Homosapien (Buzzcocks' singer embraces technology and Martin Rushent)
4. Private Lives – Living in a World Turned Upside Down (great lost U.K soul single)
5. Blue Zoo – Somewhere in the World There's a Cowboy Smiling (obscure last-throw-of-the-dice from New Romantic relegation candidates)

► chapter three

INTERNATIONAL BRIGHT YOUNG THINGS

With the sudden acquisition of such great music, I needed a way to inflict it on other people. And so, this is how I became a trainee Disc Jockey at the local hospital radio station.

After learning the ropes by sitting in on other DJs' broadcasts, I was tentatively given a show in the early summer months of 1982. The resulting 'Simon Parker Saturday Special' (snappy, huh?) was a colourful and musically astute requests programme, notable for the fact that it never actually played any requests at all. In theory, a practising disc jockey was responsible for trawling the wards an hour or two before his or her show and politely asking patients if they would like to hear a personal dedication via the magic of hospital radio. But in truth, I was completely terrified of visiting the sick and in pain, whom, I figured, would not appreciate me sticking my head around their curtained-off beds to enquire whether I could help by spinning *Bridge Over Troubled Waters* or *Seven Tears*. I'd been in hospital. It was no picnic.

So I just hung about in the foyer and invented a number of fake requests instead. This way I could play whatever the hell I wanted to. For a short while everything went swimmingly, and I routinely treated my audience to a flurry of lively tunes. The idea of collecting requests was soon nothing more than a distant memory although my playlists were careful to document that I was still including a healthy mix of MOR classics. In reality I was like John Peel's annoyingly upbeat nephew. All went well until the station controller did one of his walkabouts during my show, and sat there listening on the edge of a patient's bed as I belted out New Order's *Everything's Gone Green*. I was sacked for what I can only guess might have had something to do with possible complaints from those unfortunate people tuning in from the confines of the amputation department.

TOP TEN TRACKS PLAYED ON MY RADIO SHOW

1. Orange Juice - I Can't Help Myself
2. Nick Nicely - Hillyfields (1892)
3. A Flock of Seagulls - I Ran
4. Graham Parker - Temporary Beauty
5. The Keys - One Good Reason
6. Boomtown Rats - Someone's Looking at You
7. The Teardrop Explodes - Treason (It's Just a Story)
8. Blancmange - I've Seen the Word
9. XTC - Ball and Chain
10. The Beat - I Confess

My first brush with fame ended as quickly as it had arrived. To make matters worse, I had failed most of my mock O-Levels by a matter of two or three percent. Still, at least I had music to get me through the bad times.

AZTEC CAMERA-HIGH LAND HARD RAIN (1983)

I first became aware of Aztec Camera following the release of their brilliant *Pillar to Post* single towards the end of 1982. Having been released on an independent record label I had to search for weeks until I finally found it. But when I did (thanks Domino!) I played it constantly and Aztec Camera swiftly became my favourite new band.

In April of 1983, just a few weeks after my sixteenth birthday, a copy of the band's *High Land Hard Rain* made it to the racks of WH Smith in Chichester. This in itself was no mean feat, and I quickly gravitated to the windswept romanticism of Roddy Frame's lyrics. I would sit with headphones clasped tightly to my ears, endlessly blasting the record and picturing myself hitching all over the country, strumming a Gretsch guitar just like the one owned by the gifted Roddy. In my recurring fantasy I

33

would sleep rough in barns and enjoy brief, torrid affairs with a different girl in every town.

Of course, I never did anything of the sort, and in reality I continued to live at home with my untuneable Satellite and a frustrating keyboard that only had about one good sound on it. Just like Billy Liar, it was all in my head.

High Land Hard Rain saw me through a number of awkward teenage moments and soon became an inseparable confidante. The circumstance in which you first hear music is crucially important to your long-term emotional attachment to it, and *High Land Hard Rain* has gone on to become one of my all-time favourites. I cannot listen to it now without smiling about the clumsiness of my teenage years, with every track reminding me of some ridiculous calamity as I stuttered and stumbled my way through those earliest fumblings with members of the opposite sex. But the record also has a deep, resonant pull with *We Could Send Letters* and *Lost Outside the Tunnel* able to reduce me to tears in a matter of nano-seconds.

Even though I remained a prisoner to my abilities, *High Land Hard Rain* transported my heart and mind to other places. And that's a sign of an indisputably great body of work, right?

MY TOP 10 AZTEC CAMERA SONGS

1. We Could Send Letters (High Land Hard Rain)
2. Lost Outside the Tunnel (High Land Hard Rain)
3. Pillar to Post (High Land Hard Rain)
4. The Birth of the True (Knife)
5. Walk Out to Winter (High Land Hard Rain)
6. Good Morning Britain (Stray)
7. Head is Happy (Heart's Insane) (Knife)
8. Down the Dip (High Land Hard Rain)
9. Sun (Freestonia)
10. Mattress of Wire (Postcard 7" single)

Summer Holidays 1982: even before I had a proper band I would look for suitable locations and cajole friends into posing for pretend photo shoots. (l-r - Mark Rowe, Simon Parker, Jake Tully, Philip Bennett, Andrew Howick – photo – Philip Bennet)

MAGIC MOMENTS

Stuart Worden was the coolest of all my friends. He smoked his Marlboro Lites from soft-top packs and always insisted on wearing extremely baggy trousers to school. I tried to get my own hairstyle to resemble his floppy Edwyn Collins-style fringe without a great deal of success, as it often looked like I was wearing a motorcycle helmet spray painted straw blonde, especially if it was windy.

Stu's chiselled good looks made him unpopular with some of my own friends, so the relationship was all the more difficult to maintain. Ours became a clandestine union that only happened in cheap cafés whenever my other feuding acquaintances weren't looking. Here, Stu and I would indulge in serious discussions about music, whilst pretty girls stopped in their tracks to admire his handsome features. It was a bit like hanging out with a model from the Littlewoods' catalogue.

Stuart's older brother Ian was in an up and coming synth-pop band called Blurred Vision. BV had quickly

35

become the most important guys on the Chichester scene (make that the *only* guys on the Chichester scene) owing to the fact they were actually doing it and not just bloody talking about it. As Stu sat pretending not to notice a bevy of fawning girls staring in at him through the windows of Macari's coffee-house, through a wave of curling blue smoke he casually enquired if I would like to attend Blurred Vision's next gig at the Princess Victoria pub. I realized that I was at last cool enough to hang out with the real players. All right!

I chose not to mention the gig to my other friends for fear they might tag along and ruin this chance of a lifetime. Phil and Jake would probably make disparaging remarks about the band's fashion sense or lack of lengthy guitar solos, whilst Joey remained a not-to-be-trusted-Oxo-cube-purchasing disaster area. Rob and Andy were still only babies at fifteen years old, and they usually regarded anybody cooler than themselves as posers or homosexuals.

Back in the early 1980s, programming machines to play your parts was still outlawed in most musical circles, especially in those where the art of swilling real ale and the promise of 'keeping music live' was more a threat than a sign of good pedigree. I suspected that my friends weren't actually ready for exposure to the future of rock'n'roll just yet... but me? Well, I was already there, especially if it bought me that little bit closer to girls of my own age.

On the day of the show I took a long, unprompted shower. This immediately alerted my mother to the fact that I wasn't telling her something. For the first time in my teenage life, I stood in front of the bedroom mirror and deliberated over what to wear. I only owned four shirts and two pairs of trousers but the pressure was on to look the part. I settled for a black suit jacket and dark grey shirt, fashionably buttoned up to the neck, even though it was the middle of August. I also chose to wear a pair of comically baggy (and strangely itchy) woollen trousers that I had recently rescued from a Red Cross jumble sale. In the clueless manner of a true fashion failure, I considered this outfit something that John Foxx might have chosen for a night on the tiles. But thinking about it now, I probably looked more like Rik from The Young Ones.

Before I could impress anybody at the gig, I first had to figure out how I was going to slither in past those troublesome bouncers who patrolled the pub like angry trolls under a bridge. I was only sixteen years old and still ages away from my first shave. To put it mildly, I was not overly confident that I was going to get in.

Escaping out the back door before an inquisition into my whereabouts could develop. I set off from home like a young soldier to an electro-pop war. Knowing next to nothing about licensing laws, I arrived at the pub a little after six o'clock. Of course, this being the early 1980s meant that the place was resoundingly shut. I hadn't planned for this and was forced to beat a hasty retreat (what if someone saw me?) to a nearby park to take stock of the situation. It was at this moment that I first wished for a packet of fags to look cool with.

After daydreaming about copping off with Tracey Scott for longer than is healthy when out in a public place, I nightmarishly espied Phil and Jake approaching on bicycles. Forced into an awkward conversation about where I could be going in such an overdressed fashion, the bastards hung around for ages whilst trying to guess which girl I was meeting with half a tub of economy hair-gel plastered to the top of my head. Eventually, they got bored and peddled off to Phil's house to resume dropping you-know-what from the balcony of his parents' well-appointed flat.

I made my way back to the Princess Victoria for the second time that evening. Drawing a deep breath, I rehearsed my newly-assumed date of birth and felt my legs buckling beneath me. There in the doorway of the pub stood two of the most imposing beefcakes I had ever laid eyes on.

Somebody up there must have taken pity on me that evening, because just as I braced myself for oncoming ritual humiliation, there was a minor collision between two cars on the road outside the pub. While the bouncers lumbered over to take a closer look and take the piss, I saw my chance and slithered into the bar. It's funny really, because if I hadn't managed to get in to see Blurred Vision perform, there's a small chance that I might just have crawled away and concentrated on my studies. But rock'n'roll obviously had other designs for me as I set foot inside a pub not accompanied by an adult for the first time ever.

The Princess Vic was dark, smoky and exciting. Lined with red velvet sofas and impenetrably thick draped curtains, it resembled a Victorian brothel for fans of Blancmange and Fun Boy Three. Wall-to-wall, drop dead beautiful girls drained pints of Snakebite and black, whilst ice-cool dudes hid beneath impossible fringes. There were even a couple of blokes sharing the same toilet cubicle when I nipped in for a nervous pee before attempting to get served. 'Strange', I pondered, 'because there's no one at the urinal, and surely these boys should be tucked up in bed with such a nasty case of the sniffles...'

Once back inside the hub of saloon activity, I basked in that Gulf Stream of hot, sweet air and breathed in the sights and sounds of my first illicit night out. I'm sure that my head was spinning long before I touched a drop of alcohol as I struggled to maintain my imagined cool. Embarking upon a quick circuit of the pub, at one point I nearly ended up outside with the bouncers again, so I quickly ditched this approach and scuttled over to the crowded bar like everyone else. After an absolute eternity, a pretty, blonde barmaid, whom I could have sworn was in the year below me at school, casually flicked her eyes in my direction long enough for me to order my pint of Harp lager (I'd heard that it stayed sharp all the way to the bottom of the glass). As she poured my first world of infinite possibilities, I stood marvelling at being allowed inside a public house whilst still only a wank-crazy schoolboy. I surveyed the room and recognised several familiar faces from around the school playground. Effeminate guys with way too much make up on nodded their heads at me, whilst a couple of the most beautiful girls in the world curled blood-red lipstick smiles in my direction. And like a fool, every time this happened I turned around to see if they were acknowledging someone behind me. Impressive, huh?

After a few minutes I began to feel a little awkward about standing on my own, so I sidled over to where drama buddy Stuart was holding court with a clutch of stunningly attractive females. He acknowledged me with a slight raise of his left eyebrow, in a manner similar to the one Roger Moore employed to such great effect during his esteemed acting career.

Everyone was arguing about the Cherry Red *Pillows and Prayers* album. Upon its release, this essential bible of new/fey/obscure artists famously retailed for just 99p. Stu's table of acquaintances all seemed to have a different opinion as to the compilation's best track. Heated debates raged from person to person, but my money was on Joe Crow (*Compulsion*) or Felt (*My Face is on Fire*) although I elected to keep my thoughts to myself for fear of looking like a complete idiot. Before long the subject changed and we all came to a mutual understanding that records should cost no more than 99p. Ever.

I drank my one and only pint far too quickly and was then forced to nurse an empty drinking vessel for a good hour or so until the band finally elected to take to the stage and plug into their warship-sized synthesizers. Blurred Vision exuded the same confidence that one might expect from a good-looking bunch making their Top of the Pops debut. With my mouth wide open I stood in silence whilst Ian, Mike and Kevin posed their way through forty minutes of catchy electronic pop. They even dared play an OMD cover, and as the audience roared its appreciation at the end of the set, I predicted a very bright future for Chichester's first sons of synth. Time has eroded my memory of most of their song titles (*Another Rung up the Ladder* being the only one I can actually still remember), but take it from me, they were great and should have gone far (well faraway from Chichester at least). I left the gig walking on air, inspired by ARP (it's a make of synthesizer) and intoxicated by Harp.

I finally knew what I had been born to do. I would earn my living by playing in a band. Wouldn't my parents be thrilled?

A CODA

Many years later, Stuart Worden would go on to become the Principal of The Brit School in Croydon. This esteemed pop academy has proudly nurtured emerging talents such as Kate Nash, King Krule and Adele. While researching **Road to Nowhere**, I caught up with my old school friend for the first time in approximately twenty four years, and we quickly found ourselves reverting back to those old roles of co-habiting music junkies. We've even started making each other compilations again, although this time they are on compact disc and not cassette. It's great to be sharing the old and the new with someone who is inflicted with the same infatuation. Back when we first met, I gave Stu XTC and he opened my ears to New Order. More recently it's been Earlimart and John Murry. The music might change, but for us it's just like old times.

I've even been able to catch up with Stu's big brother Ian, who also became a teacher. When we met for a few drinks I told him that it's his fault I'm a penniless musician. But he's having none of it.

If the Brit School had been around in 1983, I'm sure I would have tried to lie my way in. But career opportunities were still very antiquated in the early 80s, so the best that I could hope for was another ten months avoiding the real world in the sixth form at Chichester High School for Boys.

BACK TO SCHOOL - BACK TO REALITY

Phil and I quickly found a very good reason for playing truant. The Sixth form shared its facilities with the previously out-of-bounds Girls' school. Studying duly took on a new meaning. After decamping to our educational counterparts' common room at precisely 9.15 each and every morning, we could then spend the rest of our school day prancing around the building looking like the Millet's version of David Bowie (Phil) and Simon Le Bon (yours truly).

It was as if we had stumbled upon an educational Shangri-La. For the first time in my life I had a fool proof excuse for being in the same room as a member of the opposite sex.

CIGARETTES AND ALCOHOL

Joey was still hell-bent on getting wasted, even though he now spent most of his time purchasing garish paisley cravats from Oxfam to enhance his 'hippy' image. By the end of 1983, our gang of marauding virgins were enjoying the full effects of booze and tobacco. In fact, most of us had already found part-time evening jobs in the local supermarkets and were happily relieving the shelves of as much alcohol as we could stuff into our school bags at the end of the shift. More importantly, after years of clueless dithering, we had finally come up with a way to lure girls into our lives. We had a plan. It went by the name of 'house party'.

PARTY FEARS TWO

To make this happen I ordered Phil to sweet-talk his parents into going out on a Saturday evening. This would give us the run of that very swish penthouse flat. The ladies would love this. I also convinced Andy Howick to ask his older sister Karen to spread the word throughout her numerous female colleagues in the girls' sixth form.

The brotherhood stole so much booze that we could have started our own off-licence should we have wished. Karen duly invited a wide selection of teenage lovelies to join us and the date was confirmed.

Things were looking up.

RETURN OF THE WASPS

After nearly two whole gloriously inept years together, Phil and I were still trading as The Wasps even though we would go for months at a time between ultra-lame writing or rehearsal sessions. But faced with the prospect of some serious female interaction for the first time in our pathetic lives, we finally agreed to ditch the childish 'Wasps' moniker, but dithered about its replacement.

A couple of our songs (*Faceless* and *Shine*) showed faint signs of melodic improvement, and those plans for world domination felt as if they were definitely on the right tracks. Most bands born into the 1980s used the phrase 'world domination' when referring to global success. Everybody was turning into another of Thatcher's greedy little cash slaves.

But the 'Ex-Wasps' (still thinking...) faced a steadily growing problem. Owing to the fact that so many sixth-formers now used Phil's flat as a sanctuary from the hell of advanced education, our band was never free to create music for more than a few minutes of any school day before someone was yelling "Phil, the bloody ZX-81's crashed again". It's impossible to be artistically creative when a house-full of teenage lobotomies are lounging around and laughing at your embarrassing attempts to come up with new songs.

Saturdays became our only refuge from this constant stream of interruptions. The band-formerly-known-as-the-Wasps embarked on their very own magical mystery bike rides around West Sussex, setting off in pre-arranged directions to remote or deserted minor landmarks in Chichester's countryside. When safely out of sight of the general public, Phil and I would meaningfully decant from bicycles and scrawl some pretentious lyrics about an old wall or derelict building. At this point it would invariably start raining and we would then get very wet while cycling home.

The not-Wasps (I give up) were struggling to put their dreams into action. Surely hard graft and disappointment weren't designed to be part of the musician's lot, were they? We avoided such questions and fantasised that we were already famous, interviewing each other for an imaginary NME feature. Pretending to smoke cigarettes, we lounged around in cheap sunglasses and proudly revealed our innermost hopes and dreams for world peace and the re-incarnation of John Lennon.

LIFT OFF! FIRST DOGS IN SPACE

Saturday 11th February 1984 was the day that everything changed. Excitement had finally decided to show us a good time. Thanks to those boozetastic part-time jobs, our gang of light-fingered desperados had all the cigarettes, johnnies and party nibbles one could ever wish for. On top of this we were in possession of enough alcohol to fill a modest-sized reservoir. On the evening of our first soirée, about a dozen of my closest male acquaintances congregated at the flat and impatiently awaited the arrival of those female guests of honour.

Kevin from Blurred Vision showed up and dropped some cheap speed into my green tin of Heineken. Disappointingly, the drugs didn't seem to have any immediate effect and my mind remained completely free of blue elephants and talking sideboards. While storming up and down the flat at a frenetic pace, I naively surmised that the powder must have been dud. Chewing on my fingernails, I gabbled impatiently at anyone within earshot.

By 8.35 pm, there was still no sign of our female entourage. Ed Wheatley had a strange, detached look in his eye that said all hell was just about to break loose. Either that or he was going to wee in the fruit bowl again. Joey smoked a makeshift reefer constructed from the finest mixed herbs and spices, whilst Phil shouted obscenities over the balcony. Jake lost the plot completely and poured several cans of very weak bitter over his own newly adapted Rockabilly hairstyle as Andy practised his kissing on the bathroom mirror. The troops were growing restless and my heart was beating like a hundred-metre sprinter stuck in fast-forward. I feared that our party may turn bum-fuck ugly if things continued on the same trajectory. Several acquaintances were already concerned that they may not be able to manage an erection if they carried on drinking at the current rate of knots, with one clueless novice even admitting to having already taken the precaution of attaching a rubber to his miniature member of parliament. By this time I was speaking so quickly that I needed an interpreter.

Moments before the most sexually charged alpha-male could pounce on the weakest link in the assembled teenage food chain, Phil's doorbell rang again and a relieved cheer went up from those fearing the worst for their bottoms. From three floors up on a wet winter's night, our world was just about to become a whole lot of colourful.

In truth, by the time they arrived the girls were visibly in an even worse state than the boys, and after a quick bout of Kamikaze spirits drinking the inevitable pairing off took place. Joey tactically feigned clinical depression and sat alone outside of the toilet, hoping to secure attention and a sympathy snog. Unluckily for him, everybody simply chose to avoid his indecipherable wailing and the clueless hippy ended up being used as a human draft excluder for the best part of the evening. There he lay with a bottle of gin in one hand, fake spliff in the other; still seemingly content to look up girls' skirts whenever they stepped over his prostrate body on their way to the loo.

I too, ended up in the WC, thanks to my conquest Rosalind thoughtfully throwing up every thirty seconds. The speed in my veins had led the pair of us into a detached conversation that kept me thinking I might partake in a raunchy kissing session the moment she stopped forcibly evacuating the contents of her stomach into the bathroom sink.

After what felt like an eternity, but which was probably no longer than a few minutes, I left Roz alone with the remnants of her regurgitated supper to revel in the chaos currently on display in Phil's lovely home. Discarded bottles of booze turned carpets into sodden playing fields, while valuable antiques were ripped from walls with drunken abandon. Teenage bodies wobbled about on the roof of the building in near-gale force winds, whilst several couples hurriedly disappeared into vacant bedrooms.

44

Unfortunately, I had to go back to the bathroom and resume my janitorial chores with the still-barfing Roz. But at least I could hear the devastation.

Eventually, Phil's horrified parents returned home to a sticky mess of hormonal discharge. The evening quickly ground to a halt. Shame-faced teens were banished back into the night whence they came and the rest of us were forced into helping clear up.

On the following Monday morning we re-grouped in the girls' common room to relive boozy tales hazily recalled from the weekend's activities. One evening of Herculean drinking had miraculously cured my shyness towards the opposite sex. Indeed, Phil's party was deemed such a raging success that we held several others just like it throughout the early months of 1984. Strangely, not one of the girls ever offered their own family homes for such a pillaging.

Of course, it didn't take long for me to start bragging about our band, although those wild claims that we were the best group in the world somewhat backfired when some of our new female friends asked if we would perform at the next party. Not wanting to lose face, I was forced to talk the reluctant Phil into playing our first live gig. Since meeting the girls he had become noticeably quieter, and was scared stiff of having to sing in front of an audience.

But I managed to talk him into it…

AKE

On Saturday 3rd March 1984, Phil and I played live for the first time. Dismally, we had ended up calling ourselves 'Ake'. If memory serves me correctly, it was me that suggested both the shit name and its very rock'n'roll spelling defect. Seriously? I should have been shot.

We had actually intended to make our debut at the previous weekend's party, but after downing three-quarters of a bottle of Pernod in less than half an hour, my shy friend had been able to locate neither his mind nor his guitar.

And so, at the second attempt, 'Ake' performed in a tiny living room to about eight cider-swilling friends, most of who were far too busy practising the slobbery art of snogging to pay much attention to the noisy divvies in the corner. Phil careered through every song at breakneck speed, whilst I just stood there behind my portable keyboard, trying to look bored. My only real musical function was to constantly increase the tempo on my 'Rock-1' pre-set to match the pace of my drunken counterpart. From where I stood, edging as far forwards as possible, Phil didn't seem to be enjoying himself a great deal. He forgot most of my obtuse lyrics and struggled valiantly with an out-of-tune guitar, not to mention my frequent selection of a wrong note. Still resembling a cut-price Pet Shop Boys playing different songs at the same time, naturally we cleared the room of all but the most incapacitated in a matter of seconds.

Phil developed an immediate and life-long aversion to playing live, while I revelled in the feeling of partial notoriety. Parading about the party in fingerless gloves and a pair of Andy Partridge round sunglasses, I drank superhuman amounts of Bacardi and attempted to cure lepers with my Jesus touch. At the end of the evening, I loaned out the only copy of our demo to a couple of sozzled girls who had arrived too late to see us play. This tape happened to include some of our most crap songs recorded 'live' to a ghetto blaster. On several of these numbers you could clearly hear Phil's mum hoovering in the background. Anyway, the girls lost the cassette on their way home and the memory of 'Ake' vanished along with it.

Thank God for small mercies.

FELL IN LOVE WITH A GIRL

Over the following weeks our party crew decamped to the Girls' school to drink alcohol out of thermos flasks - such a simple but fool proof way of making sure the teachers never caught us. The girls simply got on with their studies and largely ignored the giggling idiots standing on the next table.

I fell in love for the first time, but it would be months before I realized. To make matters worse, the object of my affections wasn't even the girl I was going out with. No sir, they were aimed at her best friend who just so happened to be going out with my best mate. Kate and I would meet secretly by the canal to discuss this grim teenage complication and every time we did a chemical reaction exploded in my head and heart. But we resigned ourselves to the fact that we just couldn't cheat on our partners and ruin long-standing friendships. But inside all I wanted to do was kiss her. It was a typically fraught teen love affair and after a while I just gave up and unwisely started snogging another girl from the party gang. Soon after the whole thing began to implode and in true student fashion our perilous relationships frayed and the party locations quickly dried up.

But make no mistake. It was great whilst it lasted.

► chapter four

STRAIGHT BACK DOWN TO EARTH

You remember earlier I mentioned the Tory party? Well, the very day I left school I suddenly became so much more aware of what life under the Conservatives was really all about. Strong-armed into one of those criminal £25-a-week Youth Training Schemes, suddenly I was both skint and unhappily working at Hargreaves Sports. Plans to carry on skiving at the local technical college had run aground and due to my estrangement from Phil and several other key friends, all hopes of putting a band together looked hopeless. Sure, I managed to cajole Rob and Andy into starting a group, but everybody misheard our name as 'Nice Boys' instead of 'Night Boys' (stolen, of course, from the Talk Talk song *Call In the Night Boys*). Around this time, TT's *It's My Life* album was a hugely important record for me, as it offered an escape route to the grey box I had somehow managed to lock myself inside of.

Anyway, when those Night Boy rehearsals started to get in the way of my friends' football commitments, the band went out the window. And I was back at square one. Again.

MR. DISCO

The only decent thing about working at Hargreaves was reacquainting with Mark Mason, an old school buddy that until now I have failed to introduce you to. Mark and I had sat next to each other in various lessons at school, back when his favourite artists were Blondie and Kim Wilde. During those long, slow days at the store we re-bonded over our mutual love of all things music and started venturing out to gigs together.

The Night Boys 1985
(l-r Simon Parker, Andrew Howick, Robert Wheeler)

TOP 5 GIGS I ATTENDED WITH MARK IN 1985/6

1. Talk Talk (London, Hammersmith Odeon)
2. Prefab Sprout (Portsmouth Guildhall)
3. The Housemartins (Brighton Event)
4. Psychedelic Furs (Brighton Centre)
5. Salad from Atlantis / Little Charmers (This was a very rare gig staged in our hometown at the New Park Road Community Centre. Both of these bands were locally sourced and VERY indie.)

Note: It has been bought to my attention (by Mark) **that I also attended Go West at the Hammersmith Odeon** way back in late 1985. Mark feels that I am still too much of a musical snob to admit to having been present at this show as I never mention it in public. I hope that by writing this in bold type you can all see what idiots we were back then.

It should also be noted that Mark Mason is the only living person to witness every band that I have ever been a member of. In fact, on one of his first visits to my house (for tea in 1982) I subjected the poor bugger to some thoroughly tuneless showing off on my portable keyboard.

Dressed in our Peter Stores' finest (think Millets only cheaper), Mark and I spent long, electric evenings of 1985/6 frugging to the latest offerings from Echo and the Bunnymen and Sisters of Mercy. In the company of Liza Lambert and Sue Marsh (two bored college students, who at the time were both busy rueing the fact they had ever cited Chichester as one of their study destinations), we could all be found enthusiastically hopping from leg to leg, free of the local populous and its undying love for all things Level 42 and Lionel Richie. The campus beer may have been warm, but it flowed cheaply and long into the night. The Smiths' *This Charming Man* received the most rapturous response of that life-affirming evening in the Uni bar, when the whole room suddenly came alive with would-be Morrissey's pirouetting across the dance floor as if their jeans were on fire.

THE CURE

Around this time my love affair with The Cure really kicked in. I had been orbiting their world for a good while by now, and secretly I had always wanted an exploding plant pot hairstyle like the one Robert Smith owned. But it wasn't until the video to *In Between Days* in the summer of 1985 that everything finally fell into place for The Cure and me. To put it simply, I became deeply smitten and revamped my entire wardrobe to pledge allegiance to the Crawley wonder boys. I rifled through those undiscovered charity shops for over-sized suit jackets and starched white shirts. I also invested in some Hi-Tec basketball boots from the sports shop where I was working. It was a strange look for someone selling 'Ivan Lendl' tennis wear.

MY TOP TEN CURE TRACKS OF ALL TIME
(In no particular order)

Plainsong (Disintegration)
Catch (Kiss Me, Kiss Me, Kiss Me)
A Strange Day (Pornography)
Open (Live at Bestival)
The End of the World (The Cure)
Untitled (Disintegration)
Cut Here (Galore)
Bird Mad Girl (The Top)
Lost (The Cure)
Out of This World (Bloodflowers)

Local meathead majority rule decreed that I had to withstand prolonged bouts of ridicule for daring to dress or think a little differently, but luckily man-mountain Robbie Wheeler decided to go the 'way of The Cure' at the same time, so at least pub bullies had to think twice before actually smashing my face in.

As the decade became more about plastic music and fake wine bar culture, The Cure remained a beacon of light in an oncoming tidal wave of shit. Delving into their back catalogue became the perfect antidote to the jazzy nonsense and bombastic ballads that Radio One served up on a daily basis.

Running parallel to this was a thriving singles market, spearheaded by two of England's best bands.

MADNESS vs. THE SMITHS

(THE SINGLES APPRECIATION CLUB)

The era of the 'great singles' band is most commonly associated with the 1960s. The 80s often tend to get overlooked. But from where I'm sitting (just a few feet from my record collection), there were many artists who chalked up an impressive back catalogue during this era. Obviously, we need to start with the band that made the 7" single really sexy again.

THE SMITHS

During a brief but illuminating career, The Smiths racked up seventeen utterly mesmerizing singles. These fabled recordings would quickly launch the independent attitude as a way of life for a new wave of impoverished students and thrift shop individualists everywhere. It became perfectly acceptable to be a pale, shy and skinny type with a penchant for sitting in an empty cemetery just so long as no one actually caught you doing it.

In the charismatic form of Steven Patrick Morrissey, we, the downtrodden teenage masses, had finally elected a new spokesperson - and the most influential one since Johnny Rotten re-energized a nation of wasted youth back in the mid-70s. The seismic importance of The Smiths should never be underplayed, as the band conquered hearts and charts in a decade famed for glossy over-production. But the sound of Manchester's finest owed more to a bygone golden era of the old fashioned 'beat combo'. This had absolutely nothing to do with the clunking noises modernity of Fairlights and Synclaviers. How could this be? The short-lived symmetry between Morrissey and Johnny Marr burned white-hot for a brief moment in pop history. It has still to be bettered decades after the band's untimely demise. Within just a little over four hyper-creative years, The Smiths became immortal and Morrissey as important to disenfranchised indie kids of the 80s as Elvis had been to the bored teens of pre-rock'n'roll 1950s. And let us not forget Johnny Marr who is still widely regarded as the number one guitarist of his generation.

The Smiths - every home should have one.

MADNESS

But everyone of a certain age or musical persuasion knows that The Smiths were an ace singles band, and it's worth remembering that Madness gave birth to 21 consecutively brilliant singles between September 1979 and October 1985. Far too much is made of the band's lively cartoon persona, and too little is spoken of the group's beady-eye for those tiny peculiarities of everyday life in good old Blighty. Ray Davies and Paul Weller may get all the plaudits regarding everything cool Britannia, but Madness bought just as much to this party. Once the band stopped being funny for the sake of it they released a clutch of melancholy singles that cut straight to the heart of the matter without the need for too much monkey business and flying sax players.

MY TOP FIVE MADNESS SINGLES

1. Michael Caine
2. One Better Day
3. The Sun and the Rain
4. Our House
5. Grey Day

History reminds us that The Nutty Boys were just a fond memory by 1987. Coincidentally, The Smiths disappeared in the same year. Pop music's nadir, maybe? From what I remember the general public was far too busy turning its attentions toward the mindless conveyor belt grot that would soon drag the rest of the decade into disgrace.

And this was why independent music stepped up and announced itself.

WHY I LOVE INDIE MUSIC

By the mid-80s, the UK music scene was undergoing something of a mini-revolution. Part funded by the comparative ease of signing on during the era of Mrs Thatcher's unemployed scrapheap, D.I.Y. bands were busy trawling the country in untaxed transit vans, where they played in dingy clubs and cellars to small clusters of like-minded music enthusiasts. A lot of this audience was also unemployed and busy with their own fledgling groups. It felt like a secret community for creative people. We laughed at the very idea of 'Yuppie culture'. Idiots. The burgeoning independent spirit so well documented by NME's 'C-86' compilation fast attracted new recruits up and down the country. Indie became street cool and the thing to aspire to, even though this meant little more than a floppy fringe and two or three haphazard chords thrown together on a slightly out of tune guitar. It was all about the attitude. Fuck those chinless wonders in their ugly suits and expensive cars!

This was also a time when music papers were crucial to one's musical knowledge. Without the aid of the Internet we all religiously followed and never questioned NME, Melody Maker and the soon to be kaput, Sounds. And even when their reviews were woefully wide off the mark (i.e. quite often) I would never hold it against the magazine in question. This is what being a fan of indie was all about. A communal spirit and a never say die (or tune up) attitude...

Fanzines were the information centres for those horrified by mainstream shockers like Paul Hardcastle and Chris De Burgh. Being indie marked you out as someone happy to take a stand against the greedy, soulless Tories. And this is kind of why I pledged allegiance - obviously it helped that the music was so great, but being indie offered a sense of identity and the reassurance that no matter how crap I might have been feeling about existing in a dead end town like Chichester, I was always safe amongst invisible friends up and down the country.

Although I had not yet been able to form a proper group of my own, at least I now looked the part. The shambling ethos of indie pop gave every struggling musician hope for the future. And that was a lifeline to people like me.

TOP TEN 'SPIRIT OF INDIE' BANDS

1. The Smiths
2. Primal Scream
3. The Pastels
4. New Order
5. Tallulah Gosh
6. The Wedding Present
7. The Soup Dragons
8. The Chesterfields
9. The Shop Assistants
10. The Brilliant Corners

Drinking became a vital distraction from the day-to-day drudgery of working for a living. By now I was earning a half-decent wage after somehow enlisting as a Civil Servant at the Ministry of Agriculture. I knew that my life was seriously off-track but Chichester's endless succession of drinking establishments delayed me from actually getting off my arse and doing something about it. Therein lies the tale of many well-intentioned souls who get hopelessly side-tracked from their dreams by the lure of pub culture. Between the years of 1986-8 drinking would continually plague my own progression.

Eventually, my indie attitude would save me from the abyss. But before that could happen, things had to get considerably worse.

STRANGE DAYS

Following a chance encounter in the town centre, Phil Bennett and I belatedly resumed our friendship and occasional song writing duties. By now Phil's parents were renting out the penthouse flat to a collection of grubby students, with Phil resolutely entrenched in one of the bedrooms. Even though the place was literally falling apart around us, within the sanctity of his four walls we started work on a primitive batch of demos that cast us as Simon and Garfunkel sporting a personality disorder. Jake pitched in with some stellar guitar work and we became a 'proper' unit for the first time. Alas, Phil's mental state had remained rather delicate, with a mixture of bad trips and a genetic tendency for depression bearing down on him. He was always nervy and on edge - like he was waiting for something very bad to happen. This began to affect how I was feeling and without realizing it, my own state of mind became foggy. Something wasn't quite right.

Christening our band 'October' and the demo tape *Fallen*, Phil misinterpreted my mock-up of the sleeve design and somehow we became 'October Fallen' instead. This shows just how little we were able to communicate at the time, and as town psychos and vagrants pillaged the flat for stuff to sell, things began to feel very bleak. Childhood lasts longer than we ever dare admit, but watching the Jesus Freaks and social fuck-ups routinely destroy Phil's home told me in no uncertain terms that the world in which we were now operating was very different to the one we had just departed. Our friendship struggled amongst the chaos, and once again Phil and I drifted apart. This was a real shame as some of the songs on our demo were pretty good. In particular *The Curse*, *Silver* and *The Witching Hour* showed that we had come a long way since those earliest of compositions about Yoko Ono farting on John Lennon's head.

But I made for the pubs and Phil retreated to the countryside. Once we had finished the demo there would be no more October Fallen. Mentally, neither of us was in a particularly good place, but Phil's problems were more serious and long term. Although he'll stick around this story for a little while longer, Phil had little desire to pursue music as a way out of his personal demons. And that became the major difference between the pair of us. I soldiered on with the day-to-day, questioning whether I really wanted to spend the rest of my life in meaningless employment, but always hopeful that music would find a way to rescue me. My favourite albums were *Infected* by The The and The Cure's *Pornography*. Family and friends remarked how ill I was starting to look, so I avoided being in anyone's company for longer than was absolutely necessary.

Depression is a powerful yet subtle beast. Its only desire is to destroy you from within. Loved ones become problems best not faced, whilst well-meaning friends are regarded as the enemy. In your head, nothing is as important as the solitude you crave, and the illness steadily grows by feeding off of an estrangement that develops between your personal problems and interaction with other human beings.

Although I had been vaguely aware of a growing sense of unhappiness, I would never have dreamed that I was experiencing an actual depression. In truth, I was running away from the fact that I had made such a mess of my young life. If it hadn't been for my mother's intervention it's pretty certain I would have become a real lost cause. But, by talking things through and confronting issues, I started to see a way forward even though my hopes and dreams looked as though they were never going to happen. Drinking was still very appealing to me and within the social whirl of bar hopping lay the inevitable romances. I ended up in a two-and-a-half-year relationship with Joanne from the Catering Course. What started as an innocent pub conversation steadily became ever-more suffocating as the weeks turned into months. In the end I was only saved from marriage by a bizarre case of mistaken identity at one of my locals. One afternoon I got talking to Sally, the new copper-haired barmaid from the White Horse who lopsidedly confessed to harbouring a secret crush on me since school days. The only problem with this was that I absolutely knew we hadn't been at school together. She was at least three years younger than me and didn't even go to Chichester High School. Try as I might to tell her she was getting me mixed up with someone else (ok, I didn't try that hard), Sally flatly refused to believe me and we ended up arranging to meet after she finished her first shift at the pub. At around seven that evening, just a mere four hours after our first encounter, Sally's dad rang to say that his daughter had indeed made a grave error and that she would not be going out on a date with me now, or at any time in the future. Brilliant.

Unfortunately, five minutes prior to our date I had finally summoned up the courage and telephoned my girlfriend Joanne to let her know that we were finally over. Sally's unexpected interest had thrown back the curtains on how dysfunctional our relationship really was and it felt easy to call and impart the bad news knowing somebody else was interested. The relief I felt in ending our doomed romance far outweighed the disappointment of being dumped so unceremoniously by the possibly insane Sally and I never actually got around to being angry with her. I simply took it to mean that an invisible guardian angel had decided to call time on Joanne and me from the warm and hazy confines of the White Horse pub. Soon afterwards I was offered a job as the Manager of Linkins Sports (which sold cool surf and ski wear) and things started looking up. My bosses loved drinking and thought nothing about 'borrowing' the previous days takings and spending them in the pub, and it's accurate to say I had the perfect job - not to mention a cheap way of purchasing Converse boots for all my friends.

HERE COME THE GOOD TIMES

We have reached the summer of 1988, and against all odds my musical prospects are about to improve dramatically. What follows is a musical expedition that will span the remainder of the 20th century and then further on into the next millennium. Some of the groups that I am about to inhabit will be destined for more than their fair share of bump and grinds up against the record industry's flabby torso. In fact, I will come perilously close to penetration on more than one occasion.

At last I had arrived at the rusty gates of rock and roll. Now all I had to do was figure out a way of breaking in...

TOP 10 1980s ALBUMS NOW DUE FOR CRITICAL RE-EVALUATION

1. Kate Bush - The Dreaming
2. XTC - Mummer
3. Pale Fountains - From Across the Kitchen Table
4. ABC - Beauty Stab
5. Aztec Camera - Knife
6. Big Audio Dynamite - This is Big Audio Dynamite
7. The Chameleons - What Does Anything Mean? Basically
8. Psychedelic Furs - Forever Now
9. Del Amitri - Del Amitri
10. Julian Cope - World Shut Your Mouth

TOP 10 VAGUELY OBSCURE 'FOLLOW UP' SINGLES PURCHASED IN THE 1980s

1. The Members -Working Girl
2. Split Enz - Nobody Takes Me Seriously Anyway
3. The Mobiles - Amour Amour
4. It's Immaterial - Rope
5. ABC - S.O.S.
6. Intaferon - Steamhammer Sam
7. Dollar - Give Me Back My Heart
8. China Crisis - Scream Down At Me
9. Thomas Dolby - I Scare Myself
10. Furniture - Love Your Shoes

▶ chapter five

START!

My determination to get a proper musical project airborne suddenly shifted up a gear. The time had finally come to harangue various friends into buying instruments and learn how to play as we went along.

THE NAME OF THIS BAND IS…FRANTIC HEADS (1988)

Andy Howick decided that he quite liked the idea of being famous and recklessly blew the best part of his first decent pay packet on a second-hand drum kit. Ed Wheatley appeared keen to learn the guitar and was drafted in at the same time. Importantly, Ed and I also embarked upon reconnaissance missions to the nearby South Downs where we would smoke pot and hatch plans in his Fiat Rustbucket.

Incidentally, 'Ed' wasn't our guitarist's real name. Oh no. He was born 'Ian', but unfortunately, the poor bugger happened to look strikingly similar to Prince Edward, Earl of Wessex. And so the nickname stuck.

Jake Tully bore little resemblance to any member of the royal family past or present, but was still hovering on the outskirts of our social circle and stepped forwards to offer his considerable services as lead guitarist. I even managed to delicately cajole Phil Bennett into contributing part-time keyboards with a solemn promise that he could stand at the back in complete darkness. I ended up with the bass guitar for the simple reason that no one else had any interesting in learning how to play it. But at least it came from the guitar family and I could indulge my Simon Gallup bass worshipping activities, so I willingly gave it a go. During our first rehearsal as a five-piece, we recorded one of my songs, *The Return,* as an instrumental because nobody could play and sing at the same time. Despite suspect time keeping issues and the bass player hitting several wrong notes, the track came out a bit like The Cure and I was transported to heaven. Why hadn't I tried this approach earlier? After years of dithering, Frantic Heads had come together in just a matter of days.

Of course, Frantic Heads was an awful name, offspring of a combination of Andy Howick and me if memory serves, which in this case it clearly doesn't. Anyway, I'm not taking all the blame for this one. At the next rehearsal, Ed gallantly stepped up to the microphone (another of Jake's buzzing monstrosities, but hey, beggars can't be choosers) and suddenly we were a fully functioning noise machine.

Among the first songs we ever wrote were *Spinning Out*, *The Girl from Last Summer* and *Waiting for the Next Move*. They weren't classics - but they were certainly a big step in the right direction.

She came on a promise, from a whisper on the wind
She took my breath she took my heart on the last day of
Spring
Wo-oh-oh, send summer through my veins
She's with me now she's everywhere again.

('Girl From Last Summer'. Simon Parker/Frantic Heads. 1988. With thanks to Vaughn Hewitt for his drunken assistance with the song title).

Like most new bands, Frantic Heads relied heavily on other people's material. Hence the slightly rickety version of The Cure's *The Perfect Girl* and a virtually unrecognizable take on The Monkee's *I'm A Believer*. Andy had real trouble with the rhythm on this one and often used to end up putting a snare beat where the kick drum ought to be, lending the song a peculiar lurching quality not apparent in the original.

Undaunted by our lack of ability, we diligently rehearsed once a week in a classroom at the back of the Arun Leisure Centre. It was here that we struggled with the basics of keeping in time while trying not to laugh at Joey Rowe's funny little Mod dance, the poor guy now dressed in what looked suspiciously like Rob and Andy's old cast offs.

ONE ABSOLUTE CLASSIC 80s ALBUM LONG SINCE FORGOTTEN...

Big Dipper - Craps [Homestead Records 1988]

Ok, so I know it isn't exactly the greatest album title in the world, but *Craps* was/is a record of sublime indie pop. Generally overlooked since its brief appearance in the racks during 1988, I constantly referenced this album whilst attempting to learn how to play and write with Frantic Heads.

At the time, Big Dipper was pretty much unknown outside of the indie inner circle. Part of a loose-knit scene based around Boston, U.S.A, most of the band members had been in other bands with exotic names like Dumptruck. The Pixies were spawned from the same scene and, of course went on to get signed, while most of the other Boston bands remained in obscurity. But Big Dipper stood out, if for no other reason than the fact that they had good songs and tasteless shirts. Which back in the 80s was a total must in indie.

To these ears Big Dipper were distant musical cousins to the (then) fairly oddball R.E.M. Thoughtfully sparse and harmonically left of centre, *Craps* pitted lean and off-kilter melodies against some wilfully obscure lyrical references that weren't so far removed from Michael Stipe's cryptic way with a non-rhyming couplet or three. In part Johnny Marr jangle (*Meet the Witch*), Big Dipper mixed psychedelic pop (*Semjase*) with a blast of Pixies savagery (*A Song to be Beautiful*). My favourite track was *Bonnie*, a wistful and understated gem that still has the ability to reduce me to a blubbering wreck.

Over the next few months I kept meaning to write to main man Gary Waleik at the correspondence address detailed on the sleeve, but I could never actually think of anything interesting to say above the usual 'I bought your album and liked it very much' nonsense. Knowing this just wouldn't do, I ended up forgetting all about it. But as the years rolled by *Craps* remained a firm favourite, and I began to regret not having scrawled a note in clumsy praise to a record that still occupies a little corner of my heart all to itself.

Hopefully, I've just rectified that.

As a post-script to this love letter to Big Dipper, a while back I stumbled upon a fan-site in the overcrowded cyber world. Thinking that very little would come of making contact and adding Big Dipper as a Myspace friend (outside of a cursory email from an obsessive uber-fan located somewhere outside Bumboil, Nebraska), I was amazed when lead singer Gary Waliek responded to my email. I duly sent him my review of *Craps* and finally got to show the guy just how much his band's record had meant to me, some nineteen years after I had first thought of dropping him a line. For the record, Gary seemed quite pleased with my belated review, but is firmly of the opinion that both *Heavens* and *Boo-Boo* are the bands best works.

You can now make your own decision because the ever-reliable Merge Records have recently released a tasty career-spanning compilation called *Supercluster*. Remarkably, just as I was finishing this story the band released their first new album since 1990. So go check out the excellent *Crashes on the Platinum Planet*. It's great to have them back.

LIVE! TONIGHT! NOT SOLD OUT!

On a pleasant Friday afternoon in September of 1988, Frantic Heads were hard at work on a particularly tricky section of The Cure's *Boys Don't Cry* (you know, that bit where it goes dah-dah-dah-darr right at the end). Mike Monk, the Leisure Centre's cavalier general manager, suddenly appeared at the classroom door and sidled in to nod along with our lumpy but promising take on the song.

I have a feeling that the poor man was blissfully unaware that we were playing a cover version, and this may explain what happened next...

MIKE MONK: (tapping his foot and acting in the manner of an annoying Uncle pretending to be the hip relation at a family wedding) 'Great song guys-don't suppose you fancy playing a gig here at the Leisure Centre, do you?'
FRANTIC HEADS: (trying not to look shocked) 'YEAH!!'
MIKE MONK: 'Fantastic! I'm trying to update the image of this place and reckon that live music is the way forward. You dudes dig?'
(Disclaimer; I can't swear that these were his actual words, but there was always a sprinkling of outdated 'jive talk' threatening to capsize the conversation whenever Mike engaged us in meaningless pleasantries on our way in and out of the centre).
FRANTIC HEADS: 'Errr, pardon?'
MIKE MONK (leaving the room): 'Ha ha! That's the spirit. Anarchy in the United Kingdom, right? Oh, one little thing - I take it that you have enough songs to play for about an hour and a half?'
ED {lying): 'Oh yeah, sure thing Mike... Don't suppose there's any chance of a free can of coke each is there?'
MIKE MONK (flatly, and from a distance): 'No.'

My band had just been booked for its real first gig. And we didn't even have to beg. When Frantic Heads arrived for their next rehearsal, Mike dropped in again to proudly unveil a poster that he had just designed for the show.

There, for the first time ever, sat the immortal words FRANTIC HEADS right at the top of the page. Resplendent in big, bold letters, it even appeared that the centre was going to charge people to come in and watch us. At this rate we were going to be rich and famous by the end of the year.

Still, it was a bit of a shame that the rest of Mike's creative efforts depicted a very cosmic-looking rainbow erupting out of the end of a twin-headed electric guitar. And even more of a shame that this hackneyed image was glued to a disproportionately tiny cut out figure of a grimacing hairy rock singer (circa 1973/4), wincing painfully as though he had just disturbed a particularly irritable case of bum grapes. No sir, this certainly wasn't the image that an up-and-coming indie band should ever think of employing.

But being the nice blokes that we were, we said 'Thanks very much' and left Mike to skip off and stick up a couple of his hilarious monstrosities around the centre. Of course, our entrepreneurial friend was blissfully unaware that such an unsightly creation would almost certainly scare off any potential gig-goer foolish enough to gaze upon his photocopied disaster. But we never thought that at the time. Amazingly, we also failed to question the fact that Frantic Heads had been booked to perform in a sports hall some ten miles east of our hometown. We naively imagined that a large and appreciative audience would simply materialise out of thin air and take us to their hearts... in a place where they never staged anything other than squash tournaments or the occasional coffee morning for the over 65 brigade.

I ask you, we deserved to be humiliated, didn't we?

This then, was how Frantic Heads came to play their first show to seven people, five of whom were our most faithful mates. The 'rest' of the audience turned out to be a slightly unusual young couple that remained frozen right at the back of the impossibly large hall for the whole evening. From the spaced-out looks upon their glazed white faces, it was possible that these mysterious lovebirds had ingested a mind-altering drug of impressive stature earlier in the day. Still, as Eddie rightly pointed out, at least they had paid to get in.

Undeterred by such trivialities as not being very popular, Frantic Heads began the gig by employing a trusty old rock cliché. Taking to the stage one at a time, we made our audience feel obliged to applaud each individual member as they walked out from behind a see through curtain and start to play. With the lights still off, Phil slid on incognito and treated everybody to some psychedelic keyboards that only really made sense inside his own tortured head. Andy Howick took to the drum stool and crashed in when those Eno-esque parts started getting a little bit too avant-garde for their own good. At this point, the song sped up by at least ten beats-per-minute. I was next to grace the stage and lumbered on to share the minimum of musical ability with my faithful friends in the front row. Actually, come to think of it, this was the only row. I enthusiastically hacked at the 'E' string on my bass for all I was worth as it would be a fair while before I knew where any of the notes on those three thinner bits of metal were located. At this point Andy and I became locked in a heated battle to see who could reach the end of the song the quickest. When Ed missed his cue to join us, I looked around and realised that he must have buggered off for a last minute pee. God knows how many times we repeated *The Return*'s four-chord introduction before our singer eventually appeared onstage with the ends of his shirt sticking out of his flies. But, some five or six minutes after Phil's enigmatic entrance, Frantic Heads were in full flight and howling through the Sports Centre like a detuned radio broadcasting the sound of the end of the world.

It should be mentioned at this point that Jake had suspiciously cried off at the last minute due to a 'forgotten' family engagement. In the absence of our lead guitarist's ability to deftly take control whenever Eddie wasn't singing, Phil did his best to fill in the many holes in our sound via a vast array of squelching and fizzing synthesizer noises that, at best, conflicted with the vocals, but which also scared the life out of those mortified sweethearts cowering in the shadows at the very back of the hall.

Bathed in the flickering whispers of a set of borrowed disco lights, I quickly forgot all about any disappointment at playing to a carload of mates who had one eye on last orders back in Chichester. Instead, I felt the God-given power of live music surge through my veins and furnish me with the ability to rock like a mutha-humpa. Throwing some nifty moves into the equation whenever I got the chance, this hindered my ability to hit the right notes, but did give the impression that I had a donkey's dick swinging between my legs.

The complete Frantic Heads repertoire actually consisted of less than twenty minutes of live material (including those unrecognisable cover versions I told you about). So, to 'pad things out a bit' we were forced to repeat the whole bloody set to get anywhere near the time Mike had requested. By the end of the third version of *The Return* it felt as if Frantic Heads had the entire audience on their side, or rather, would have done if five out of seven of them hadn't been already been heading towards the car park, united in the vain hope of catching that final round of the night back at the Hole In The Wall in Chichester.

An hour or so later, the band was still buzzing on the after show adrenalin and chatting excitedly about playing live again in the very near future. But by the following morning, when our enthusiasm had been dampened by the stark realisation that the show had been an under-achieving disaster, we couldn't even bring ourselves to darken the leisure centre's doorstep again. Although this wasn't too much of a hardship (most of Frantic Heads went pale at the very thought of exercise), disappointingly we had just lost our much needed rehearsal room.

Still, it had been a beginning for Frantic Heads. I had a band at long last.

Frantic Heads 1988
(l-r Simon Parker, Ian 'Ed' Wheatley, Andrew Howick
- Philip Bennet not in shot)

TALK TALK - SPIRIT OF EDEN

Monday September 24th 1988.

Following the success of the *Colour of Spring* album, tour and associated singles, there had been very little news from the Talk Talk camp. Rumours of a live record and an accompanying video had come to nothing, with a small army of anxious Mark Hollis fanatics like me nervously awaiting another batch of shows. As it would later transpire, I had already witnessed one of the bands last-ever gigs, way back in May of 1986.

So, by the autumn of 1988, an uneasy feeling had started to take root. What if Talk Talk had simply split up and not thought to tell anybody? It was quite possible, as lead vocalist Mark Hollis always seemed to be arguing with everyone.

Advertisements for the group's fourth album, due to be released on 24th September 1988, and preceded by the words 'other-worldly' and 'ethereal', went a long way to placating my fears about the band's imminent demise but only added to the mounting suspense and apprehension. Would I like their reputed new direction? Would they be using more unpronounceable instrumentation? And, perhaps more importantly, would Mark Hollis ever take off his sunglasses again?

On the morning of release, I purchased both the vinyl long player and chrome cassette of Talk Talk's fourth offering on my way to work at the sports shop. I then spent nine very long hours thinking about nothing else but what *Spirit of Eden* might sound like when I eventually got it back home. In my head I was worried: I couldn't help but notice that the album only had six songs on it. Had I waited over two years for so little? What if all the tracks were rubbish, or worse still, very short?

At approximately 5.37pm, I finally wedged the cassette into my cheap car stereo system. The drive home from work usually took me no longer than a few minutes, but on this memorable evening I would end up driving in circles for ages.

Spirit of Eden unfurled with one long, slow and mysterious swish of the curtain. Well, it did after I had saved those delicate spools of tape from the savage jaws of my ruthless car stereo every time I took a corner at too steep an angle.

First impressions told me that the songs on *Spirit...* were very different to what I had been expecting. Side one contained three 'pieces' that eerily morphed into one another. This gave listeners the impression they were listening to one very long song. Apparently, these three tracks utilise key-changes similar to those found in opera. Alas, this tiny piece of information would have been totally lost on me back in 1988. All I could tell was that there were no rousing choruses or familiar Talk Talk trademarks. In fact, I might very well have been listening to another band entirely if it hadn't been for Mark Hollis' voice. And even that resembled a ghostly apparition beaming in from another planet. On first inspection, *The Spirit of Eden* appeared to have been made by spectral beings with no

69

regard for pop songs. I was confused but intrigued to go further, realizing that here was another of those musical 'eureka' moments.

As darkness swallowed the early evening sky over Parklands, I found myself careering up and down the estate like a lost lunatic. Eventually, I dared turn the cassette over to side two. When *I Believe in You* drifted through the speakers, I froze in stunned amazement, prisoner in my car and automatically rewinding as the last choral voice faded away into the tape hiss. Never have I been so instantly floored by a piece of music. If anyone asks, *I Believe in You* is the track that I would most like played at my funeral. Well, that and *Thoughts of You* by Dennis Wilson.

Spirit of Eden is a maverick work of fragile beauty and brave experimentalism, created at a particularly soulless time in pop history. Stock, Aitken and Waterman may very well have been suffocating the life out of good music with its jaunty jig of shite, but Talk Talk stood firm and defiantly raised its middle digit to all and sundry, seconds before sailing over the edge of the world forever. Of course, in a decade as mercenary as the 80s EMI didn't have a clue how to market an album with no radio singles, and *Spirit...* quickly disappeared from pop's consciousness. I remember seeing copies in the bargain bins of just about every record shop I ever visited during the next couple of years. Nobody was particularly interested in the band's new direction and I had to stop buying copies in the end as I ran out of people to bestow them on. Still, they are worth a fortune today though...

Happily, the album has gone on to cult status with lovers of ambient and progressive music. Talk Talk's fourth album is now routinely regarded as something of a lost classic. It was difficult to see this ever happening at the time, but music is nothing if not full of surprises. Way back then on that woozy September evening in 1988, my musical horizons suddenly freed themselves of borders and rules. Black notes became as important as the white ones. I was ready for the next thing.

ONION JOHNNY [1988/9]

It's mortifying to have to follow details of Talk Talk's single-minded masterpiece with the embarrassing news that I was just about to rename our band 'Onion Johnny'.

Late 80s indie street fashions usually dictated the wearing of a black and white striped t-shirt, standard issue black Levi jeans, poncey beret or cap and the obligatory pair of Doctor Marten shoes. Around this time, Sarah Records was in full-flight and bands like Tallulah Gosh were not to be sniffed at. So I toed the party line and chose to dress accordingly.

Unfortunately, Andy Howick's father wasn't particularly clued up to the preferred alternative music uniform of the day and duly nicknamed me 'Onion Johnny', largely on account of the fact that he thought my outfit looked a wee bit French. Latent racism? Well yes, possibly, but you should have heard what the French were calling us Brits back then.

Onion Johnny 1988/9
(l-r Philip Bennett, Ian 'Ed' Wheatley, Andrew Howick, Simon Parker)

In April of 1989, Onion Johnny made its Chichester debut at the Fernleigh Centre in North Street. In a poorly lit basement cellar, complete with a deaf old biddy selling chocolate and pop from behind the tuck shop bar, we were about to show the world what we could do with four chords and a shared infatuation with The Cure.

Before show time, all five band members steadied that peculiar feeling of cart-wheeling seasickness with a few swift ales at the Hole In The Wall pub. My mind raced at the prospect of playing a gig in front of a local crowd. Would Ed remember all the lyrics? Would Andy get his beats all upside down again? Would there be enough room for me to throw more cool shapes? Or would we simply get laughed offstage for not being punk rock enough? After all, our band image certainly left a lot to be desired.

Jake (yes, he actually turned up to this one) had elected to wear a homemade pink and yellow psychedelic shirt that looked as if someone had just violently honked up an ocean of raspberry ripple ice cream all over his chest. If this wasn't bad enough, our lead guitarist's effects unit was malfunctioning and fizzled like a bowl of electrocuted Rice Krispies. Ed was unwittingly showing off his genitals thanks to a pair of tatty old jeans that he had been busy growing out of for the past five years, while Andy merely looked like something out of the Next catalogue. Alas, he had nervously splashed on an ocean of boy racer aftershave. It was quite a gusty night and we all quickly learned not to stand down wind of him. At the other end of the scale, Phil hid in an old woollen jumper, slowly going blue in the face thanks to a knotted scarf that his sister had thoughtfully garrotted him with for good luck.

But, worst of all, I had turned up in a pair of multi-coloured surf pants and proto-type Onion Johnny T-shirt, unevenly stencilled with one of those not-very-effective home-printing kits.

When we returned to the venue an hour or so later, around fifty people had already crammed into the tiny cellar and were inquisitively gorging on Lion Bars and Tizer. We literally had to fight our way through the crowd to get to the stage, and for stage, read 'corner of the room where the pool table usually lived'.

With the five of us collectively shitting in the pair of Onion Johnny underpants, we took to the stage (this time minus the prolonged introduction) and blazed through thirty-five minutes of Goth-lite indie pop in roughly a quarter of an hour. It was on this evening that we experienced our first sightings of proper mosh pit action, not long after a bunch of local teenage delinquents dared tangle with our own hard-core gathering of sugar-rushing best mates.

Such a warm reception came as something of a surprise to us, especially when those people that we weren't on first name terms started clapping as well. Sure, we fluffed a few endings and watched helplessly as Ed's vocal microphone stand got knocked over every ten seconds, but nobody left whilst we performed and the cheers were definitely louder than the boos.

Celebrating with a can of cream soda and half a Crunchie after the show, I felt as if we had made an important breakthrough in establishing our name around Chichester. Well-wishers enquired about the possibility of other local gigs, whilst a couple of the more overly keen attendees even asked if I had any more of those smudged Onion Johnny T-shirts for sale.

But from the mothballed darkness of the venue's cloakroom, Phil confided to me in no uncertain terms that he hadn't enjoyed the experience of playing to a room full of people in the slightest. In fact, my fragile friend had hated performing to what he saw as a bunch of 'strangers'. It was at this moment that I realised it would be cruel to try and make Phil stay in the band if he didn't enjoy being up there for everyone to see. My friend's days in Onion Johnny were coming to an end after just one decent performance.

As Phil quietly slid out of the venue with various members of his immediate family still working to free him from his neck scarf, I consoled myself that at least we had accomplished what we set out to do some eight years previously, when cheating at the cross-country race had inadvertently bought us together for the very first time.

Onion Johnny had officially arrived at that first platform on a long journey towards Pop Central, but for Phil this was already the end of the line.

CH-CH-CH-CH CHANGES

In the next few weeks we made other changes to the line-up. Ed drafted in his best mate Rich Salmon to help share lead vocal duties, simply because the guy owned a van and a small PA that we would be allowed to use if we let him join. Andy Howick was eased out after new boy Richard confessed that he rated our drummer amongst the worst he had ever seen. 'Dick' Salmon (I mean, come on, with a name like that he was born to be in Onion Johnny, wasn't he?) went on to casually mention that he knew a stack of better tub-thumpers should we ever want to be taken seriously.

Andy had recently shared a drunken embrace with a girl that I was meant to be seeing. Although we hadn't fallen out over the incident to any degree, things had remained slightly awkward ever since. Of course, years previous to this I had been in a similar situation with his then-girlfriend Kate, but had chosen not to get involved for fear of destroying our friendship. Funny how these things come back to haunt you, isn't it? My desire to push the band forwards at any cost went squarely against Andy's wish to spend equal times playing football and posing down the pub. The rest of the OJ's took a secret vote and our original drummer was consigned to the dumper.

Andy and I had been mates for the best part of our lives, from baby boys to baby men. Finally, we were about to veer off down different forks of that dusty old road. Andy would soon begin a job for life with the local Council, while I decided to gamble everything on music. I knew that my options were limited and success a very long way off. But I would have ended up depressed or terminally drunk if I had not allowed myself to take this opportunity. Being in a band was the only thing that didn't make me shudder when I thought of the future. Jobs, mortgages and kids weren't high on my list of priorities at twenty-two years old.

As I would learn to my cost over the next few years, it's much wiser never to be in a band with your closest friends. Issues regarding loyalty, money and commitment will drive a dagger through the heart of any beautiful relationship. Andy Howick was replaced by a succession of boisterous drummers that all suffered from slightly worrying drug problems. It seemed that Dick wasn't a particularly good judge of character, possibly because he spent most of his waking hours either very pissed or stoned.

Just what had Eddie let us in for?

Onion Johnny's period of self-imposed change also led us into demoting Jake to lowly keyboards and second guitar. With the best will in the world, Ed was completely rubbish at soloing and Jake should have challenged him to an axe duel or something. But because the guy was so unnaturally quiet and non-committal, Jake found himself pushed to the side-lines, where he then contributed even less than he normally did. I continued to throw the bass around simply because no one dared try prising it out of my hands.

Dick wasted little time in teaching us some of his hippy meanderings, most of which appeared to be in praise of the good Lord upstairs. Worryingly, Dick was soon

75

claiming that he had recognized a similar religious bent in some of my compositions. This was patently not the case, as I was far too busy worshipping at the altar of Robert Smith.

Not to be discouraged, Dick thought that *The Return* was about the reincarnation of Jesus Christ. It was at this point that I began to worry things might be veering off the road a little...

Despite such apprehension, Onion Johnny (now featuring a speed-freak drummer by the name of Mark Greenaway) rehearsed for a second show at The Fernleigh Centre, knowing that they would have to be seriously bloody good after these personnel upheavals.

Many dreams have passed since we
Searched the skies for distant stars
And gave them names the same as ours
Holes now gape in heaven's sky
We came too late the rivers dry
We say 'the world looks big tonight' and cry

I'm waiting for a sign
Summer kiss me blind
My skin begins to burn
But I'll wait for the return

(First verse and chorus to *The Return*.
Simon Parker/Onion Johnny. 1987/8).

L'ENFANT WISH

Summer 1989 found me spending long, stoned evenings round at Simon McKay's house. We had met in a local pub (where else?) and my partial namesake happened to be a fellow struggling musician. We drunkenly talked about forming our own band should the situation arise. On warm, vibrating evenings I would haul my acoustic guitar round to his place before inhaling a lot of hashish. This was how our first songs were born and most evenings usually descended into a messy sing-along with the rest of the clan. Scotty, Graham, Chris, Mike, Julie and Julia would all actively encourage our early attempts at

76

song writing. I wasn't used to this. And our late night version of *Imagine* was virtually unrecognizable. Simon was employed at one of Chichester's top Architectural Partnerships at the time, but my convivial drug buddy also harboured a secret desire to have a crack at the rock'n'roll lifestyle.

Si McKay happens to be one of the most naturally gifted musicians I have ever had the pleasure of working with. From the little time we had already spent together at this point, I knew that it was going to be so much more fun working with him than with the new look Onion Johnny line-up, so I quickly installed our hastily put together 'L'enfant Wish' duo to the bill for the upcoming OJ re-launch show. By the way, in case you're wondering, our name was stolen from one of those syrupy 1980s Athena posters that were all the rage at the time.

Good to see those awful band names were still coming thick and fast...

SUMMER, THE FIRST TIME

At approximately 8.25 pm on Saturday 22nd of July 1989, the music-hungry populace of Chichester was trapped in a snaking line that stretched back nearly twenty yards from the Fernleigh Centre entrance. How about that then? We were becoming popular. By the time L'enfant Wish took to the stage, there was already a big crowd of people squished into that tiny airless cellar. The old lady at the bar sold out of Curly Wurly's in record time and the toilet overflowed with discarded cider bottles, courtesy of those punk rock teenagers last seen sicking up in the car park.

L'enfant Wish played five original songs, including one about cold sausages and beef burgers on a plate by the bed, before I left the stage to let Simon finish things off with a solo rendition of Pink Floyd's *Wish You Were Here*. This would not be the last time we ever shared a stage together.

Next up were those friends from student disco days, Sue Marsh and Liza Lambert. Under the name 'The

77

Biffas', they had chosen a mixture of choice covers such as The Cure's *In Between Days* and The Go-Betweens *Streets Of Your Town*. Unfortunately, Liza's evening was somewhat marred by the fact that her on/off relationship with Mark Mason was now officially off/off, due to the fact that he had just sneaked in with a new lady friend in tow. Consequently, Liza played most of the gig looking like a 'bulldog chewing a wasp' (thank you Viz Comics). From where I was standing it looked as though the stage was the very last place Liza wanted to be at that precise moment in time. It was left to Sue to try and win over the audience, whilst Liza's reticence made Morrissey look like Coco the Clown. Rounding the evening off with the Saturday boy from Linkins, Liza tested the suspension of Sue's Citroen 2CV while we all pretended not to notice.

In front of its biggest paying audience, the new-look Onion Johnny had delivered a forty-minute set of surprisingly coherent songs in sub-tropical temperatures. Thanks to the antics of our saucer-eyed drummer, these latest creations were book-ended by flashy drum rolls and bombastic crescendos. But the audience seemed to like it and only Dick's frantic head wobbling (maybe we should have reverted back to the old band name?) caused any real concern. He looked like David Gray in a hurricane, all wobbly of head and voice.

But, by the end of the evening, when the 2CV stopped rocking, I was convinced that Onion Johnny was starting to get somewhere. The next morning I flew off to Corfu with Mark Mason and spent seven nights drinking for England. When I returned, the band took the next logical step and booked time in a proper recording studio. A few weeks later we set off to the countryside, excited at the prospect of making our very first demo tape.

Dick knew a producer and arranged the session without any input from the rest of the band. What were we thinking? Somehow he neglected to mention that the studio was located at the bottom of a steep, disused quarry. It was whispered that the owner was being chased by the Taxman and had chosen to set up in a place where he would never be found. Unfortunately for us, this meant that an old corrugated works office now doubled up as a makeshift recording studio. It looked like something out of those Mad Max films, all post-apocalyptic and fucked up. This tiny tin shack was virtually inaccessible and we couldn't even fit the drums in through the front door when we finally negotiated the near-vertical slope. This meant that Onion Johnny was forced to use the 'in-house' electronic kit that instantly made us sound ten years out of date. I asked Sue March to sing backing vocals and she stood atop a box to complete this task. Despite the weirdness, it was good to hear the songs 'properly' recorded and we sent out a few demo tapes to local radio stations and south coast venues before everybody on the planet habitually ignored us.

JIMI HENDRIX SAVES MY ARSE

Things took another turn for the worse when Eddy booked us a show at the cavernous Bognor Regis Centre. Thanks to our singer's unusual bartering skills, we stood to lose around £400 of our own money should we not sell a frightening amount of tickets in a horribly short space of time. Suddenly, it was all about the need to round up lots of our mates to help pay for the costs. Being an acquaintance of an unsigned band can be a real pain in the arse and wallet for unsuspecting friends. The OJs struggled to offload little more than half of the required number before turning up and sound checking in front of two of the world's grumpiest engineers. There's at least one in every town across the world, but Bognor Regis had two in the same venue. This particular strain of failed musician is the nemesis of wide-eyed starlets everywhere. Overweight and over-opinionated, such a degenerate life form generally gets its kicks from making young bands look (and sound) stupid. When faced with this grim scenario, the best you can do is to try and placate the beast with a couple of well-timed pints. Do not cross them at any cost, especially when you are just about to play your biggest gig to date.

On the night in question, Onion Johnny was saved from impending financial ruin and musical ridicule by an inquisitive bunch of local indie-kids who arrived en-masse and were happy for something to do in their ailing seaside town. Regrettably, we turned in a shocker of a performance largely due to the fact that the venue had furnished us with our very first backstage dressing room, in which we got far too wasted to play. The only thing that stopped the audience from demanding their money back was Jake's textbook rendition of *Purple Haze*. In fact, so warm was the response to this classic Hendrix cover that we drunkenly played it three times that sorry evening. If it hadn't been for Jake's togetherness and the fact that he neither drank nor drugged before show time, those smirking sound engineers would almost certainly have dragged us offstage.

Of course, in the run up to the show I hadn't been particularly happy that we had resorted to cover versions to bolster our set, but I was resoundingly outvoted 4-1 by my fellow band members (which now included a devil-worshipping drummer called Nick Bennett). But stubborn as I was, even I could see that Jimi Hendrix had just saved my pretty pink bottom from a right royal roasting.

Cheers Jimi. Cheers Jake.

BREAKING US IN TWO

In a remarkably short space of time, Onion Johnny had turned into a drunken, under-rehearsed mess. Had complacency set in so soon? Nick the mental drummer was more interested in upsetting old age pensioners with his numerous cries of 'Satan' and left the band almost as quickly as he had joined it. Jake was so distraught with our behaviour that he promptly cut all ties with music and has refused to play live since. Suddenly, things felt a little ropey in the world of Johnny. We limped on as a three-piece, complete with replacement drum machine and a sulking bass player. Onion Johnny even secured a support to London punksters Snuff at 'Thursdays' nightclub near Chichester. Alas, an inebriated member of the audience mistook the headliners drum kit behind us as a signal to get up and jam throughout our entire set, even though he had never heard our music before. Consequently, each and every song quickly degenerated into farce. We skulked off after four numbers and promptly split up in the car park outside the club. It was November 1989.

Dick Salmon toiled on the heartless pub-covers circuit throughout the early 1990s, before later becoming a music teacher in Surrey. He and Ed remained good friends and played in a short-lived duo called State of Mind, but today Mr Wheatley earns considerably larger sums of money as an air traffic controller at a major London airport. There is a very good chance that he has seen your plane down from some far-flung holiday destination. How scary is that? Even more frightening is the fact that he still looks just like Prince Edward.

I recently bumped into ex-devil worshipper Nick Bennett at a rock show in Brighton. He was there with his teenage son. Nick appears to be a well-adjusted chap these days, and the only nod to those demonic obsessions of the past is a well-groomed goatee beard.

Andy Howick never returned to the drum stool and still works in Chichester, where he lives with his wife and children. Robbie Wheeler and Vaughn Hewitt also have kids and are living in or around Chichester. We occasionally meet up for a beer and throw insults at each other. Nothing has changed really. People just lose their hair and put on a bit of weight, don't they?

Mark 'Joey' Rowe remained faithful to the bible of Mod and went off to train as a chef. Since then he has travelled extensively and is now a part-time resident of Thailand, where he (presumably) enjoys good quality drugs and under achieving motorcycles.

Real life: you couldn't make it up...

▶ **chapter six**

GRABBING THE BUCKET BY THE SHOE
THE VIOLET TRADE 1989-93

A few days after the Onions went to seed (again, I'm sorry but these puns are comedy gold), Simon Mckay and I finally got around to forming a band of our own. By December of 1989, we were sharing a townhouse and living next door to a quiet hostelry. Whenever there was too much washing-up, we would simply go and buy food in the pub rather than contemplate doing the dishes. Life was good.

My managerial responsibilities at Linkins Sports still revolved around copious trips to The White Horse with owners Simon and Michael Jennings. In fact, as long as I could get up and open the shop at 9am every day, they seemed very happy to keep employing me. Greg Saunders was a local drama student who had just started at the shop. When I told him I was forming a new band he offered both his musical services (adequate) and ability to show-off (second to none). Within days, two of his college buddies had also expressed an interest in joining. Gary Capelin (pale, skinny, Gothic) was a fellow thespian who liked to play drums, while Dezmond Carter (pale, ginger, Neanderthal) couldn't actually play anything but knew where to score great drugs. He quite fancied a go on the bass, so I happily moved myself to second guitar and swiftly arranged for some 'auditions' back at our house.

The five of us congregated in Simon McKay's unkempt bedroom, where we braved an unsightly collection of grubby underpants drying on a noisy radiator. Avoiding the previous night's takeaway curry that was still fragrantly leaking its contents into the threadbare carpet, we made our introductions and held a competition to see who could skin up the biggest joint. Dez won and I came last. But I still got very stoned, so who really lost? The first song we attempted to play was a wildly improvised version of The Cure's *Just like Heaven*, and, despite our best efforts, we never officially made it through from start to finish without someone cocking it up. But, by the end of the rehearsal, or rather, when the neighbours started hammering on the wall with their foreheads, I knew that we were onto a winner.

The Violet Trade (come on, you didn't expect a good name, did you?) formed just a few days short of the end of the eighties. I was twenty-two years old and finally about to take a great musical leap forwards. VT would quickly become a real band in every sense of the word.

As a group we collectively listened to REM, The Beatles, Talk Talk and The Cure. However, as individuals we were all into wildly differing styles of music. Dez was partial to a bit of 1970s space rock, whilst dark lord Gary was more in thrall to pasty-faced staples such as Bauhaus and Alien Sex Fiend. I knew of at least four Status Quo albums lurking in Simon Mackay's record collection, whilst Greg just went around pretending he was Prince.

But the one thing that united us all was the age-old art of getting stoned. And so, this is what we did every day for the next three years.

REM-REMEMBERED

For the uninitiated it had all started with *Murmur*, a mumbled introduction to strange, chiming apparitions. I pondered the relevance of a vocalist who didn't want to be heard and made a mental note that lyrics didn't really have to make much sense just so long as they sounded good.

NME informed me that there had already been an earlier REM release, so I backtracked to *Chronic Town*'s beguiling mix of melody and mystery, just prior to second-album proper, *Reckoning*, giving birth to a cluster of bleached out country rock songs playing in a parallel existence. REM's artwork was cryptic and messy, with random numbers strewn about the sleeves. This appealed to me as I have always found myself idly sketching the number '3' in moments of distraction.

Fables of the Reconstruction was both angular and beautiful. Bookended by *Feeling Gravity's Pull* and *Wendell Gee*, and recorded here in the UK, it at least proved to me that this band really existed, but their videos left me scratching my head. Were there more clues in the artwork? What did it all mean?

Life's Rich Pageant was another favourite in the mid-80s, especially during those early stages of struggling to improve one's own song writing skills. Being able to muddle my way through *I Am Superman* gave me untold encouragement. 'Look everybody; I can play an REM track...' I bragged, unaware that the band hadn't even written the damn thing.

By now it felt as if other people were looking in, although the bands mystique remained intact even after *The One I Love* fleetingly graced the airwaves during 1987. 'But it's not a love song' I protested. Parent album *Document* continued an upward sales trend and was played until the needle skidded right across both sides of the record without pausing for breath.

1988 spoiled us. *Eponymous* came first and carried with it constant reminders of earlier triumphs. This was followed just a few weeks later by the band's first release on a major label. *Green* was, and still is, my definitive REM moment: my favourite body of Berry, Buck, Mills and Stipe. Housed in an alluring but mysterious sleeve, complete with symbolic references to the number '4', I loved every track on that very special record.

Green was also important for a new wave of American alternative guitar acts that were able to use REM's momentum to infiltrate the U.S mainstream. It also brought to light the fact that REM had succeeded by being true to their art. Proof that it can still be done, we all thought.

Lost in a private worldview, but somehow clearer and more accessible, the band was performing on Top of the Pops in 1988/9. REM's transformation was almost complete, their moment very nearly upon them.

REM - AN IMAGINARY COMPILATION

Welcome to the Occupation (Document)
World Leader Pretend (Green)
Shaking Through (Murmur)
The Great Beyond (The Great Beyond)
So. Central Rain (Reckoning)
Man on the Moon (Man on the Moon OST)
Supernatural Superserious (Accelerate)
The Flowers of Guatemala (Life's Rich Pageant)
Fall on Me (Life's Rich Pageant)
Imitation of Life (Reveal)
Harbourcoat (Reckoning)
I Remember California (Green)
Perfect Circle (Murmur)
Swan Swan H (Life's Rich Pageant)
The Wrong Child (Green)
All the Way to Reno (Reveal)
Wendell Gee (Fables of the Reconstruction)

THINK I'LL KILL THE RADIO...

As the 1980s wound down, the charts began to smell of the regurgitated dross thrown up by artists like Sonia and Rick Astley. Everybody seemed to be buying songs that had first featured in adverts, whilst bland cover versions ruled the airwaves over at Radio One. TOTP had been overrun by an endless succession of perma-grinning, fake-tanned twats. Music lovers groaned outwardly.

As if this wasn't bad enough, a lot of the more successful independent artists were now seeking pastures new at the home of larger record companies. The Wedding Present, Mighty Lemon Drops, Pop Will Eat Itself and House of Love had all been expected to make the leap into 'Simple Minds' territory and shift units. All were busy failing to do so. By 1990, major record companies were greedily devouring independent record label rosters by luring acts away with big wads of cash. You couldn't really blame the artists for taking the money and running, as niche acts like Stump and That Petrol Emotion took their chances without diluting their sound. But virtually none of the indie acts re-housed on majors would ever live up to the sales expectations of their new paymasters. To put it bluntly, if you weren't Phil Collins, Wet Wet Wet or Simply Red, you were well and truly fucked, no matter how garish and expensive your wardrobe might have been.

This sorry state of affairs would accelerate throughout the 1990s, with independent record labels finding it progressively harder to fight the power. When Creation finally sold out to Sony in 1998, this effectively bought down the curtain on indies competing with the big guns.

But Goliath wasn't going to get everything his own way. After a lifetime spent feasting at the table of price-hiking and relentless profiteering, the corporations were caught with their trousers down come the advent of digital music. Rather than embracing the oncoming technological innovations, every major record company in the world chose this moment to stick its head in the sand and pretend nothing was going to change. This left the back doors wide open and a whole new team simply rode into town and claimed digitized music as its own.

Stepping forward to the present day for a moment, major labels now have to pretend to be indies in order to win some highly valued street-cred from the on-line world of bloggers and tastemakers. Only then is it deemed safe to release new artists out into the downloadable world. Most new acts can usually be traced back to a parent company that is in fact one of the few remaining multi-nationals. Pseudonyms and smoke screens have become the most effective way to launch major label bands to a generation that wrongly assumes it is avoiding a little nibble on the corporate cock.

But this was all set to happen in the future. Back in 1990, most of us were still blissfully ignorant as to what a music corporation actually was. In fact, although we might have complained about the rising prices, we were all happy to keep buying records, tapes and compact discs in order to keep the industry swimming in its obscene lake of money.

NME pointed to the North where The Stone Roses, Happy Mondays, James and Inspiral Carpets were part of an exciting 'baggy' scene spilling out of Manchester's hedonistic underbelly. If that wasn't strong enough for your taste buds, Sub Pop was waging war on the world and busy introducing us to a new strain of American Punk Rock, soon to be rebranded as 'Grunge'.

UK daytime radio's refusal to acknowledge the presence of alternative music meant that indie lovers everywhere had to be content with a brief refuelling courtesy of the Channel Four/ITV Saturday morning Chart Show. Since the demise of The Tube, this programme had become the only way of catching a look at something slightly more appealing than the ailing Top Of The Pops, which of course was only capable of reflecting the diseased corpse of the Top Forty. Who knows, without the Chart Show I may never have heard the likes of The Dave Howard Singers, The Motorcycle Boy, Big Black, Circus Circus Circus or The Man from Delmonte. And then my world would have been just that little bit darker.

As the new decade got underway I had every confidence that within the next few years I too would be getting rich from my involvement with music.

Oh dear.

TOP 20 UNDERRATED 1980s SINGLES

1. The Beat - Save it for Later
2. Wah! - Come Back
3. The Keys - I Don't Wanna Cry
4. The Very Things - The Bushes Scream While My Daddy Prunes
5. Julian Cope - The Greatness and Perfection of Love
6. The Pale Saints - Sight of You
7. Psychedelic Furs - Love My Way
8. The Jesus and Mary Chain - Just Like Honey

9. Camper Van Beethoven - Take the Skinheads Bowling
10. Cardiacs - Is This the Life?
11. Microdisney - Town to Town
12. Stump - Buffalo
13. Altered Images - Don't Talk to Me About Love
14. B-Movie - Remembrance Day
15. Orange Juice - What Presence?
16. Husker Du - Could You Be the One?
17. The Chameleons - Tears
18. Felt - Primitive Painters
19. Win - You've Got the Power
20. House of Love - Destroy The Heart

Lest we forget; Private Lives - Living in a World Turned Upside Down, The Church - Under the Milky Way, Kitchens of Distinction - The First Time We Opened the Capsule, Laid Back - Baker Man, Mick Karn featuring David Sylvian - Buoy, Pop Will Eat Itself - Beaver Patrol, Floy Joy - Until You Come Back To Me, New Musik - Sanctuary, Terence Trent D'arby - This Side of Love, Shannon - Let the Music Play, Ultra Vivid Scene - The Mercy Seat, Graham Parker - Temporary Beauty, Jesus Jones - Info Freako, The Smithereens - Behind the Wall Of Sleep, The Blue Nile - Tinsel Town in the Rain, P.I.L. - Rise, The Fat Lady Sings - Arclight, Nick Heyward - Blue Hat for a Blue Day, The Sundays - Can't Be Sure.

TOP TEN UNDERRATED 80s ARTISTS

1. The Chameleons
2. Felt
3. The Sound
4. The Associates
5. Nick Nicely
6. The Close Lobsters
7. The Field Mice
8. The Brilliant Corners
9. The Pale Fountains
10. The Chesterfields

They also served; The Bodines, The Triffids, The Razor Cuts, The Farmers Boys, The Popguns, Bradford, The Flatmates, Goodbye Mr Mackenzie, Icicle Works, Circus Circus Circus, Shop Assistants, The Jack Rubies, The Big Dish, China Crisis, The June Brides, The Pastels, Immaculate Fools.

TOP 20 UNDERRATED 1980s ALBUMS

1. David Sylvian - Secrets of the Beehive
2. Orange Juice - You Can't Hide Your Love Forever
3. The Icicle Works - If You Want To Defeat Your Enemy Sing His Song
4. XTC - Skylarking
5. Brilliant Corners - What's in a Word
6. Edwyn Collins - Hope and Despair
7. Immaculate Fools - Dumb Poet
8. The Pale Fountains - From Across the Kitchen Table
9. The Waterboys - A Pagan Place
10. New Order - Republic
11. Julian Cope - World Shut Your Mouth
12. The Lover Speaks - The Lover Speaks
13. Thomas Dolby - The Flat Earth
14. The The - Soul Mining
15. American Music Club - California
16. Close Lobsters - Headache Rhetoric
17. Railway Children - Reunion Wilderness
18. The Wonderstuff - Hup!
19. The Chesterfields - Kettle
20. The Housemartins - London 0 Hull 4

Also ran: Felt - Forever Breathed the Lonely Word, Band of Holy Joy - Manic, Magic Majestic, The B-52's - Cosmic Thing, Lloyd Cole & The Commotions - Easy Pieces, The Go-Betweens - 16 Lovers Lane

Guilty pleasures: Rick Springfield - Tao, Then Jerico - First (The Sound of Music), Blue Zoo - Two by Two.

1990

There was something in the air... there really was. The first few days of 1990 felt positive, welcoming and inspiring. Who knows? Maybe this time I was going to be in the right place...

TOP TEN ARTISTS WHO WERE MOST DEFINITELY IN THE RIGHT PLACE AT THE RIGHT TIME

1. Elvis Presley
2. The Beatles
3. The Sex Pistols
4. The Stone Roses
5. Oasis
6. Spandau Ballet
7. Franz Ferdinand
8. Coldplay
9. James Blunt
10. Alvin Stardust

Ok, so I threw one of those in for a laugh - but I expect fans of Franz Ferdinand might have already noticed that.

DANCING WITH MYSELF

The advent of acid house and free parties scared the Government into devising suspect new laws to help combat the rave nation. Politicians became concerned about those pesky 'repetitive beats' and hastily furnished the police with new powers to help stamp out illegal gatherings. Dancing like a ninny in a field peppered with cowpats and potholes was suddenly considered to be a threat to the moral fabric of our society. Youth culture had evidently found its edge again.

But congregating in an out-of-the-way location somewhere off of the M25 held no such allure for me, especially after good friend Scotty Macdonald returned home from one free festival sporting a nasty dose of scabies. So instead, I frequented some of the better indie nights stashed away in those towns that were considerably less boring than Chichester.

1990 was a time when friendly and unthreatening faces populated the dance floor, even in notoriously punch-drunk Portsmouth. It was here that I loped like a long-armed gibbon to the grooving beat of Ocean Colour Scene, years prior to their reinvention as Mods (I wonder if they ended up with any of Rob and Andy's hand-me-downs?). Amazingly, my crap moves raised not one eyebrow or terse comment. Alcohol had been upstaged by Ecstasy and bottled water, with fighting scratched from the agenda until further notice. Everybody in the club was simply intent on having a good time.

INTRODUCING THE BAND

Simon and I wrote the Violet Trade songs and the band just sort of fell into place. Greg played about a thousand notes a minute and had to be reined in on excessive keyboard antics. The only tune he was proficient at was the old chestnut *Blue Moon*, which he often tried to shoehorn into our own compositions when he thought we weren't looking. Gary had been a good find and was a decent drummer, now unexpectedly playing 'baggy' inspired break-beats for the first time in his Gothic existence. Dez simply did what he was told, although rehearsals were frequently interrupted so that he could skin up or sell drugs to a steadily growing number of student visitors.

Before long our bathroom became a makeshift crash pad to those who were too stoned to go home. On any given evening it would be necessary to pee in front of glassy-eyed strangers who were simply too fucked to vacate the toilet. Simon was suitably inspired and managed to turn these strange lavatorial affairs into one of Violet Trade's best-loved songs.

Bucket Bong Ant it's funny how you look so odd in pants...

(*Bucket Bong Ant*. Simon McKay/The Violet Trade 1990).

The band thrived in this Bohemian atmosphere and soon became a six-piece when Simon introduced backing vocalist Emma Finlay into the line-up. Perhaps unwisely, she and I embarked upon an afterhours' lust affair, with Emma then constantly having to put up with a gang of star-spangled stoners and their endless knob-gaggery. Such was the pull of this lifestyle, I would always find myself making excuses to return to that den of iniquity after a dose of late night raunch even though it would have been more romantic to stay. Yes, I know. How very male of me.

It became difficult for Simon and me to make it into work on time, and some mornings most of the drama course was prostrate on the living-room floor as we tried to tiptoe our way out of the house. I was now living the student lifestyle that Mrs Thatcher's YTS scheme had so cruelly robbed me of all those moons ago.

Mobile phones were still the size of house bricks and the grapevine was in no way global. So I continued to spread the word about our band via the underground network at Linkins. Such was the cross to bear when alerting the world to your musical presence at the arse end of the 20th century.

Emma quickly tired of our relentless marijuana exploits and thought it cool to mimic us in her best 'Neil from The Young Ones' voice. This upset some of the lads a little and contributed towards me dumping her just in time for our first hometown gig. Of course, this in turn upset her, and I then had to apologise and promise to set up on the other side of the stage just to get her to agree to show up. Despite such tenuous beginnings, The Violet Trade was ready for its first blurred crusade by spring of 1990.

Due to the heavy spliffage, we missed a chance to include covers by, say, Pixies and Stone Roses and dropped in tracks by Frazier Chorus, Del Amitri and The Hothouse Flowers.

Our logic was indeed fuzzy...

PLAY TO WIN

Much like their predecessors Onion Johnny and Frantic Heads, The Violet Trade chose to play in the Fernleigh cellar. At the time, there really was nowhere else. And so it was here in those familiar choc and pop surroundings, that we delivered a set of immaculately stoned indie dance to a packed room. A fair percentage of our audience had to wait until the very last song of the evening before we played anything remotely aggressive enough for them to 'mosh' about to. Somehow, all attempts to rock out to Frazier Chorus' *Typical* had proved frustratingly unsatisfying to those in the mood for a little bit of sweaty male-bonding. But we pulled it off and word soon spread that The Violet Trade were the local band to go see.

Of course, Emma soon washed her hands of the whole affair (on both counts) and Dez decided that he preferred selling drugs to practising with the band. He was officially kicked out a few weeks later and replaced by the afore-mentioned Marc Gallup, who joined us just in time for that ill-fated Lavant Village Hall show in May of 1990. Unfortunately, Marc lived too far away to ever be considered a full-time member of our group, so once again I gave up my aspirations of becoming a guitarist and returned to bass duties.

We continued to develop our indie dance sound, buoyed by the fact that bands such as The Charlatans were riding high with a similar musical style.

TOP-TIP THREE:

WHEN FORMING A BAND, BE SURE TO AVOID COPYING A GENRE THAT IS CURRENTLY COMING INTO FASHION. BY THE TIME A RECORD COMPANY HAS GOTTEN ROUND TO DISCOVERING YOU, YOUR MUSIC WILL ALMOST CERTAINLY BE YESTERDAY'S CHIP PAPER.

We were served notice to quit the rented townhouse not long after two unidentified drama students were crushed under the collapsed weight of unloved washing up. It was definitely the right time to move on, and in doing so we rapidly accelerated the bands creative growth.

OUR HOUSE

Just weeks before that beautiful summer of 1990, The Violet Trade and assorted acquaintances moved en masse into a large, disused house that was situated to the north of the city in leafy Summersdale. Our new five bed-roomed house was cheap, spacious and (most important of all) detached. For a bunch of degenerates trailing their own P.A. around, this was a golden find. My friends, I think it's fair to say that even Jesus loves a stoner.

Peggy Bottles, Peggy Bottles
With your glass eye, green and mottled

(*Peggy Bottles*. Simon McKay/ The Violet Trade. 1990).

Summersdale is a well-to-do corner of Chichester and The Violet Trade caused a great deal of consternation among its nearest neighbours by taking up residence. Some years earlier, a group of 'concerned' local house owners had successfully argued that the site of our abode overlapped a public alleyway by all of a couple of inches. Remarkably, this had resulted in the house sitting empty for years on end as the builders could find no way to legally sell or rent it. But the appeased citizens of Summersdale were soon horrified to find every local drug addict, wino and squatter breaking in and dossing down. In the event, the house was soon a graffiti covered eyesore, with every window completely smashed in and a wild, unkempt garden reminding everyone what a pigsty they had helped create. When VT moved in, our first job was to re-glaze the whole building. I remember that we ran out of putty quite early on, so my bedroom window was held in place with copious amounts of Blu Tack.

94

To this day I'm not exactly sure how we were allowed to rent the house, but I do know that a private contractor with big plans had recently acquired the land rights. So we were always on borrowed time. We snuck in under the radar and those concerned neighbours then had to sit and watch as drums, amps and glazed stoners moved in right under their snooty noses.

Of course, with us came the whole fraternity of Chichester pot smokers. Ex-bass player Dez wasted little time in setting up 'shop' and continued to ply his trade by selling soft drugs to students and degenerates. People would turn up at all hours of the day and night to purchase his wares. I have it on very good authority from a friend who used to work for Chichester Police that the only reason we weren't raided was the fact that the local rozzers felt it better to have the majority of the city's major dope smokers together under one roof. This way, the problem was contained in one very run-down building.

Somehow this was where the band flourished. It was like living in a never-ending episode of The Monkees. Sure, Dez harboured a bit of a grudge about being chucked out of the band, but he still sold me hash so all was cool for the time being.

New Order released a footie anthem and the English national team looked like a good bet for that summer's World Cup. It was a glorious few months.

TOP TEN NEW ORDER TRACKS

1. Temptation (Substance)
2. Weirdo (Brotherhood)
3. All the Way (Technique)
4. Age Of Consent (Power, Corruption and Lies)
5. Run (Technique)
6. Bizarre Love Triangle (Brotherhood)
7. Love Vigilantes (Low Life)
8. Paradise (Brotherhood)
9. Mr Disco (Technique)
10. Krafty (Waiting for the Siren's Call)

A NIGHT OUT WITH THE VIOLET TRADE

Coincidentally, we found ourselves living next door to a pub again. The Wellington was one of those quiet places frequented only by stony-faced OAPs during the daytime and then nobody in particular at night. Of course, we would soon change all this and for a while it felt as if we had our own drinking club and private gig venue. Things just kept on getting better.

And so it was that on a balmy summers evening in June 1990, The Wellington filled up with a number of inquisitive friends and family members, all keen to check out this new-fangled 'indie-dance' thing. Encouragingly, there was also a large turnout of underage cave dwellers who had forsaken the usual cider guzzling rituals in the Fernleigh Centre car park to walk up the hill and check us out. Even the reclusive Phil Bennett put in an appearance, although he chose to stay at the back of the room hiding behind his pint glass.

It had only been a couple of months since those first Violet Trade shows, yet the band's sound and style had altered a great deal. Trimmed down to a four-piece, we were tight, danceable and fun to watch. But most importantly, we wrote really catchy pop songs. It really was a no-brainer. The audience loved it and swiftly took us to their parts. People couldn't help but head for the dance floor and over the next year or so audience participation would always be the barometer of how well we had performed on any given evening. Ask any new band and they will tell you it's nigh on impossible to get people to dance. But impressively for an unsigned act, we always managed to get at least two-thirds of the crowd up out of their seats, even though any song I contributed was virtually impossible to jig about to in a straightforward manner.

On that first landmark evening, we ploughed through our entire repertoire before inviting the whole audience (not forgetting the pub landlord and his hollow-legged wife) back over to our tatty house for some after-hours hospitality. The party raged until the early hours of

Sunday morning, and this set the tone for a run of similar debauched shows at The Wellington throughout that memorable summer. After a couple of weekends, there were just as many people dancing in the pub's garden as there were crammed inside the bar itself. Sales of Snakebite and black went through the roof, and the dodgy landlord even offered to manage us. We politely turned him down after first asking for, and securing, an extra twenty quid a night.

This was how we became a popular draw in our hometown. One of the proudest moments of my entire musical life came when I first heard members of the audience enthusiastically yelling my own lyrics back at me.

You know you drive me mad she said - I said
I'd drive you anywhere
To the end of the road, to the end of the world,
come on I'll take you there...

(*Ribbons*. Simon Parker/The Violet Trade 1990).

Actually, when I come to think of it now, most of Violet Trade's audience knew the words to our songs much better than Simon McKay ever did. But that only served to endear our singer even further to those enthusiastic new fans. To paraphrase one of Talk Talk's finest moments, I was living in another world.

FREAK SCENE

It wasn't long before we needed somewhere else to play. The Wellington gigs were chaotic and enjoyable, but if we were going to get noticed VT needed to shift up a gear. After blank looks from landlords of several local pubs, Mark Mason and I drove out to the Coach and Horses at Westhampnett, where they hosted occasional heavy metal nights. Mark became de-facto band manager around this time and took his role very seriously. Importantly, he wasn't into drugs, so we always had someone with a clear head in the ranks. But, put a pint in his hand and all hell would break loose...

Andy at the Coach turned out to be a decent guy and offered us a speculative mid-week booking with the promise of a coveted Saturday evening slot should the first night go well. Obviously, we were taking a bit of a chance invading a known rock haunt with our new-fangled indie dance sound, but confidence tends to surge through those intrepid bands with a decent local fan base. In the event, VT would help transform this unassuming pub into a thriving musical hotspot, whilst also creating our very own Chichester indie scene.

Although the Coach and Horses was situated a good couple of miles outside of the town centre, this didn't stop south coast revellers from finding us and packing the venue every time we played. When we started it felt as though we were the only local indie fans in the area. But word spread like wildfire and fellow music enthusiasts cottoned on pretty quickly. Around 75 people showed up for that debut Wednesday evening appearance at the Coach and most dragged hangovers to work or college the next morning. Despite Greg setting up too close to the front of the stage (an alarming trait present in all keyboard players) VT was an immediate hit and we were elevated to Saturday evening's post-haste.

On a bright hillside
She paints me pictures of the North Star

(*Light and Shade*. Simon Parker/The Violet Trade. 1990).

Within weeks of our first Coach and Horses show, other indie bands started coming out of the woodwork. Evidently, we were not alone. Just like the Stone Roses, The Violet Trade had arrived at the right time. But very much unlike the Stone Roses, The Violet Trade had decided to launch their careers from a ghost town where live music was considered a bit of a nuisance.

Undeterred, we battled on, confident of our glorious futures in pop.

TOP TEN UNSIGNED BANDS BASED IN THE WEST
SUSSEX AREA (1990-1993)

1. Amazing Windmills
2. Second Hand Daylight
3. The Green Ray
4. Waterfall
5. The Daniel Grade
6. Pyramid of Johnny (See also: The Pink Garden)
7. Wonderful Green Circles
8. Stone Cold
9. The Love Blobs
10. Bully's Special Prize

MONEY

One of the best things about the Coach and Horses was that whenever VT played we got to keep all the door money. I became band treasurer and diligently banked a huge pile of £1 coins in a shoebox under my bed. This money would go on to finance future recordings and a rusty old band van that refused to climb hills when fully laden with gear.

PARTY OUT OF BOUNDS

Keen to put our house to good use, we decided to stage the mother of all parties. In late September of 1990, The Violet Trade hosted their own mini music festival from deep within the bushy confines of their spacious back garden. At a conservative estimate, around 250 people would join us for a night of drinking and drugging under the stars.

First, we took delivery of a stolen marquee and assorted barrels of slightly out-of-date beer, courtesy of our friendly publican from just across the driveway. Then, Simon McKay successfully improvised some makeshift stage lighting simply by attaching a string of puny light bulbs to the washing line. Simple but surprisingly effective. Everyone else pitched in to help clear the necessary space and even resident drug terrorist Dezmond contributed to the cause by thoughtfully emptying the contents of his motorbike's petrol tank over the neglected garden. After a copious dowsing with second-hand two-star, the ginger lunatic merrily set light to the assorted jungle, torching everything in sight with just one match. This experimental form of gardening was particularly effective, although the whole area became acutely prone to spontaneous bouts of bushfire long after the gig had officially ended. Following the party, we were forced to abandon several footie matches on nearby Oaklands Park when we saw black smoke rising from our back garden on particularly hot summer's days.

On the day of the party, news of live bands, cheap beer and copious amounts of puff offered an attractive alternative to young fuck-ups everywhere. In a town as cosseted as Chichester, it felt as if we were pushing things as far as we could. The first guests of the evening arrived with looks of total disbelief as 'Tradestock' hit Summersdale, unhindered by local Constabulary or patchy English weather. It was as if we had cloaked ourselves in an invisible force field. By rights, we should have been busted within thirty minutes of the first band going on, but the evening went off without a hitch despite the fact that you could clearly hear the music well over half a mile away.

Following a great set from Portsmouth's Amazing Windmills, The Violet Trade took to the stage and plugged in beneath a cloudless, navy blue sky. Friends and fans instantly made for the mosh pit and kicked up a thick plume of dust and charred grass particles that drifted into our eyes and mouths as we careered through our set. Who needs dry ice when you have a dirt cloud to hide behind? Simon McKay was spitting grit balls for days. We played for around an hour and left the stage to a huge roar from the officially high as a kite crowd.

The party carried on until dawn, with many new faces turning up once the pubs had kicked out. I awoke on my bedroom floor early the next afternoon, partially clothed and with absolutely no recollection of how I had ended up there. A sure fire sign of a great night out.

Now all we had to do was to clear up.

FRIDAY I'M IN LOVE

This legendary evening cemented The Violet Trade's reputation as a decent band with a sweet tooth for fun and illegal substances. Our notoriety continued to grow around pubs and local colleges, with VT shows becoming riotously sold out affairs.

I had managed to avoid getting myself into serious relationships for a while now, but finally, in the autumn of 1990, I fell in love with a Cure acolyte called Lisa.

I had first noticed her during the earliest days of Onion Johnny gigs at The Fernleigh Centre. In fact, we had often said 'Hi' whilst purchasing melted confectionery at the tuck shop bar. But it wasn't until the evening of our garden party that I finally plucked up the courage to ask her out on a date. Luckily, we were both rather drunk and she said 'yes'. Thank God for alcohol. Lisa claimed that Robert Smith lived at the bottom of her road and at first I thought she might be a little bit unhinged. But upon closer inspection, her boasts turned out to be absolutely true. What other sign did I need that we were made for each other? And so, during the latter stages of 1990, Lisa and I hit it off in a big way. Our relationship was conducted around her College studies and my musical commitments. In the process we ended up staying together for almost five years.

24-HOUR PARTY PEOPLE

On any given evening, another group of new acquaintances would drop by to score hash and then stick around and smoke most of it. And, as the joints rolled on enthusiastically into the misty nether regions of 4 or 5am, Simon and I finally lost all will to go to work. Our world was sound-tracked by The Beatles *White Album* and Talk Talk's *Spirit of Eden*. LSD entered the equation for the first

101

time. Our minds became suitably elastic. The Violet Trade appeared to be living out the rock'n'roll fantasy way before it ever went anywhere near a record company's front door.

I was living on a lager and shortbread diet seldom known for its slimming qualities. My days of looking like the indie Jason Donovan were coming to an end. With long, straggly blonde hair scrunched back into a ponytail (not forgetting that little lager potbelly resting on top of my trousers), fellow work colleagues began to question whether I portrayed the correct image for a sports' shop manager. The Jennings Brothers knew all about the colourful lifestyle I was pursuing and began to lose faith in me. I tried to balance a boozing day job and the surreal goings on in an indie commune, but usually found myself crawling off upstairs in the shop for a quick lay down amongst the ski jackets. On one particularly memorable occasion I obeyed the harsh tones of the morning alarm and struggled off to work only to find that my housemates had crept into my room and wound my clock on by three hours. After turning up at the shop at 6am, I staggered off back home to a standing ovation, and then grimly overslept by a good hour or so. Of course, nobody at work would believe my protestations when I tried to explain that I had already been in once that day.

At 23 years of age, I was sailing somewhere up that crazy river with neither a paddle nor a return ticket. Life was wonderful.

OPPORTUNITY KNOCKS

But summers like this can never last for long, and soon Mark and I were entertaining the idea of taking our band up to London to secure a record deal. Dad knocked up some headed notepaper to make it look as if our manager really knew what he was doing, and we were off. No game plan, no meeting; just a friend who used his work's telephone every time he got the chance.

Mark's first success was to secure us a slot at the prestigious Rock Garden venue in Covent Garden.

Encouragingly, this also happened to be the first London venue that The Smiths had ever set foot in. According to the excitable bloke at the other end of the telephone, record labels were always sending scouts to check out the new talent at his establishment. Indeed, many artists, U2 included, had gone on to bigger and better things after first playing on the Covent Garden Piazza. 'Sold', to the gullible band from the provinces...

Naïve as we were, The Violet Trade willingly agreed to the rather one-sided terms dictated by the Promoter. Blinded by the dazzling lights of pop immortality, we prepared for our inaugural Saturday evening slot in London.

TOP-TIP FOUR:

UNSIGNED ARTISTS SHOULD NEVER CONSIDER PLAYING IN LONDON AT THE WEEKEND. RECORD COMPANY SCOUTS WILL ALMOST CERTAINLY BE ELSEWHERE - DESPITE WHAT UNSCRUPULOUS PROMOTERS MAY TRY TO TELL YOU.

In return for the opportunity to impress the world at large, we had to agree to hire a coach and sell a minimum of fifty tickets. If this wasn't bad enough, it was also The Violet Trade's responsibility to supply a drum kit and amps for the other artists to use, even though we were on stage quite early and would end up having to wait around for several hours to retrieve our gear at the end of the evening.

Like many other unsuspecting bands looking forward to their first London show, we learned the hard way. The harsh reality of being booked onto a showcase night in the capital was considerably different to that of the romantic notion floating round my head. In fact, it was more like being repeatedly hit around the face with a diseased trout. The Rock Garden turned out to be the last place on earth that record label scouts and lovers of live music would be seen dead in. Unbeknown to manager and band, most of the acts on offer at the Rock Garden were cheesy covers or cabaret outfits and not, as we had been led to believe, the next wave of indie hopefuls.

On the evening of our first London performance, four non-descript bands of wildly varying musical styles (and very little musical equipment) all benefited from playing in front of fifty-plus of our best mates. Obviously this didn't include that handful of Japanese tourists who spent the best part of the evening trying to negotiate a refund after wandering in by mistake.

Undeterred, we tore through our set like paparazzi through a scandal. Simon McKay celebrated in style by wearing a dress for the occasion, and even though I broke a bass string during the third song, nothing could have stopped us from having a whale of a time in front of so many familiar faces.

SIMON MCKAY'S TOP 5 DUBIOUS VIOLET TRADE OUTFITS

1. Those beloved 'MC Hammer' style trousers
2. Testicle-revealing shorts and a psychedelic Mambo t-shirt
3. An old man's roll neck sweater and cardigan combo
4. A football kit
5. A purple waistcoat with little mirrors sewn into the fabric

By the end of The Violet Trade's first foray into London, we had spent over £300 for the 'fun' of it. And this was before Gary discovered that some heartless bastard had stolen his set of very expensive borrowed cymbals. Unbelievably, we went back for more, simply because it was London.

SLIVER

You learn quickly or go bust. On subsequent London trips, Mark hired a beaten-up mini-bus to help transport a dozen or so of our most fervent supporters to a number of dilapidated venues. The Violet Trade would soon go on to grace the stages of The Islington Powerhaus, Euston Rails Club, Ladbroke Grove Subterrania, Fulham Kings Head and various other grim and grimy dungeons that were still on the unsigned band radar back in the early 1990s. Incidentally, most of these sticky-floored back rooms have long since been sold off and re-developed as Building Societies or Coffee Emporiums. It is rumoured that if you listen very carefully, the cries of long-forgotten indie musicians can still be heard as you order overpriced skinny lattes in various prime locations throughout London's inner sanctum.

We grew steadily accustomed to shifty-eyed venue promoters slipping away with the door take long before the end of the evening. The Violet Trade had been caught in a venue flytrap, and although we knew we were being exploited, there was always the outside chance of performing in front of someone from a record company to keep us coming back for more. And should The Violet Trade have ever turned down such a booking, there would have been countless other bands scratching each other's eyes out to step into our pungent trainers.

London music promoters had us all over a rusty barrel. There was not an unsigned musician amongst us that didn't have a forest of tiny splinters sticking out of their sorry-looking behinds.

The Violet Trade 1991 – backstage at the Powerhaus in London with our friend Lindsay Churchman.
(l-r Lindsay, Greg Saunders, Simon McKay, Gary Capelin, Simon Parker – photo Mark Mason)

VIOLET TRADE IN THE CHARTS

Over a very long weekend of getting stoned and sitting in front of Greg's hi-fi unit, I ran off about forty copies of *Give Me the Happy*, which was a sort of ragbag compilation featuring Violet Trade's best demo and live recordings to date. The quality was pretty ropey, but once housed in the Simon McKay designed sleeve, these artefacts looked halfway decent and were the only product our band had to sell. Mark duly struck up a deal with the local Our Price store and delivered our cassette only release in early 1991. A few days later we received a call informing us that VT were outselling every other artist that week and could they have some more tapes. This kept happening for the next few weeks and by the time it stopped selling I had broken most of the buttons on Greg's stereo.

LONDON, CAN YOU WAIT?

Frustratingly, by the spring of 1991 it was becoming increasingly difficult to talk Simon and Greg into wasting time and money on fruitless gigs in the capital. Like Mark and me, Gary the Gothic drummer was fine with the situation because he agreed that this was going to be the only way of getting a band from Chichester noticed. Unfortunately, Greg and Simon were considerably lazier and quickly went off the idea of trawling round the various hellholes of London in the vague hope of bumping into a record company scout. Our music had quickly moved away from indie dance and each new song we wrote was better than the last. Pitched somewhere between Oasis and Blur, it was a pity that we adopted this sound a few years before the advent of Britpop.

Despite such setbacks, I remained insanely confident that a label would soon pounce on one of those demo tapes Mark was busy forwarding with stamps swiped from his job at good old Hargreaves Sports. Violet Trade was a band with potential. So what more did those record labels require? Disappointingly, the phone wasn't exactly buzzing with enquiries...

A&R

This is how it generally works. A&R (Artist and Repertoire) departments are the semi-mythical creatures that act as the first point of contact between the artist and the slobbering corporate beast. Once in a blue moon, a scout will think to contact you after receiving a demo that he/she finds mildly interesting. But, more often than not, lines of communication will open only after another label's talent-spotting fraternity drunkenly brags about its latest new discovery.

Unable to keep even the simplest of promises -like turning up to a gig when put on the guest list- the majority of this grubby little species are well-versed at finding endless excuses for not attending whenever you are booked to perform in London. Constantly in fear of losing

107

their jobs to someone younger and more dynamic, those few A&R scouts that do go on to find success achieve this feat by suspending any last vestiges of musical integrity. Usually, this will mean adopting the futile policy of getting excited about the same type of artist their bosses signed to the label twelve months previously. Sadly, the days of sticking one's neck on the line for an act that didn't fit the corporate criteria of any particular record label had all but vanished by the early 90s.

Of course, in 2013 record companies, A&R departments don't exist in the same way that they did in the cash-rich early 90s. These days, there's hardly anybody actually employed to discover new bands, save those unpaid interns slavishly searching the Internet for artists with ten thousand Facebook likes. Every major label in the land has had to make huge cutbacks in order to stay afloat in these changing times, with the A&R department always one of the most hit areas. Whereas once upon a time there might have been a dozen or so people in the main office, now there are only one or two. For those of you wanting a real eye-opener into the grim and grimy world of 1980s/90s A&R subculture, be sure to buy a copy of John Niven's excellent *Kill Your Friends*.

Meanwhile, back in my story, The Violet Trade was about to enjoy a little skirmish with the A&R department of Chrysalis Records.

THE ONE AND ONLY

By the summer of 1991, The Violet Trade resembled a bedraggled mess of longhaired layabout not unlike the indie Canned Heat. Partying in a derelict building littered with dead washing machines and rusting car parts, it's fair to say that the constant tomspliffery was eating into our collective sanity and momentum. Nevertheless, we had stockpiled an impressive collection of songs and our live shows were still popular affairs.

The A&R incident began when one of our friends turned up to a Coach & Horses show armed with an eye-catching female companion in tow. This got us all interested. The girl in question happened to be a junior employee at Chrysalis Records. Pattie Parsons was a curvaceous nineteen-year old who liked our music enough to ask for a demo tape. This was a promising start. Over the course of our first evening together, it became apparent that Ms. Parsons was connected to rising bands of the moment like EMF, Poppy Factory and 35 Summers. If I'm honest I should admit that I was distracted by her magnificent cleavage and probably wasn't paying enough attention to what she was saying. And neither was our manager.

A few days later, the first of many packages carrying numerous records and CDs procured from her label's impressive roster arrived at band HQ. In handwritten letters on company-headed notepaper, Pattie referred to several lurid encounters with members of other popular early 1990s acts. In short, she was a bit of a name-dropping sexy machine. But that's par for the course, right? It's the music industry. Not the church. Over the next few weeks Pattie stayed in constant touch and one evening excitedly phoned Mark at home with the rather bizarre news that a certain Mr Chesney Hawkes (then signed to Chrysalis) was now a big fan of the band. Even more improbable was the titbit that Sir Chez had apparently gone on air at Radio One to proclaim his undying love for an unsigned group called The Violet Trade.

I never managed to fully substantiate this most interesting of rumours, although another friend swore blind that he had heard the tail end of this story on the very day of its original transmission (circa August 1991). Stranger still, a few years later I would bump into Chesney at a gig in London, where his sister was singing with the (then) newly signed Transistor. Coincidentally, my band just happened to be the support act. When I spotted Sir Chez lurking in the corridor outside the dressing rooms, somehow I lost my nerve and couldn't bring myself to ask whether the Violet Trade story had really been true.

Open up your eyes and see the person I call me
We could take a walk and pick some
blackberries for tea.

(*Blackberries*. Simon McKay/The Violet Trade. 1991).

Pattie returned to watch us perform several times. Apparently, the Head of A&R also liked the VT demo tape. Pattie stayed over at our house and seemed totally oblivious to anything strange about her surroundings, content instead to regale us with her X-rated tales of record company rumpy. We could never keep her on the subject of the band for long enough to ascertain just how much Chrysalis really liked us.

And so it continued. Violet Trade would play a gig and Pattie would turn up and take photographs. Decked out in a pukey collection of floral shirts (all except Gary that is, as he remained resolutely in washed-out Goth black) we did our best to impress.

Anticipation grew like an expanding balloon at a birthday party. Of course, time responded in its usual fashion by immediately slowing to a deathly crawl. Every ring of the telephone could have been the Managing Director at Chrysalis summoning us to Shepherds Bush for our shot at fame and fortune. Alas, it always seemed to be the landlord asking us to hurry up and move out.

The freebies kept arriving and it felt as if something truly amazing was just around the corner for The Violet Trade. We were at the peak of our song-writing prowess in 1991, and it would have been poetic justice should we have gotten signed at this moment.

Real life rarely plays out the way you want it to. It was time for that next kick in the goolies...

DEAL OR NO DEAL?

Suddenly, all communication between Pattie and the band came to a grinding halt. Our blonde bombshell inexplicably disappeared from behind her desk and nobody at the label seemed to know where she had gone or, more importantly, when she was coming back. Mark's polite but desperate inquiries went unanswered and it began to feel as if we had all imagined Pattie's existence. Surely we couldn't have been that out of it, could we?

Pattie eventually resurfaced a few weeks later and called Mark from her flat in Chelsea. We arranged to meet at a Blue Aeroplanes' show at the Town and Country club in Kentish Town to find out what was going on. Things started to go wrong almost immediately when we found that that our names weren't on the guest list as promised. In fact, Mark ended up paying for all three tickets, and as we stood haggling at the box office, other members of the Chrysalis A&R team flashed their passes and cast Pattie derogatory looks as they breezed in to the venue. Blur arrived and poured themselves out of a taxi, steaming drunk. Pattie made a beeline for Graham Coxon, who bolted towards the sanctuary of the backstage area. If alarm bells were ringing, both Mark and I couldn't hear them above the excellent noise of the Blue Aeroplanes, who turned in a belter of a set. This culminated with about ten band members thrashing away at guitars during the final encore of *Breaking in My Heart*.

MY TOP 10 BLUE AEROPLANES TRACKS

1. Growing Up Growing Down (Friendloverplane 2)
2. Beautiful Is (As Beautiful Does) (Altitude)
3. Yr Own World (Beat Songs)
4. Your Ages (Swagger)
5. Up In a Down World (Altitude)
6. Broken and Mended (Life Model)
7. Disneyhead (Friendloverplane 2)
8. Mercury (Hold-Protect-Love) (Life Model)
9. Breaking in My Heart (Warhol's 15)
10. ...and Stones (Swagger)

After the show we gave Pattie a lift back to her flat. Once ensconced at chez Pattie our uneven host refused to talk about what had happened at Chrysalis and informed us that she was now going to be a professional dancer. She also intimated that she was up for a threesome. Mark and I cast each other a quick glance. This was a bit unexpected. On my way back from the loo I took a quick peak inside her bedroom. Plastered all over the walls were those photographs of Violet Trade. Houston- we have a problem. Mark and I left before anything stranger could occur.

We persisted with phone calls to Chrysalis and eventually Mark managed to corner the Head of A&R, who confessed in the strictest confidence that Pattie had been recently dismissed for 'unsuitable' behaviour. In a business as filthy as the one of music, this didn't exactly fill in a great deal of the blanks.

Of course, nobody at the label had ever heard of our band, but the A&R department did offer to listen to a demo tape by way of an apology. Mark duly forwarded a cassette, and once again we held our breath. A few days later, a standard issue photocopied reply detailing how we 'weren't what Chrysalis were looking for', dropped unceremoniously through the letterbox at 68, Summersdale Road.

This neatly curtailed our first disappointment with a major record company and it also heralded the start of a slow decline for The Violet Trade.

DOWN THE DIP

After months of rumours, our house was finally demolished, and with it went that all-important rehearsal room. Mark and I were actually travelling around Europe in a car when it was bulldozed to the ground, but I returned to find all of my belongings, and most of my bedroom wall, in the back of the band van. After too much time living on friend's couches, Gary and I finally managed to locate a landlord foolish enough to rent us another place. My old mate Robbie Wheeler moved in as well, although we had to keep him hidden from the owners until the tenancy had been well and truly inked. By now Rob was a strapping mass of unwashed hair and army surplus clothing. He looked a bit like Cousin 'It' gone grunge.

Because we were no longer all living under the same roof, the band split into two friendship camps. Gary and I wanted a record deal at any cost, and as we continued to live together, would spend most of our waking hours plotting VTs next move. But Simon and Greg could only feign interest in the future of the group and the good ship Violet Trade started to list violently. The Pattie episode had left us all feeling slightly stupid, and I could see the enthusiasm visibly draining out of Simon and Greg.

Had a look in your bottom drawer of broken things to see
In amongst the photographs - a future there for me.

(*Velocity Street*. Simon Parker/The Violet Trade. 1991).

The drugs made it hard to focus or move forward, and I grew frustrated with playing the same set over and over again. Simon's confidence in our newer material seemed to be diminishing, even though songs like *All I Hear Is Music*, *Bad Day* and *Meringue* were all excellent proto-Britpop anthems.

MY TOP TEN ACTS OF THE EARLY 1990s
1. Teenage Fanclub
2. Ride
3. The Boo Radleys
4. Dinosaur Jr
5. Trash Can Sinatra's
6. The Band Of Holy Joy
7. Julian Cope
8. The Rockingbirds
9. Power Of Dreams
10. Ned's Atomic Dustbin

Living in Chichester meant that we had absolutely no chance of being spotted by a record company. Worryingly, by 1992 Simon had started to resemble a bearded and less communicative version of Shaun Ryder. We did the rounds of playing the Mean Fiddler venues of the early 90s, where emerging acts like PJ Harvey, Suede, Senseless Things, Pooh Sticks, Mercury Rev, Pulp, Laverne and Shirley (soon to be Spearmint), Thousand Yard Stare, Candyskins, Venus Beads and Kingmaker all regularly gigged. But because we weren't from London and could no longer promise a busload of fans to attend, Violet Trade languished on unsigned bills with other unheard of entities.

I DON'T LIKE CRICKET...

In case you're wondering, part of the Mean Fiddler booking process of the early 90s involved demo tapes and a cricket bat. If a member of the booking team caught a cassette as it flew across the office, chances are this band might be offered a gig. A rather drunk ex-member of staff told me this in confidence a while back.
We really didn't stand a bloody chance, did we?

NEVERMIND

Meanwhile, back in Chichester, acts like 'My Cousin Rachel' and 'Oba Topei' had started to build up their own sizeable followings. Even Robbie Wheeler had gotten in on the act and was now enthusiastically thrashing away behind the drum kit for a rock band called 'Squelch'.
I couldn't help but notice that Violet Trade was starting to sound a little flimsy in comparison to those longhaired oiks that the NME and Melody Maker were championing. The first wave of grunge had washed ashore on a punk rock coastline and was busy sticking it to Messrs. Hucknall and Collins. But VT made mannered indie pop which was diametrically opposed to the spirit of grunge. When Squelch got the chance to support Midway Still, Gary and I were left to gravely ruminate on our own growing misfortunes from the back of the Coach & Horses. Nirvana had re-opened every aspiring teenage musician's eyes and ears to the possibility of playing very loud electric guitars again.

Here we were at the dawning of another musical year zero. Somehow The Violet Trade had ended up on the wrong side of the fence. Now I knew just what Emerson, Lake and Palmer must have been feeling when punk first appeared. The only trouble was, I had never wanted to be in bloody ELP.

It was at this point that my Gothic drumming buddy and I decided to prove that we weren't quite musical dinosaurs yet. Yet, despite our heartfelt battle cry, we spectacularly failed in our mission by forming a band that was even less noisy than The Violet Trade.

THE WHISKEY GIRLS (1992-3)

Over many a can of Bavaria Super Strength, the short-lived Whiskey Girls project was born into a world of testosterone and Pearl Jam. For some reason Gary and I decided to form a folk-pop band. Even though we knew it was all about the rock in 1992.

Together with Sue Marsh and the mild-mannered vocalist Steve Tett (once of Amazing Windmills), we wrote a number of melodic tunes that were augmented by the unexpected arrival of a classically trained violinist called Shelley Britton. The Whiskey Girls then descended upon south coast venues during the summer of 1992, with a sound that owed more than a little bit to The Wonderstuff's *Golden Green*. Clutching a tin of 8.6 % proof in one hand and a half-smoked reefer in the other, Gary and I enjoyed the spontaneity of playing with a new band, despite the fact that we hadn't actually moved any closer to approximating grunge's bad tempered racket.

Alternative and indie music was a hugely popular subculture by this time. The Cure had gone straight into the charts at number one with their *Wish* album, dethroning the likes of Jimmy Nail and Right Said Fred forever. Well, nearly forever.

The Whiskey Girls turned out to be great fun, not least because the glamorous Shelley had a habit of under dressing for gigs. Consequently, whenever we chose to play live, our violinist's side of the stage was always populated by a disproportionate number of male on-lookers.

Our violinist quickly became attracted to the booze-and-spliff-related lifestyle that followed Gary and I from house to house. Inevitably, things took a turn for the messy when she and I wound up alone in my underground lair after a rehearsal. At the time, I was living amongst the amps and drums in a damp cellar, and following one too many cans of the devil's brew, she ended up staying over and we shared a bed together. Somehow we managed to avoid playing the inevitable hide the sausage game, although I was forced to lay there in the darkness trying my best not to think of anything remotely sexy.

It was a very long night.

The Whiskey Girls' star burned brightly under the spotlight of its one and only London live appearance. Gary certainly didn't do us any favours by telling an A&R scout that we were just doing the band 'for a laugh'. The guy cast Gary a surprised look shortly before scuttling towards the exit faster than I could shout 'don't listen to him-he's only the bloody drummer...'

TOP-TIP FIVE:

NEVER LET YOUR DRUMMER DO THE TALKING

The Whiskey Girls
(l-r Steve Tett, Marc Russell, Simon Parker, Shelley Britton, Sue Marsh, Gary
Capelin – photo Mark Mason)

NEW PUNKS AGAINST TROMBONES

Violet Trade wearily regrouped in September 1992. Only this time we were a five-piece. Whilst the drummer and bass player had been fiddling whilst Rome burned, singer and pianist had recruited a new member. It was just a shame that they hadn't thought to mention anything to their band mates first.

Ted Tedman (I kid you not) was the lucky man invited to join VT, and he trailed an electric guitar, trombone, bongos and harmonica behind him. Ted was busy studying music at the local college and decided to bring the baggage of musical theory with him. Whereas in the past our best ideas had always sprung from happy accidents or a cup of mushroom tea, now I was faced with having to explain my songs in order to get him to play something relevant. I have long believed it is less about how many notes you use, but much more about how passionately you play the few you do select that really makes all the difference.

Such a transformation for our band made for awkward rehearsals back in 1992. Ted was only really able to add something of worth if you told him which band to imitate the style of. And as we did this, every other group in the country simply turned their amps up to eleven.

EARTHBOUND RECORDS

Pyramid of Johnny (the only group in the world to regularly cover our songs) gave me the address of a small record label called 'Earthbound'. Amazingly, this tiny indie loved our demo and called with an offer to release *Salvation* as a twelve-inch single, should we first agree to re-record it. This song had long been a classic VT moment at gigs, complete with its surging, circular vocal motif and a drumbeat slightly reminiscent of a messier version of Talk Talk's *Life's What You Make It*. Unfortunately, the indie-dance heyday was now some way behind us, but who was I to argue with the first label to show an interest in us since the Chrysalis catastrophe? I told myself that this was not the time to be nit picking. Besides, we could always record something fresher for our second single... couldn't we?

So, The Violet Trade scrimped and saved to pay for the necessary recording time at the label's miniscule studio in Reigate and emerged with a heavily edited version of the track. Listening back to it now, *Salvation* is marred by a spectacularly 'wine bar' piano solo. One of the problems with smoking dope during recording sessions is that you invariably make bad choices and wrong decisions.

Still, Earthbound seemed pretty happy with the results and instructed us to rehearse for imminent live shows whilst they manufactured the record. Weeks passed and an old familiar feeling started to set in. This was a road I did not want to be on.

Of course, we never heard from Earthbound again. The ruse was that the label never intended to put out our (or any other bands) records, but they did make a nifty little profit from the recording time that we agreed to pay for. All we had to show for our £300 investment was a stolen cassette copy that was rendered unusable when the tape accidentally twisted in my stereo system the first time I played it in the band van.

Following this, VT rehearsals became even more infrequent, with many cancelled at the last minute for the flimsiest of excuses. Our rusting mode of transport sat on Simon's driveway and continually refused to start, leaving us unable to play even the most local of shows. Some fifteen years later, our singer finally admitted that this might have had quite a lot to do with the fact that he used to disable the engine's spark plugs just minutes before we arrived to load up for anything band related...

GOING NOWHERE

Gary and I knew that we had to get out of Chichester. We owed a small fortune to the local garage for van repairs and were perilously close to breaking up.

Ex-Whiskey Girl Sue Marsh was now working at Thames Valley University and booked us to play a lucrative show during Fresher's Week in October of 1992. Unfortunately, the gig was called off minutes before we took to the stage thanks to a volley of complaints from local neighbours. Impressively, we were still paid and drank rather a lot of beer. Somehow, several crates of Ribena which had been destined for the raffle, ended up in the back of our van. Perhaps not surprisingly, Sue never booked another band during her time at the University. However, she did offer to run the fan club for both Phillip Schofield and Bobby Crush, but sadly, both turned her down.

119

Sue Marsh still lives in London and can regularly be seen with her head wedged in the doors of the tube train, where she enjoys those breath-taking views along the District line. When not commuting in this strange manner, she records music under her 'Mildred Bleak' alter ego. In case you're wondering, she did eventually forgive me for my part in that soft drinks heist, but not until quite recently when I offered to play on her album for nothing.

ASHES TO ASHES

The Violet Trade eventually called it a day in December 1992. Gary and I decided to leave Chichester far behind us (well, at least forty miles or so) and make the life-changing pilgrimage to music-savvy Brighton.

My Gothic buddy and I spent Christmas formulating a number of grandiose plans on how to take Brighton's burgeoning scene by storm. Our proposed move may only have been a short drive along the coast, yet it still felt as if we were about to depart for another planet. Legions of small-town idealists often harbour lofty plans about how they are going to take on the world, yet when it comes down to it, few uproot to a new hostile environment for fear of failure and ridicule. I was 25 years old and knew that if I didn't get out of my hometown at this precise moment then I would probably never leave at all.

In January 1993, The Violet Trade played their final gig at the Coach & Horses. Due in part to the venue's sudden acquisition by a Chinese restaurant, we were forced to play on a quiet Monday evening. Consequently, there were only thirty or forty people in the audience that night. It was a sad occasion and an ill-fitting tribute to a band that deserved a better send-off. The show included numbers spanning those three full years of partying for the hell of it. As we took to the stage, I realised that these songs would probably never be heard again. Each number bought back memories of a better time when just showing the rest of the band how to play a new tune felt more important than trying to figure out a way of luring A&R sloths along to another treacherous London show.

The very last song of this poignant evening was a spirited rendition of Camper Van Beethoven's *Take the Skinheads Bowling*. From behind a screen erected to the side of the stage, the four original members of Violet Trade swapped instruments and stage attire. Gary squirmed into Greg's garish threads and prodded enthusiastically at that battered keyboard as it wobbled atop an old ironing board. Simon McKay wedged himself into our Gothic timekeeper's skin-tight black uniform to keep a steady beat behind the drum kit. The diminutive Greg Saunders drowned in one of my over-sized shirts, whilst I wrestled with Simon McKay's questionable wardrobe for approximately two minutes and thirty-five seconds of my life. Believe me that was quite long enough.

Suddenly, I was getting my first taste of what it was like to front a band. Despite the fact that I was only singing to friends and family, it felt electrifying. For those of you wondering, Ted simply remained Ted Tedman, the boy with the dented trombone. And then it was all over and we were no longer in a band together anymore.

YOU SHOULD ALWAYS KEEP IN TOUCH WITH YOUR FRIENDS

The following afternoon, we sold the beaten up band van for an eighth of hash. The five members of The Violet Trade then spent one final evening getting very stoned. After this, Gary and I would rarely see or hear from our ex-band mates for the next couple of years. In that time we would cover a lot of ground.

The Violet Trade with Ted Tedman
(l-r Ted, Simon Parker, Simon McKay, Greg Sunders, Gary Capelin)

THE LETTER

A short while after we departed for Brighton, a letter appeared in the back pages of NME. Or was it Melody Maker? Anyway, over a couple of heartfelt paragraphs, an anonymous individual outlined the closure of The Coach & Horses pub, pointing out that Chichester was now in the grim position of having precisely nowhere for bands to play. This letter then went on to name-check The Violet Trade as being one of the two best local bands that the 'scene' had thrown up. This would become the one and only time that VT ever made the hallowed pages of the national music press. Alas, we had just gone our separate ways.

Whoever that mystery letter writer was, may I thank you on behalf of The Violet Trade. At the time I suspected that it was either Mark or Gary's handiwork. But it was nice to know they cared...

VIOLET TRADE ADDENDUM

Fast-forwarding to 2013, Ted Tedman continues to make the odd appearance in pubs around Sussex armed only with a trusty harmonica. Simon McKay never formed another band after his time in VT although he continues to write and record at home. Nowadays, both he and keyboard player Greg live and work in Brighton as well, where the diminutive ivory-tinkler has been rather more successful in business than he ever was in music. We occasionally hook up for a beer and hazily recalled memories. It's very true what they say about hash smoking and the short-term memory isn't it?

Recently, it's come to light that the former members of Violet Trade could never watch my peculiarly jerky stage movements during our gigging days, as it would completely throw their own sense of timing out of whack. Embarrassingly, I am aware that this particular trait has followed me through just about all of the bands I have been in. That I have somehow managed to execute (reasonably) accurate bass guitar throughout my performing days is nothing short of miraculous to those that have watched me dance like a stiff Uncle with a swarm of angry bees swimming around in his underpants.

LIFT THE NEEDLE FROM THE RECORD
AND FLIP OVER TO SIDE TWO ▶

► chapter seven

MOVING

COLOURBURST MK. I 1993

The first thing I noticed about Brighton was that there were so many amazingly beautiful girls. The second thing was the pace of life, which felt much quicker than sleepy Chichester. For example, I started work at the HMV store on a Friday morning, and by lunchtime had already located a new guitarist. Fate obviously wanted me to get on with it...

I had just turned 26. Brighton was a fashion conscious town, so I quickly lost the stoner mullet, which at the time had none of the ironic fashion status that it went on to enjoy in later years. I even lost the beer-belly, although this had more to do with the fact that I was thrust into a job better suited to two people. Back when people were still willing to spend their disposable income on recorded music, I would spend my days running round like a lunatic frantically ordering chart CDs.

Still, at least there were a million and one pubs to get drunk in. Armed only with a monthly pay packet and new guitarist James Portinari in tow, my new friend and I would embark on lager-fuelled sessions, trying to outdo each other with lists of ever-more obscure indie bands. We also talked about The Cure, James being another big fan. We quickly found that we had a lot in common and formed a strong allegiance.

Ex-Whiskey Girl Steve Tett was drafted in as vocalist for our new line up, even though he was then still in the final few months of his degree at Lancaster University. During his absence Gary, James and I spent a couple of months figuring out a brave new sound and then faithfully posted cassettes of rehearsals to the other end of the country every time we needed some lyrics written. We

125

held our first rehearsals in the cellar of Cobra Sports on Western Road, where ex-Violet Trade manager Mark Mason was now in charge. Indeed, it was my friend's enthusiastic reports of live bands and late night drinking which had been a major factor in the relocation to Brighton.

At first, it was daunting to be the small fish in a big pond. I knew that we would have to work hard to get noticed in a town as musically astute as Brighton. Accordingly, Gary and I drew up a new agenda. It was very different from the one that we had adhered to in The Violet Trade. I like to think that this is still a good blueprint for any new band, although, in our case we weren't able to adhere to item number two for very long.

A NEW AGENDA

✓ Meet like-minded musicians. Ask them to be in your band.

✓ Stop smoking hash. It slows you down.

✓ Rehearse at least three times a week.

✓ Put the importance of the band before your own personal commitments.

✓ Don't let each other down.

✓ Suffer for your art if you want to make it.

✓ Have nothing to do with any particular musical style or genre.

✓ Make good use of a distortion pedal.

Despite grunge's best intentions to infiltrate the mainstream, 1993 was full of nasty little blotches like 2 Unlimited and Ace of Base. There were still far too many

Bon Jovis and Annie Lennoxes to go round. Groups like American Music Club (*Mercury*), The Posies (*Frosting on the Beater*) and Jellyfish (*Spilt Milk*) all released quality albums that barely scraped the lower reaches of the charts.

MY AMERICAN MUSIC CLUB & MARK EITZEL ALL TIME TOP 10 TRACKS

1. Western Sky (The Ugly American)
2. Home (Love Songs for Patriots)
3. If I Had a Hammer (Mercury)
4. One Step Ahead (The Golden Age)
5. I Love you but you're Dead (Don't be a Stranger)
6. Go Away (Caught in a Trap...)
7. I Broke My Promise (San Francisco)
8. Johnny Mathis' Feet (Mercury)
9. Why Won't You Stay? (Everclear)
10. At My Mercy (Engine)

The British record buying public seemed fixated on Culture Beat and Shaggy, so it was left to REM to carry the torch of alternative rock with their *Out Of Time* and *Automatic for the People* records. Most major labels went about their business believing they were living in the 1980s. Consequently, old farts like UB40 and Wet Wet Wet continued to sail to the top of the charts, despite what our noisy American cousins might have been advocating. So it kind of still felt like the previous decade, really.

Around this time NME started recommending Suede and The Auteurs as the hot new indie bands to adore. Both possessed a knack for welding decent tunes to a twisted pop psyche that would go a long way to help revitalise British-based alternative music in the continued absence of the gone-to-seed Stone Roses or bombed-out Happy Mondays. Suede's impressive taste in trousers would also aid and abet their rise to the front covers of various important U.K music publications throughout 1993, with the band going on to become the biggest alternative group in the country by 1994. Just a few months prior to all of this, Suede was just a bunch of skinny guys from Haywards

Heath who were often performing at those very same empty London venues as the luckless Violet Trade.

I began to see what was required of us, if we were to succeed.

TOP-TIP SIX:

DEVELOP AN IMAGE. MOVE TO LONDON.

SUBCULTURE

Grunge quickly sold out to the corporations, who, displaying their characteristic greed and misunderstanding of a popular underground scene, then simply decided that they would dress down a bevy of rubbish heavy metal bands and sell them on as 'punk rock' to the disenfranchised middle-class children of the Western world. And it worked, for a while.

In the UK, the so-called 'shoe-gazing' movement hailed those with loud, floating guitars and quiet, dreamy vocalists. After an initial bout of fervent swooning by the music press, 'the scene that celebrated itself' was callously laid waste by an army of bitchy journalists, with only Ride, Lush and The Boo Radleys seeing any notable chart activity. Such groups as Chapterhouse, Revolver, Slowdive and Swervedriver all continued to struggle as the music press bit down hard on its own poisonous tongue.

The early 90s were a worrying time in English pop music. From the confines of the HMV sales counter, I witnessed an unexpected shift in musical tastes during this uncertain period. A new breed of record buyer seemed far more interested in BPM than a soaring chorus. Hardcore, rave, jungle and techno twelve-inch singles flooded into the store via a bewildering array of tiny dance labels. Nobody seemed that bothered by the latest release by Moose. Well, nobody except for me.

EARLY 90s SHOEGAZE/DREAM POP TOP 10

1. Swervedriver - Duel
2. Moose - Little Bird
3. Slowdive - Souvlaki Space Station
4. Disco Inferno - It's a Kid's World
5. AR Kane - When You're Sad
6. Ride - Like a Daydream
7. Catherine Wheel - Black Metallic
8. Swervedriver - Never Lose That Feeling
9. Kitchens of Distinction - 4 Men
10. Drop Nineteens - My Aquarium

Brighton has long enjoyed a strong association with dance music and club culture, with this scene truly exploding in the early 90s. This meant that, somehow, I had successfully transferred myself to the best indie music town on the south coast just as it decided to lose all faith in guitar bands.

On top of this, Gary and I soon discovered that the local music scene was not quite as cutting edge as we had first suspected. Indeed, the unsigned Brighton demographic seemed to be populated by sub-baggy stoners clinging to the past in their blim-burned T-shirts. The only new thing in town involved dreadlocked traveller types playing super-long flute jams through delay pedals. Imagine an army of Jethro Tull look-a-likes busking in the subways. It wasn't pleasant. To make matters worse, a fair percentage of Brighton's wannabe population seemed utterly oblivious to the fact that we were living in the 1990s and dressed as though Quadrophenia was just about to happen all over again. If rock wasn't ragged jeans and plaid shirts, then it was horrible funk bullies in basketball vests. This was both distressing and distasteful. The Spin Doctors were becoming massively popular out there in the charts and beards were making a comeback amongst lazy unsigned musicians for the first time since the mid-seventies. Sprinkle in the usual proliferation of ultra crappy local heavy metal outfits, and I suppose it's not hard to see why dance music suddenly became so appealing.

GIANT STEPS

Back in the rehearsal room, Gary, James and I took refuge from this shit storm and auditioned possible second guitarists. We talked about creating a vast melodic emptiness with most of the noise channelled into short bursts of frenzied disgust. Or, in layman's terms, we simply wanted to have quiet and loud bits in our songs, just like the Pixies. Unfortunately, most of the musicians that we encountered were far too busy emulating The Levellers, then the City's biggest musical export. So whilst the world was busy going raggle-taggle gypsy-folk and nailing bits of carpet to its guitars, my band mates and I prayed for something a little bit darker and glamorous. As would-be accomplices pranced around the sports shop cellar on one leg shouting 'hey nonny nonny', we glanced at each other with barely suppressed contempt for new hippies. This was most certainly not where we were heading.

I became obsessed with The Boo Radleys' *Giant Steps* album, and was intrigued by the bands kaleidoscopic sound. Many years later, ex-Radley singer Sice would make my day by sending me an email detailing his liking of some of my very own musical creations. I love that sort of stuff.

MY TOP 10 BOO RADLEYS TRACKS

1. Lazy Day (Everything's Alright Forever)
2. Lazarus (Giant Steps)
3. Towards the Light (Everything's Alright Forever)
4. Upon 9th and Fairchild (Giant Steps)
5. Stuck On Amber (Wake Up)
6. Does This Hurt? (Everything's Alright Forever)
7. The White Noise Revisited (Giant Steps)
8. Find the Answer Within (Wake Up)
9. Barney and Me (Giant Steps)
10. Kingsize (Kingsize)

Jim and I often surveyed the Brighton music scene. After three or four pints of 'old-fight-yourself', we regularly stumbled into arguments with people for the way they revered and encouraged the importance of the disc jockey. Now, both Jim and I have gone on to spend a fair amount of time as indie DJ's... so maybe we were just jealous, but this is what we always preached back then.

TOP-TIP SEVEN:

DJ'S SHOULD NEVER HOLD COURT OVER MUSICIANS.
EVER.

WHO ARE YOU?

Up in Lancaster, Steve's initial response to our new sound had been very encouraging. Indeed, he swiftly turned in some stinging lyrics to a song called *Minor Character*. But when he stalled his move to Brighton I began to wonder what could be going on in his mind. Surely this was the chance of a lifetime, right?

As the weeks rolled by, our vocalist became harder to track down and without mobile phones or the Internet, all we could do was wait for a letter or phone box communication as some sign of vague reassurance. It gradually filtered through that Steve had accepted a summer job in Germany, where he would be labouring on a building site much like those motley characters from 'Auf Wiedersehen Pet'. One look at the effeminate and cack-handed Mr Tett would have told you this was a highly unlikely scenario. I hazarded a guess that he was busy playing nudie prod games over in Bristol, where his bad-news girlfriend was carrying out her own studies.

Following a fraught couple of months, Steve very hesitantly joined Gary and me in our tiny third-floor flat near the town centre. Giving our vocalist absolutely no time to settle in or find his feet, we booked a recording session with the legendary Terry Popple at Bloomsbury Studios in Kemp Town. This big-hearted Northerner had previously played drums with the likes of SNAFU and Van

131

Morrison. No, I wasn't particularly sure if this was a good or bad thing either, but the big guy convinced us that he could make a decent job of recording our band's first demo, so the offer was graciously accepted.

Oh, and we finally had a band name...

COLOURBURST

It had taken months to whittle down a vast array of possibilities to an under-whelming bunch of no-hopers that included the likes of 'Rainmouth', 'The Framing of Archie Clay' and 'The Face Lickers'. Via a democratic voting system, we had somehow voted out all the good ones and were now left with just the most amusing or stupid, not unlike electing politicians, when you come to think about it.

Fearing that we may become 'The Trouser Uncles' at any moment, Steve and I went out for a walk and spontaneously fired words at each other until 'colour' (me) and 'burst' (him) fell out of our mouths in quick succession. Honestly, it felt as if we had just scored the winning goal of the Cup Final in the ninety-third minute.

And then, without warning, one of my all-time favourite albums was released...

THE TRASHCAN SINATRAS – *I'VE SEEN EVERYTHING* (1993)

During a spot of inter-railing back in 1991, I had fallen in love with *Cake*, the debut album by Scottish band The Trashcan Sinatras. *Obscurity Knocks* still reminds me of late night adventures in Paris, when Ed Wheatley nearly got mugged in a back alleyway whilst Mark and I drunkenly staggered on, blissfully unaware of any commotion behind us. When *I've Seen Everything* came out in 1993, I had no idea it was going to have such a big impact on my life. In the event, the Trashcan's second album would soundtrack my transition from confident small-town know-it-all to melancholic indie drunkard.

The Trashies are a hugely underappreciated group who excel in crafting sad and glorious music. Back in 1993,

132

those minor chords and snowy melodies perfectly suited my changing frame of mind. I would often go late night walking nowhere in particular just so that I could load *I've Seen Everything* into a Walkman and explore my new hometown in the company of those terrific songs. Listening to the Trashies made me feel reflective. Drinking exacerbated things, but I was never a loud or aggressive drunk. In fact I quite liked this new Simon. Years later, that same bottomless, melancholic feeling is still with me and forever leading me into self-inflicted trouble. I have the Trashcan Sinatras to thank for this, for it all started when I fell in love with *I've Seen Everything*.

The album opens with *Easy Read*, which is possibly one of the most beautiful songs ever written. It swoops and glides, changing key as it shifts up through the gears. The word 'exquisite' was possibly invented to describe this track. I dare you not be moved. *Orange Fell* transforms from hushed beginnings to a beautiful lullaby for the lovelorn, whilst the record's title track is as world-weary as one could ever wish to be without actually running over the edge of a cliff. Guitars jangle and vocals purr. The drums caress and melodies gently coerce you into submission. The Trashies second long player is a powerful seductress, once experienced never to be forgotten. Unfortunately, it happened to be released at a time when the words 'measured' and 'tasteful' were severely outlawed in music. By comparison, everything else sounded cheap and crass to me, but of course it was TCS who failed to sell. This only increased my respect for it, and I made sure to order up various 'spare' copies for HMV whenever I could.

Twenty years after it was first released and I still feel exactly the same about *I've Seen Everything*. A giddy mixture of romance and sadness pulses through me every time I play the album. I recommend that you go and investigate it now.

I'll wait here for you...

IN THE STUDIO (Pt. 1)

I could have been a child star
When I look back now I could have gone so far

(Minor *Character*. Steve Tett/Colourburst. 1993)

The night before our first Colourburst recording session, Steve Tett sheepishly admitted that he hadn't actually managed to get around to finishing any of the lyrics yet. Cue panic and endless lakes of coffee whilst the pair of us soldiered on through the night to revamp the missing or crap bits. Luckily, I had pages of drunken scribble for us to choose from, and even Gary got in on the act by recycling an ancient poem, stolen from a distant family relation.

If heartache bought fame in love's mad game
I'd be a legend in my time...

(*Within Without*. Ray Moore/Colourburst. 1993)

Despite the suspicion that our singer was only running on half-power, we were all very excited with the results of our first trip to a proper recording studio. To be fair, Steve had been dropped in at the deep end but it was clear for all to see that he didn't share our insane hunger for band life. To the delicate singer, this was merely something to do before he was forced into paying off his student loan. But it was a very different story for Gary, James and I, as Colourburst was our only means of escape from lives spent in dead-end jobs.

After rehearsing without a vocalist for the best part of six months, the three of us had stumbled upon an interesting sound, far removed from Violet Trade's shiny three-minute smiles. Bass and guitar were sparse, brittle and argumentative. Gary was at the peak of his playing abilities and propelled the songs with deft precision. Over the top of this Steve could have been reciting the phone book and it would have still sounded fairly interesting. It's possible that if we had focused on this atmospheric side to our nature we would have attracted more comparisons to

Radiohead, who, at the time, were only just starting to break through. But my straight-ahead indie nature allowed us to include just a few too many breezy numbers that went against the grain of our darker alter ego. Damn those pop songs!

The six-track *Nova* EP was released in October 1993. Fanzine reviews were encouragingly good, and we started playing live shows soon after. Beginning with a support slot to Orange Deluxe (who had just morphed out of the much-hyped but short-lived 5.30) and then a second booking at the impressive Pavilion Theatre in Brighton, we chose to throw in bloody-minded cover versions of Wham's *Freedom* and The Divinyls *I Touch Myself* which, although bastardized, again only served to confuse our new audience.

LOCKED OUT

We built for the big time by playing a handful of non-descript shows around the East Sussex area. It must be said that these gigs took place without a great deal of enthusiasm for our (bad) tempered new sound. On one such memorable occasion, I somehow managed to lose the keys to our hired Transit van in sub-zero temperatures. Cleverly, we were still about twenty miles north of the nearest area of civilisation. As the four of us huddled together for warmth, praying for the arrival of the only twenty-four hour locksmith in the South of England, Steve looked as though he was living a particularly hellish nightmare.

PLAYING TO AN AUDIENCE CALLED 'MARK'

Colourburst ended 1993 with a low-key acoustic show at The Princess Victoria pub in Brighton. Coincidence nudged distant memories of that fabled Blurred Vision show I had attended at Chichester's' very own Princess Vic all those many moons ago. In fact, over ten long years had now evaporated since that momentous decision to give my life to music. But was I really any closer to fulfilling the dream?

Not on the evidence of this gig, because an impressive crowd of just three people turned up to watch us sit like silly sods atop wobbly bar stools whilst we earnestly strummed our way through a clutch of first demo material , not forgetting that obligatory-at-some-point-in-your-career cover of The Jam's *That's Entertainment*. Apart from the ever-present Mark Mason, the only other punters in this evening's three-strong gathering were two very pissed strangers. Strangely, both shared the same Christian name as my best friend. We were playing to an audience of 'Marks'. It was as sad as it was funny.

At the end of the gig, the thin Mark rambled on about how he used to be in North of Cornwallis whom I had seen supporting The Housemartins back in the mid-eighties, whilst the larger Mark offered a business card and slurred something about the Irish three-piece The Frank and Walters, then riding quite high. Eventually, the thin Mark finally staggered off into the night with his rotund mate trailing behind, inelegantly falling into skips and lamp-posts whilst trying to negotiate his way towards the nearest taxi rank.

Unbeknownst to the band, but we had just experienced our first meeting with the soon-to-be manager of Colourburst...

OVERVIEW OF AN UNDERWHELMING YEAR

Despite a list of minor gripes, Gary and I knew that we had made the right decision to relocate to Brighton. Just nine short months after leaving Chichester, we were back on track and praying that 1994 would turn out to be the year that we finally got noticed. Even though we were no closer to a record deal, our plan was sort of working.

Colourburst got ready to welcome in the New Year much like everybody else with equal measures of booze, drink and a little bit of alcohol. But, on the morning of December 31st 1993, we awoke to find a 'Dear John' note taped to the TV set. Detailing Steve's dramatic late night exit from the band, our singer's wily girlfriend had managed to convince the unsettled singer to slope off and shack up in Bristol. And so, on the very last day of the year, Colourburst had become suddenly useless again.

I'm sure that I'm not sure
I left my point of view with a good friend, in a dead end

(*Gravitate to Me*. Simon Parker/Colourburst. 1993)

COLOURBURST (MK. I) ADDENDUM

Whilst gathering information for this book, I did one of those Google searches on the word 'Colourburst'. Here, I stumbled upon a seemingly harmless post on Billy Bragg's message forum that slowly unfurled as a description of our ex-singer's departure from the band. When I realised it was Steve using an Internet pseudonym, I read on with interest whilst he described his fearless escape from a 'tyrannical bass player'.

Steve and I had been in touch via the net for a couple of years before I discovered this most revealing of posts. By the early 2000s, the ex-singer of Colourburst was a teacher, living and working in Denmark with a wife and young family. After being reminded of his colourful description of me, Steve apologised for the use of the word 'tyrannical', which, the more I think about it, was probably pretty accurate at the time.

Evidently, I had come a long way from those misty days of being easy-going and forever stoned. My determination and commitment were obviously starting to get the better of me. In private moments I was, of course, a sad drunk, but to my band mates I was the one who would bulldoze his way through any obstacle and give confidence to his fellow partners in crime.

So where to next?

Colourburst (Mk I) 1993
(l-r Steve Tett, Gary Capelin, Simon Parker, James Portinari
– photo Mark Mason)

► chapter eight

Regrouping with the inevitable nasty New Year-induced hangovers, the three remaining members of Colourburst swore to bounce back super-fast. We just needed a couple of Resolves first. I located that dog-eared business card given to me during our acoustic performance in front of the three Marks, and on dialling the number quickly found out that the larger of the two Marks was in fact the Tour Manager for the Frank and Walters. Things didn't feel as if they were going to slow down anytime soon.

As I pumped ten-pence pieces into the hungry callbox slot, Mark Marable filled me in on his own career in music. Once a member of legendary Brighton band 'How Many Beans Make Five?' he was now actively on the lookout for artists to manage. In my haste to further our career, I somehow neglected to mention that Colourburst had just lost their singer. In fact, I heard myself invite Mark to a show at the Prince Albert, which had actually been my next phone call - you know, the one where I cancelled our appearance. An educated guess told me that Mark had been too wasted to remember exactly what he had first seen, and this made me confident that we could find a new singer, write and rehearse a new set and be ready for the gig which was a little more than three weeks away. I took this news back to my band mates and we swiftly posted some adverts around Brighton music shops and coffee bars.

It's funny what comes out of your mouth when someone shows an interest, isn't it? It was also pretty weird that of the three people who watched us play at the

Princess Vic, two of them turned out to be reasonably connected to the music industry.

> **TOP-TIP EIGHT:**
>
> NO MATTER HOW SPARTAN THE CROWD - ALWAYS PLAY AS IF YOUR VERY EXISTENCE DEPENDS UPON IT. YOU NEVER KNOW WHO MIGHT BE LURKING IN THE SHADOWS.

Following crisis talks in the lounge, we decided that our new front man was to be no older than twenty-five and must still possess a full head of his own hair. Colourburst certainly didn't want a wrinkly old baldy at the front of their band. It was bad enough that James and I were already in our mid-twenties. Surely, this was as old as indie-rock was ever going to tolerate before it finally put us out to pasture in some nice, clean covers outfit, wasn't it?

So those three intrepid explorers of Colourburst set sail for a few nights in the pub, where we earnestly navigated a colourful cross-section of Brighton vocalists. But after horrific meetings with assorted freaks, couch potatoes and Meat Loaf look-a-likes, Gary decided to bail out and leave the very last candidate in the questionable hands of Jim and myself. With the benefit of hindsight, this turned out to be pretty ironic.

John Smith was an intense individual. He even gave us a false name the first time we met him - but that turned out to be something to do with worrying about benefit fraud more than any personal vendetta against the collective members of Colourburst. Those would come a bit later.

Within moments of his arrival at the pub, some thirty minutes late and without a single word of apology (which at the time I thought displayed characteristically good front person charisma), we were quickly impressed with John's extensive knowledge of music. Indeed, this skinny, unshaven individual didn't put a foot wrong all evening, and I steadily grew to admire the way he kept his woolly hat pulled hard down over cranium, even when the beads of sweat started dripping into his eyes. Damn it! This boy had style! By the fifth pint of the evening, John Smith had been declared the new singer of Colourburst (Mk.II).

I thrust a tape of 'must learn' songs into his hands, explaining that we had just ten days until a prospective manager with career-enhancing properties would be coming to watch us play live. John left us with a promise to nail the songs quickly.

Jim and I stayed in the pub until long after closing time that night, royally celebrating the fact that we had just found ourselves a new front man. We talked excitedly about impressing Mark Marable with our new line-up, and pictured that first Frank and Walters support slots taking place at a swanky London venue in the not-so-distant future.

But then a nagging doubt sat down at the table and joined in the discussion. Just why had John elected to keep his hat on all evening?

When I got home I reassured Gary in my best 'I'm not drunk' voice that we had just found the perfect replacement for Steve. After falling into the fireplace several times, I crawled off to bed, where the ceiling spun around the room like someone had just strapped it to helicopter rotor blades. All the while, I was acutely aware that Jim and I might just have made a calamitous mistake. In 1994, baldy singers were still somewhat of a rarity in music, Buster Bloodvessel and Sinead O'Connor notwithstanding, and I worried that I may have let the side down by examining a potential front man whilst sporting a pair of Elton John-sized beer goggles.

TOP-TIP NINE:

ALWAYS STAY SOBER AT BAND AUDITIONS

Band rehearsals started two days later, and my worst fears were partially eased by John's already-sound knowledge of our back catalogue. Indeed, the guy was studiously rewriting lyrics and melodies to a number of the songs, including some that we definitely didn't want to change. Still, top marks for commitment. Let's hear it for singers on the dole.

It had taken Steve Tett approximately six months to scrawl what John swiftly redefined in those couple of evenings. Such unbridled enthusiasm came as a huge relief to the other members of Colourburst. We tried to make John feel as comfortable as possible, even though the hours were counting down towards our first gig like a pair of comedy hands whizzing round a malfunctioning clock. The subtle arrangements were thrown out and replaced with a reckless punk abandon. This was largely inspired by the alter ego of our new singer. Every time John picked up a microphone it looked as if he was being electrocuted by the spirit of Punk. These sessions were so intense that I treated each practise as if it was to be our last, returning home physically exhausted but elated to know that our singer was a fully-fledged nutter.

Colourburst never intended to re-invent itself as a punk rock band but that's exactly what happened. Of course, the balding theory turned out to be spot on. There's a joke in there somewhere. So fill your boots and have a good laugh. John's woolly hat flew off during one particularly frantic bout of self-harm to reveal a large dome of stubbly headspace. Bollocks.

'Chrome-dome' Smith (as he was never called) informed us that he was gay at the third rehearsal. Asked whether this was going to be a problem, we loudly assured our new singer that it didn't make the blindest bit of difference to the equal opportunity employers at Colourburst PLC. Mind you, the bottom jokes were out, but other than that, nothing felt much different really.

John, on the other hand, certainly did have a problem with his gayness, as lyrics to future songs like *Bender* and *Found Dead* would scream at the world in no uncertain terms. A certain amount of pussyfooting and tiptoeing around our volatile singer would ensue, but for those first few weeks at least, we were the most excited pups in the Andrex toilet.

FIGHT FOR YOUR RIGHT

We took to the stage at the Prince Albert in front of a packed room of interested on-lookers. Testosterone levels were already cranked up way too high on one of those kinetic evenings where anything could happen and most certainly did. By the start of the second song a fight had broken out in the middle of the crowd, inspiring us into a petulant, uptight performance that finally saw the whole room erupt into violence as tempers frayed and thuggish behaviour came looking for a place to party.

From my vantage point (laying on the stage floor amongst broken beer bottles whilst barking into a discarded microphone), the scene was reminiscent of one of those spaghetti Westerns where comedy chairs splinter over thick skulls and sprawling bodies sail unconsciously down the bar. Alas, after only four songs the power was pulled and the police summoned.

In amongst the mayhem stood Mark Marable, grinning from ear to ear and carefully protecting his pint from flailing bodies. By the end of this lively evening we had saddled ourselves with both a manager with a bit of a booze problem and an emotionally unhinged lead vocalist.

Job well and truly done...

Things happened quickly, as they always do when you are onto something interesting. We came close to signing with a small label called 'Les Disques De Popcor'. Their other acts included S*M*A*S*H, Spacemaid and These Animal Men, all of which were part of that doomed 'New Wave of New Wave' movement. Perhaps we got lucky there, but at the time we would definitely have signed should they have asked us to. Alas, Popcor always appeared to be terminally broke, so we ended up giving them one of our songs (*Happy*) for a compilation that they then handed out for free at a show with Crawl Limbo and The Dakota Stars. No wonder they were so skint! Unfortunately, the 'NWONW' scene lasted but a few short weeks before the arrival of an oncoming juggernaut called Britpop.

Colourburst went on a spree of terrorizing local venues with a set of high-octane punk pop that barely made it past fifteen minutes. We recorded three abrasive demo tapes, and in the spring of 1994, were cordially invited to play at the annual 'In The City' event.

'ITC' is generally considered to be an unsigned artist's best chance of bringing itself to the attention of the music industry. Once a year, every record company in the country would ritually decamp to Manchester to survey the talent. Like a plague of ravenous locusts, hundreds of label scouts eagerly crawled all over a myriad of venues to suss out which bands they think the competition was having a sly look at.

Coincidentally, and at exactly the same time, John started having a personality crisis and stubbornly refused to share the details of it with anyone except poor, unassuming Gary. Jim and I compensated by spending lots of time in the pub, where we rode a wave of lager madness and local recognition.

THE BOY WITH THE THORN IN HIS SIDE

Mark Marable was the first to feel the wrath of our volatile singer. John quickly ditched with the pleasantries and wielded his power like Adolf storming through the Hinterlands. In truth, our easy-going manager didn't really have much of a master plan outside of the occasional support slot with his best mates The Popguns, also fellow residents of Brighton, and at the time re-launching their own career. They fell in love with our *Bender* tune and used to play it just before they went onstage.

Opportunity always knocked, while he was out he supposes
And each time one door shuts somewhere, another one closes

(*Bender*. John Smith/Colourburst. 1994)

144

Mark's brief stint as band manager was nipped in the bud following a fraught weekend of shows where John's self-harm started to cause us all a little concern. Our singer had swiftly developed opinions on everything from politics to pop. The rest of us just stood in his shadow and prayed for the day when we might finally secure a record deal and stop having to borrow money off of our parents and girlfriends.

But all was not well within John's world, and this caused Jim and I to speculate on what possible problem could be making our front man so miserable. Although I felt a little betrayed that Gary had become so preoccupied with John's tales of woe, I figured that this was just part of the price to pay for working with a fire-cracker front man. I had never been an angry musician before and consoled myself by drinking endless oceans of lager with the hilarious Jimmy. We frequently upset resident DJs in the trendier alternative nightclubs by making them play long-forgotten Spandau Ballet and Duran Duran tunes. Scaring off the other clubbers with a series of ludicrous moves last seen in Wham videos some ten years earlier, we would turn up for work with the grottiest hangovers imaginable. Meanwhile, Gary and John's idea of fun was to stay in and watch re-runs of Apocalypse Now.

It wasn't long before cracks started to appear in our inter-band relationships. Eventually, I just gave up caring and washed my hands of the whole tortured singer charade. I suspected that a culmination of debts and possible hard drug use were at the root of John's evil, but reasoned it would be difficult for the guy to talk openly about such subjects.

As it turned out, my theories were woefully wide of the mark. Well, so much for cod-psychology, eh? We all lent John various denominations of never-to-be-seen-again cash, which partially bailed him out of a myriad of personal crises. But our singer's mood only seemed to further darken as the weeks rolled by. Rehearsals became fractious affairs and the atmosphere within the band deteriorated accordingly.

John and Gary talked left wing politics and equal rights for travellers, whilst Jim and I discussed our favourite A-ha records.

Something had to give...

SUMMER FUN

Colourburst (f)unwisely decided to take a band holiday at Gary's parents' house in Cornwall. Our objective had been to get away from Brighton and relax before that all-important 'In The City' date. Instead, we spent most of the week falling foul to our singer's unpredictable mood swings. Thanks to the various potions he had procured just before we set off, John rattled like a tube of black market Smarties.

Upon our arrival at that remote country idyll, Jim and I made straight for the pub. The bar staff at 'The Crow's Nest' cast us uneasy glances as we attempted to blend in with the regulars, the youngest of which would have been about seventy years old and down to his very last tooth. We sat in a corner of the saloon bar and pretended to play dominoes, half-drunk on some fearful local brew that grazed the roof of the mouth whilst crippling your ability to speak.

The cottage was on the edge of Bodmin Moor, next to an old disused tin mine and not much else really. We quickly grew bored of our tranquil surroundings and set off on a daytrip to a stone circle, thinking this might help cheer our listless singer up a bit. Gary and John had both become increasingly attracted to all things Pagan, thanks to Julian Cope's *Peggy Suicide* and *Jehovakill* albums, so traipsing round Neolithic tourist attractions was particularly high on their list of things to do. Sitting cross-legged on a big hunk of rock that looked suspiciously like it hadn't long left a local quarry, our pseudo spiritual singer tried to summon up some unpronounceable Olde English spirit.

Unfortunately, Jim and I were just inches away, enthusiastically trying to relive some magic moments

146

recalled from football history via a bevy of overhead kicks and tremendous volleys. Barnes! Fashanu! Hooodddlllleee! John's withering looks quickly shamed us off the field and back towards the sanctuary of our car, where we tried to blot out the New Age goings on with a can of Red Stripe and a serious discussion about our forthcoming date in Manchester.

Jim and I were totally convinced that ITC would lead us to the oasis of a record deal.

TOP-TIP TEN:

WHEN SUBMITTING A DEMO TO AN EVENT SUCH AS 'IN THE CITY', BE SURE TO PUT YOUR **MOST ANGRY** SONG AT THE START.

Our particular foul-mouthed moment managed to include the word 'fuck' shouted triumphantly at least four or five times within the tracks' 1:35 duration. *I Can't Sing* was one of those songs that sounded so angry it was in danger of punching itself in the face. Thanks to that handy 'f' word, it also gave the impression we were wild-eyed stallions intent on ripping up the rulebook. It was all quite anarchic and 'spirit of 76'.

Anyway, I am pretty sure this was the sole reason that our band was asked to play at the 1994 'In The City' showcase. Unsigned bands - feel free to try this approach, but not when submitting songs for radio play, as I'm pretty sure this won't work.

AN ASIDE

Colourburst (Mk. II) had recently supported a fast-rising female-fronted act. As most aspiring hopefuls are want to do on such occasions, we had thoughtfully furnished the most sociable member of this band with a tape of our music, doing so in the slim hope that these mystery artists would then pass said item on to their record label and help to get us noticed. Obviously, we thought no more of it when the label in question forgot to call.

However, just a few months later, this self-serving bunch of bastards happened to enjoy a big hit single with a song that sounded remarkably similar to our *I Wasn't Invited*. Of course, this track had been one of the three that we had innocently slipped the conniving poo bags at Brighton's Zap Club on the evening of our one and only encounter. Huh!

THE SHAPE OF THINGS TO COME

From deep within those flinty confines of our rustic retreat, we continued to drive each other mad and came together only to listen in shocked awe as Chris Morris baited Cliff Richard about the Devil's cock live on Radio One. Amongst many other topics, we drunkenly argued about the ups and downs of being in a band at the tail end of the 20th Century.

August 1994 was a particularly hollow moment in the history of pop music, with TOTP reduced to a shadow of its former glorious self. The institution's long-suffering arteries were now clogged with unsavoury cover versions, bland remixes, faceless club anthems and general major label grot like Maria Carey and D:Ream. Nobody seemed to care anymore. Artists, audiences and record companies all wore the same clueless expressions that indicated music was certainly in the hands of business corporations more used to maximising profits for global fast-food bullies than the caressing of the rock'n'roll palate. A musician's career had become a ridiculously short-lived affair. If you couldn't sell a million copies of your debut album there was a very strong chance you would be unceremoniously dropped before your first-week chart position had been disclosed to the public.

Indie bands found themselves banished to the foothills, with established acts like Morrissey and The Cure disappearing into the middle distance without so much as a whimper. 'Riot Girl' managed a quick stamp of its foot, whilst journalists desperately tried to resuscitate the twitching corpse of alternative music with half-hearted bleating. Records entered and left the charts at an alarming rate of knots. Most singles typically commanded a shelf life of about seven to fourteen days, as desperate record companies spent huge amounts of money in pre-release campaigns just to ensure their artists gate-crashed the Top 10 for a solitary week. Accordingly, the charts no longer felt as if they stood for anything.

Thankfully, the Blur and Oasis snowball was beginning to gain a little momentum. *Parklife* had already been released to glowing reviews and *Definitely Maybe* was just weeks away from helping to create the next musical phenomena. In the event, this would furnish the industry with its final hurrah.

COMPUTER WORLD

The period between 1994-7 would, in time, be recognized as the last unchallenged period of major label profiteering. Since the mid-nineties, the widespread advancement in computer technology has steadily torn an ever-widening hole in the lumbering hull of the good ship Greedy Bastard. But before this, the music business had been reaping the rewards for longer than it needed to remember. With such abundant wealth came even greater waste, and thanks to a never-ending line of disastrous acts, the industry wantonly frittered away huge sums of money rather than invest in its future. Even though the digital era was knocking on the door, the music business just kept doing what it had always done best and snorted, boozed and squandered until its little heart gave out.

As the mid-nineties UK braced itself for the advent of Cool Britannia, the Labour Party installed its youngest ever leader and the music industry proudly reported another bumper year of profiteering. Nobody would have believed what was just around the corner.

LONDON CALLING

It was around this time that Colourburst decided to boycott all London gigs. 'Let the scum come to us' we reasoned, unreasonably. Unbeknownst to such lofty twerps as ourselves, we adopted this attitude at precisely the moment when it became fashionable and career enhancing to do so again. Indeed, clueless A&R managers with keys to the company chequebook were happily signing anything with a pulse in good old Camden Town, just so long as there was some vague element of 'Britpop' sell-ability to the artist in question. Such a vast umbrella covered a multitude of sins, and legions of instantly forgettable bands were loudly hailed as the next Beatles, despite the fact that most sounded more like Arthur Mullard on acid.

Major labels were literally stapling money to the heads of regulation indie bands. If you happened to play at The Camden Monarch or drink in The Good Mixer, a stranger would dart out from the shadows and offer you a sizeable record deal no questions asked. For some strange reason, everybody in the record business mistakenly thought that North London had all the answers.

THE TRUTH WILL OUT

Many miles away, back on that ill-fated Cornish holiday, we were idly watching Gary set fire to himself with lighter fuel in his parents' conservatory. All four members of Colourburst had just taken half a fake tab of Ecstasy and were patiently waiting for the pill to start doing its thing.

After approximately 45 minutes of wondering whether John had purchased Paracetamol instead of Ecstasy, singer and drummer slid off to see if listening to a crappy dance compilation could perk up their dud trips. This left Jim and I alone and free to speculate. As usual, the conversation turned towards just what the hell was up with our insufferable front man.

Maybe it was enlightenment received from that recent visit to a stone circle on Bodmin Moor, or perhaps we *had* ended up with the good 'E' after all. It might even have been intelligence gleaned from those last cans of Special Brew that we had just polished off. But finally, after months of speculation, the pair of us shared an epiphany. In unison, Jim and I turned to each other and whispered 'John fancies Gary!'

My God, how stupidly obvious. We had just spent eight months tiptoeing around the world's most temperamental front man simply because he fancied a bit of rear-guard action with the little drummer boy. There was no family tragedy, no hard drugs scandal and, more importantly, no bloody good reason for treating Jim and I like second-class citizens.

Instantly we knew that we had solved the puzzle. Both of us were disappointed that something as trivial as the love that shall not speak its name had cast so much consternation over the career of Colourburst (Mk.II). But remarkably, the balance of power seemed to swing back in our favour from the very moment of this important discovery. Despite the fact that Jim and I never directly confronted John about our suspicions, the ruthless dictator had finally been overthrown in a bloodless coup.

IN THE CITY

Unfortunately, we made this breakthrough just in time for the most prestigious show of our not-so-young lives. By solving the riddle, we inadvertently lost our edge and completely wrecked the delicate chemistry that governed our band. John went to pieces and began hinting that, if the runes indicated otherwise, he might not bother to show up for the 'In The City' gig. Oh good.

On that fateful September morning of our long haul to Manchester, Mr Smith turned up resplendent in a pair of jeans that looked as if they had just spent the summer picking tomatoes off of vines. Worse still, John trailed a twisted scowl and three-day stubble that told us he really couldn't be bothered. This rather conflicted with the Britpop uniform of 'V' necked jumpers and cheeky chappie grins that Jim and I were sporting. As confused as ever, Gary was rocking a natty 'Gothic Michael Bolton' look. To a stranger, we must have looked like a very weird bunch as we hurtled up the M1.

Aside from his neat new image, Jim had just splashed out on a new Marshall head and cab for this career-defining show. Disappointingly, the poor guy hadn't made time to figure out how it worked before loading it into the back of the van.

As per usual, the other bands on our bill thoughtfully over ran their sound checks. We were billed with Fall-esque 'Ricky Spontane' and smarmy indie-pop hopefuls 'Spike'. If memory serves correctly, I think at least a couple of them were ex-members of Jefferson Airhead. Anyway, by the time Colourburst finally got set up on the stage at the Flea and Firkin, the audience was already arriving. Jim panicked and fumbled about with his new amp, but the only sound he could muster was a distant scraping that reminded me of those far off days of playing through my first ever taxi-transmitting amplifier back in Barton Road. Still, time was of the essence, so I gamely plonked at a couple of my bass strings whilst the venue engineer rushed us through the quickest sound check in rock history. On the night of our most important gig ever.

The next thing I recall is that the house lights had gone down and we are technically onstage. Within seconds of Gary counting us in to the first number, I reasoned that Jim must have unplugged altogether. Drummer, bassist and guitarist then proceed to give the impression that this was probably their first ever gig, whilst the less said about that old git frothing and gurgling into a perfectly decent microphone the better, thank you very much.

Where once we would have smashed through eight songs in sixteen breath-stealing minutes, on the evening when it really mattered Colourburst delivered an emphatically shit all-round performance. Gary pulled off some quite disastrous fills and broke countless sticks simply by looking at them, whilst I went off in search of some previously unchartered jazz notes. John avoided any semblance of melody for the entire duration of our set and barked every lyric like he was selling meat off the back of an old lorry. Meanwhile Jim might well have been playing a tennis racket.

Not even Mark Mason could think of any compliments as we hid in the corner of the venue, thirty seconds after leaving the stage to open-mouthed silence from the A&R fraternity stood at the bar.

Back in the hire van we deliberated over what to do next. John and Gary were up for driving through the night and getting as far away from Manchester as possible, but Jim and I saw this as a once in a lifetime experience. Following a quick conversation about damage limitation, Colourburst's hot-wired guitarist and bass player set off for the heart of the city with a view to gate crashing as many shows as we possibly could.

LIGGING THE LIGHT FANTASTIC

'Ligging' is the ancient art of telling everyone within earshot of the venue bar just how great your band is. It is widely regarded as the musician's most precious weapon when dealing with the likes of A&R scouts. Of course, it is also a convenient way to fib oneself out of sticky situations like the one Colourburst had just sunk themselves into.

HOW TO HANDLE AN A&R SCOUT AT A MUSIC VENUE

Gig-night conversations usually revolve around the knowledge that any interested record company representative will have probably arrived too late to see your band perform. A well-drilled unsigned musician should be able to spot the label oik stood at the bar. Tell-tale signs include the wearing of posh jeans or fashioning of empty record bag slung casually over the right shoulder. It is the musician's foremost responsibility to convince the cornered individual that they have just missed the show of a lifetime. The unsigned artist should always offer to buy the unsuspecting scout a drink, as this will help stall for time whilst possible options are sized up. Before long, the obligatory demo and phone numbers should change hands, and this will at least earn you a couple of toes in the door, even when the label in question decides that you're not really the next Coldplay after all.

Jim and I did indeed lig for England on that damp and dirty evening back in 1994. We gamely strolled past security with inappropriate passes for many bands including Gene (who were awesome), Marion and Spacemaid (who were excellent), and a lot of unsigned hopefuls that we never knew the names of anyway.

We even managed to impress a young scout from Rhythm King Records with our rapid-fire drinking. This poor girl quickly became our personal chauffeur as we forced her to drive us all over town while we searched out a procession of steadily seedier bars miraculously serving alcohol long into the Manchester night. When the early hours of Monday morning began swirling ominously overhead, our tour guide waved her magic wand and found us somewhere to stay.

We returned to the van to collect Gary and John with several new best friends in tow. After a volley of predictably catty remarks from our lead singer, I inelegantly threatened to pull his head off in front of everybody. But even as I was slurring my drunken threat, an unopened can of Boddingtons was busy making its way off of the drum cases and hurtling in my direction. It ended up smacking me painfully on the end of the nose and swiftly curtailed my life's only moment of machismo.

We set off towards a complete stranger's house in uncomfortable silence, with Jim confusing the words to *God Save the Queen*, while I nursed a bloody nose.

JILTED JOHN

The morning after our grand failure to impress the music business at large, Colourburst set off back to Brighton. John spent most of the journey describing how he was going to re-invent Colourburst in his own image. It felt as if I was already listening to the next Billy Joel record, so I

154

just stared out of the window and pretended that my nose didn't hurt.

Twenty-four hours later, John was no longer the singer in Colourburst. Jim was given the responsibility of explaining to our former vocalist that we were 'splitting up for the time being'. Obviously we weren't going to do anything of the sort, but Gary and I were far too scared to tell him the truth.

TOP SIX ARTISTS WHO WENT ON TO DO BETTER THAN COLOURBURST AFTER 'IN THE CITY' 1994

1. Deus
2. Puressence
3. Gorky's Zygotic Mynci
4. David Gray
5. Salad
6. Catatonia

Not surprisingly, I didn't see John Smith again for a very long time. Brighton can be like that. Although it's a relatively small place, you can get lost in your own thing and fall out of orbit with former friends and acquaintances. But fifteen years was going it some by anybody's standards, and when I did bump into him it was in a hardware store just fifty yards from where I live. He had been working there for ages and yet I had never seen him. OK, I'm not exactly the type who spends a lot of time in hardware shops, but you know what I'm trying to say here.

Over time we have eased back into an uneasy relationship. We've even talked about going out for a drink, but that has remained just an idea. Recently John left the hardware store and is now training to be an English teacher.

Our brief tenure with John was proof that singers need total conviction and a little something to shout about. If not, you're going to find it very hard to get noticed.

Colourburst (Mk II) 1994
(l-r Gary Capelin, John Smith, Simon Parker, James Portinari
- photo Petrina)

► **chapter nine**

NEW LIFE

(THE SHORT-LIVED LIVES OF
RAINMOUTH, CRUSH AND CLUB ROUGE, 1994/5)

I've always suspected that coincidence enjoys a good laugh, but this was a bit much. Just fourteen days after John's unceremonious departure from Colourburst, Gary, James and I were once again committed to playing an important live show. Just like the Steve Tett scenario eight months previously, Colourburst had a gig to play that they just couldn't pull out of.

Frustrated by what was becoming something of an annual problem for our band, I offered to take over vocal duties despite my only previous experience having been that final Violet Trade gig where we dressed up as each other, or even further back when I squeaked along with the school choir for one short evening in December 1979.

Not the greatest credentials by anybody's standards really. I wasn't even sure if I could hold a tune, but desperate times will always call for idiotic gestures. If nothing else, I could at least guarantee that I wouldn't be falling in love with the pretty Gothic drummer anytime soon.

At twenty seven-and-a-half years old, I had left it ridiculously late to be leaping into the spotlight, even if I did still possess all of my own hair and teeth. Showing true dedication to the cause, Gary and I both immediately left our day jobs to concentrate on the huge task of transforming me into something approaching a singer. My drumming buddy even offered himself as a freelance vocal coach, which was cheaper than one of those singing tapes that they advertised in the back of the NME. So I agreed to Gary's persistent instructions to sing from the stomach and project from the diaphragm. Things went surprisingly well. We quickly did away with the old set and came up with seven brand new songs in as many days.

I'm feeling like a poor relation at another table
Won't you spare a coin of phrase for me?

(*The Poor Relations*. Simon Parker/Colourburst.1994).

It was only when we set foot on the stage of The Crypt in Hastings that I finally realised the enormity of what I had let myself in for. Not only did I now have to sing in front of complete strangers, but I also had to think of all those witty and insightful things to say in between each song. A mixture of fear and excitement punched me hard in the stomach as I approached the microphone to shout my first 'Hello Cleveland'. I glanced over at Jim who was grinning, defiant and possibly a little bit drunk, whilst behind me Gary looked as though he urgently needed to use the toilet. We tore into the first tune (aptly entitled *Hit by a Bus*) and the next thing I remembered was walking offstage to a loud cheer.

So there you have it. I had finally discovered my true vocation despite the fact that I never actually wanted to be a singer. Inwardly, I berated myself for not having made this move a long time ago. I had wasted a frightening amount of my life in pursuit of a suitable front man and never once imagined that I would (or could) do it myself.

Determined to keep moving forwards at any costs, the band had settled on the grossly unsuitable 'Rainmouth' as a replacement for the exiting Colourburst. Thankfully, this was swiftly booted into touch when I realised that most people thought it sounded more like a grim holiday destination in Devon. 'Crush' fared little better when road tested at gigs towards the end of 1994 with a lovable bunch of Medway rouges called 'Westpier'

We swiftly became strong allies with this band and then looked on enviously as they signed to Indolent Records. Although Westpier only managed to release one single before being dropped, they at least got to tour with the awesome 'Wannadies', where they thankfully remembered to put us on the guest list.

In time, the band's handsome guitarist Carl Mann would end up playing in Kylie Minogue's ill-fated 'Impossible Princess' outfit, before stints with Sleeper and his own 'Salvador' project. Carl and I recently met up after a twelve-year absence, only to discover that we have unwittingly experienced a lot of spooky coincidences during our intervening decade of musical estrangement. Of course, my own path has had little to do with Kylie Minogue, but then Carl's has had nothing to do with Chesney Hawkes, has it?

Carl recently set off for a new life in New Zealand with girlfriend Kat. Look out for Union Jackal's *Universal Screenplay* album. It's another lost classic just waiting to be discovered.

CLUB ROUGE

Rewinding to 1994, Westpier's lead singer Simon Oxlee joined James and I in a hush-hush project called 'Club Rouge'. Secretly, Simon was just as obsessed with the 80s as the Colourburst twosome, so it didn't take much to convince him to join. With Jim and I on cheap Yamaha keyboards and Simon mincing about down the front with a microphone and headband, it was only ever going to last for one evening, especially if Mr Oxlee's more fashion-conscious band mates got wind of it.

Therefore, Club Rouge's only live performance took place without fanfare at the dingy Loft Club in Brighton, in front of just a handful of very confused looking clubbers. Unwisely deciding to vogue our way onto the stage solely to perform our seven-minute epic *Crimson Rain*, Jim resembled a prettier Ron Mael from Sparks, whilst Simon had more than a touch of the 'Le Bon' about him. I, on the other hand, just looked like a builder in drag, or at a real stretch, my sister on a very, very bad day. Sorry, Nikki. In case you're wondering, Gary declined to have anything to do with this despite the fact that Jim and I had been trying to talk him into 'doing some mime', complete with face paint and cheap B&Q plastic chains like the ones Jed used to chuck around when he was busy getting in the way of Howard Jones on TOTP.

Simon Oxlee went back to Westpier just as soon as he managed to remove the make-up. I caught up with him on-line a while back and sent him the only photographic evidence of that Club Rouge gig. At this point, all lines of communication were abruptly severed...

Club Rouge 1994
(l-r James Portinari, Simon Oxlee, Simon Parker
- photo Mark Mason)

Following this debacle, Gary, James and I stopped dicking around and resumed trading as Colourburst (Mk. III). After a few months of studiously avoiding the issue, it was time to admit that Colourburst was what we did best.

▶ chapter ten

THROW ME A ROPE

COLOURBURST (MK. III) 1995-96

There was only one problem with reverting back to the old band name, and that had quite a lot to do with the fact that every record company in the country would think we were the same bunch of clueless jokers who had performed so dismally at the previous In The City showcase, which, of course, was true - but only to an extent. That such a large number of A&R departments had witnessed this nightmare gig (or worse still, had a laugh about it back at the delegates' hotel) now meant we faced a huge uphill battle to convince anybody to take our musical endeavours even remotely seriously.

But with no shortage of spiky three-minute pop songs pouring out of us, Colourburst forged ahead with its foggy game plan. After all, we can't have been the only disappointing band in Manchester that weekend, can we now?

TOP-TIP ELEVEN:

BE SURE TO CHANGE YOUR NAME SHOULD YOU MESS UP AT AN IMPORTANT GIG. RECORD COMPANIES HAVE SUPRISINGLY LONG MEMORIES.

Taking no chances, we decided to release our own 7" single in the early months of 1995. In tribute to the 'Hawaii 5-0' character Steve McGarrett, Gary, James and I proudly unveiled The Jack Lord Foundation record label and promptly sank all of our hard-earned cash into the pressing up of a thousand copies of the *Throw Me A Rope/ Bad Hair Day* 7" single.

My father used his contacts within the bookbinding trade to obtain and manufacture the all-important sleeve. This was how our debut offering came to be housed in an expensive cardboard overcoat emblazoned with a solitary black 'Colourburst' etched into the front. Each and every copy resembled a freshly scrubbed paving stone. It was all very Factory Records, and at the time I liked to think that the legendary Tony Wilson (they just don't make them like that anymore, do they?) would have been proud of us.

Of course, we had left ourselves no budget for promoting this release and that meant we had zero chance of getting our record heard or into shops outside of Brighton.

If we sold about five copies at every gig we played, it was still going to take around two hundred shows to get rid of the bloody thing. Considering we only played around fifty shows per year (and this was quite a lot compared to other local unsigned bands that we knew), Colourburst was going to be promoting this release for anything up to four years!

TOP-TIP TWELVE:

WHEN RELEASING YOUR FIRST SINGLE, BE SURE TO PRESS UP NO MORE THAN 500 COPIES. TRUST ME; YOU'LL END UP USING THE REST AS FRISBEES AND COASTERS FOR YEARS TO COME.

COR BLIMEY, WATCH OUT

Disastrously, Colourburst chose the wrong song to launch its career. *Throw Me a Rope* had originally been written as a humorous dig at all those fake 'Landarn' accents that so many bands were lazily employing at the time. Suddenly, we were all aboard that crazy Britpop gravy train with 'gor blimey watch out' Phil Daniels peeing in the corner of the first class carriage. New to this game and still finding my vocal feet, I too adopted a fake Bow Bells twang and Colourburst were instantly marked as yet another second-rate Britpop copycat band.

TOP-TIP THIRTEEN:

HUMOUR DOESN'T BELONG IN MUSIC. WELL, NOT UNLESS YOU ARE FLIGHT OF THE CONCHORDS OR GOLDIE LOOKIN' CHAIN.

ANNIKI IN THE U.K

The only positive thing to come from self-releasing our single was an unexpected invite to play at the birthday party of an eighteen-year-old student with the unusual name of 'Anniki'. The explanation for this came from her music-obsessed father who had (of course) been a huge Sex Pistols fan. And it was this same inquisitive guy who got in touch and haggled us up to £75 for a show that we would have gladly played for free.

Performing at Anniki's birthday trebled our fan base overnight. On top of this, virtually all Colourburst shows for the next year or so were exciting affairs, with a large number of female students pushing their way to the front of the stage and dancing their merry arses off every time we appeared. This wiped the floor with other local unsigned artists, most of who were still struggling to drag more than a handful of put-upon loved ones or the odd well-meaning work colleague out on a wet and windy Monday evening.

I had only been singing for a few months, yet here I was surveying scenes of total carnage as bodies went flying through the air and pretty girls queued to talk to us after the show. So this was how Colourburst became one of the most popular draws in Brighton. Our confidence grew accordingly, and it wasn't long before both James and I were investing in some very punk rock PVC trousers. We bought a pair each in case you're wondering. It just wouldn't have looked right if we shared a leg, would it? Resembling the English Green Day, but blessed with better skin and a drummer apparently on loan from late-eighties poodle rockers 'Poison', Colourburst headed into unknown territory by becoming popular, at least locally, for the first time since the drummer and bass player had rolled into town some two years earlier.

We began employing some of those well-worn showboating techniques like throwing ourselves around the stage or dragging out the endings to our best-loved tunes. But people really seemed to like the music we were making.

Being in Colourburst was terrific around this time, and there's nothing like being in command of an audience who hang on your every word. Listen to me, I sound like bloody Bono, don't I? Don't worry, normal service will soon be resumed, but for now, Gary drummed like a man possessed by the spirit of several Keith Moons, while Jimmy balanced precariously somewhere between guitar-hero and too-drunk-to-do-the-solos. I careered about the stage playing a fuzzed up bass, doing my best to look skinny and handsome in a tight-fitting seventies shirt that Mum and Dad had been kind enough to buy for me on one of their visits to Brighton.

And if man's been on the moon
Why the hell am I still in my room...in the wardrobe?

(*Columbus*. Simon Parker / Colourburst. 1995).

Of course, before too long local acts started asking if they could support us in the vain hope of stealing our fan base. Not a chance, sonny. Whenever Colourburst weren't onstage our new army of friends simply turned their attentions towards the bar. We even had to autograph copies of our records. This was virtually unheard of in super-cool Brighton, where everybody usually just stood at the back of the room, speaking in very loud voices about how they could do it so much better if only they weren't so 'busy with their art dissertations'.

All that remained now was for a complete stranger with no music business acumen to come waltzing into the picture and offer to manage us...

CHUFFEY

A frighteningly large number of unsigned artists make the same schoolboy error of employing the services of an inexperienced manager. From what I can make out, this is usually on account of the fact that the individual band members are all too lazy, stoned or scared to pick up the phone and do things for themselves.

TOP-TIP FOURTEEN:

PLAN YOUR OWN TRAJECTORY. GIVING THE JOB TO AN INEXPERIENCED FRIEND OR ACQUAINTANCE WILL INEVITABLY END IN TEARS.

Stupidly, we chose to install an absolute beginner to propel our band skywards. Rather than embarrass him, I'll use the affectionate nickname that we used in private. 'Chuffey' or 'The Chuffster' (on account of his resemblance to a little chuffing train) officially became our financial benefactor in the late summer of 1995.

At first we weren't sure what to make of this awkward specimen, largely because he bore such an uncanny resemblance to 'Data' from 'Star Trek: The Next Generation'. All three members even took to hiding in a Tunbridge Wells KFC on one particularly excruciating occasion, not long after Chuffey's good-natured advances had led us all to believe that he wanted to feel our bottoms.

But one memorable night in East Grinstead (I wonder how many times that particular phrase has been used in a book before?), our acquaintance from another galaxy drunkenly offered to invest a sizeable chunk of money into Colourburst. We all knew that Chuffey's finance was a good-natured lifeline that would keep us pointed in a forward-facing direction, so Gary, James and I willingly agreed to this arrangement, even though we all harboured a number of nagging reservations about our rich acquaintance. Beggars just can't be choosers, right?

Within weeks of Chuffey picking up the gauntlet, our new sponsor could be found at every Colourburst show, chatting up a succession of underage lovelies with the aid of his trusty credit card. At most gigs, the guy would drink himself senseless and pass out long before we even arrived at the encores. Yes, we were even doing encores by this point! Sinking endless bottles of posh red wine, our new manager stuck out like a pensioner in a break-dancing competition. Worryingly, this strange man/machine dressed like Gary Numan circa *Replicas* way before it was cool to do so again.

Still what the hell? We were getting stuff for free.

Gary, James and I got used to bundling Chuffey into the back of a taxi and sending him off in the direction of Haywards Heath with a twenty-pound note sticking out of the pocket of his jacket. In the absence of a proper record company, our manager's drunken condition felt a small price to pay in return for such a financial injection.

Gary was so happy that he finally got around to cutting off all his hair. Gone at last, was the mid-80s footballer look. Instead, our drummer belatedly discovered the joy of burning his scalp with the aid of those do-it-yourself bleaching kits from Superdrug. Classy, huh?

LIKE A VIRGIN

I've not mentioned much about my love life since we met Lisa a few chapters ago. She and I enjoyed one of those comfortable relationships where the other partner did exactly what they wanted to do. I was in a band and Lisa knew nothing would make me deviate from this path. For my part, I understood that my girlfriend's studying was vitally important to her future and then watched as she had set sail for three years at not-so-close-by Hull University.

But when the job centre started hinting that they were going to send me to work in a Supermarket, I hastily applied for a part time vacancy at the local Virgin Megastore. Such an innocuous gesture had life-altering consequences. The only position available at the store involved working just six hours a week on a Sunday, so I went back to music retail comforted by the knowledge that only a tiny fraction of my creative life would be eaten up by such a pathetic commitment. But it was here that I immediately struck up a friendship with Jennie Cruse, the hot-looking in-store display girl who was forever up a ladder or dangling precariously in one of the shop's many windows. In truth, I think I fell in love with her at first sight, but was mindful to suppress my feelings as we were both in long-term relationships and, perhaps more importantly, both trying to make it in music. Colourburst quickly became her go-to boys when she discovered we were an indie band.

A few days later, rehearsals began with Jennie and we did our best to emulate early-period Blondie, but probably sounded more like Sleeper. Still, she thought we were great and promptly booked time at Worthing's Old Pink Dog studios. The session went pretty well and I was impressed at Jen's ability to stack vocal harmonies. These lent the recordings an air of accomplishment missing from Colourburst demos.

It was at this point that she disappeared to the US with her boyfriend and my heart started doing strange things.

BIZZARRE LOVE TRIANGLE

During Jen's month long stay in the States she was never far from my thoughts. My mind raced with the possibilities of us becoming lovers, but this seemed totally out of the question.

On the evening of her return to the UK, Colourburst played at the Mean Fiddler in London. My heart jumped up into my mouth as I took to the stage and spied Jen in the audience. This made the art of singing even more difficult than it usually was for me. Something unplanned and cosmic was most definitely occurring. And I willingly let it happen.

Soon afterwards, on a magical May evening in 1995, Jennie and I stayed up all night and admitted that we were falling in love. It was like being on the very best drugs in the world. And then some...

To cap it all, the morning following our nocturnal heart to heart Teenage Fanclub released their career-defining *Grand Prix*, and this swiftly became the soundtrack to our relationship. Every song on *Grand Prix* spoke directly to J and I about how we were feeling. Isn't it bloody marvellous how music can do this? Songs written by a complete stranger resonate to such a degree that you are convinced they are describing your own situation.

MY TOP TEN TEENAGE FANCLUB SONGS OF ALL TIME

1. The Concept (Bandwagonesque)
2. Don't Look Back (Grand Prix)
3. I Need Direction (Howdy!)
4. Sparky's Dream (Grand Prix)
5. Everything Flows (A Catholic Education)
6. Norman 3 (Thirteen)
7. My Uptight Life (Howdy!)
8. Sometimes I Don't Need to Believe in Anything (Shadows)
9. Your Love is the Place That I Come from (Songs from Northern Britain)
10. = Some People Try to Fuck With You (B-Side to Mellow Doubt)
    = He'd be a Diamond (B-Side to I Don't Want Control of You)

This romance happened totally out of the blue, and before Jen and I consummated our relationship we made a pact to finish with our current partners. So, a few days later I travelled up to Hull to end things with Lisa. I knew instinctively that I had to be with Jennie.

Unfortunately, I had no choice but to break the news to my (ex) girlfriend on the very last day of her Finals. Not my finest moment. As you might expect, Lisa didn't take this particularly well, and I slunk out of Hull guilty as hell but utterly convinced that I had done the right thing. In my gabbled break-up speech I chose to leave out the part about Jennie and I, fearing that Lisa would think we were already entwined. Of course, this turned out to be a bad move because when Lisa saw us together a short while later she just presumed the worst anyway. Note to self: always tell the truth in love.

Lisa leaves the story at this point, and I can only hope everything turned out well for her. Years passed, and I eventually found out that both Lisa's family and Robert Smith had left their seaside pads for bigger places in the countryside.

Don't worry. I'm not about to go breaking into any more back gardens...

JENNIFER OH JENNIE

Our first summer was an idyllic sun-kissed affair enlivened with plenty of getting-to-know-you trips to the bedroom. Here I was at 28 years old and still not burdened by real life. Could things possibly get any better?

Surprisingly, the answer was yes.

THE FREE BUTT

British guitar music was enjoying its own Indian summer after a couple of years out there in the pop wilderness. Pulp, Blur, Gene, Elastica, Supergrass, Paul Weller and Oasis were but a long sentence-worth of Britpop legionnaires railing against grunge and dance. Suddenly, indie guitar bands were back in vogue again. Eat my shorts DJ culture.

Brighton's unsigned music scene was suitably re-invigorated throughout the summer of 1995, and everybody chose this moment to descend upon the unsuspecting Free Butt venue. Managed by the Gollum-like Will Moore (not really, mate!), the Butt was one of those ancient pubs that had been around since the dawn of time. Populated by no more than five or six hard-core geriatrics during the morning session, come 6pm this miniature musical heaven underwent a magical transformation simply by erecting a makeshift stage in the place where the pool table usually sat.

The Free Butt quickly became the hippest place in town for yet another procession of next generation indie hopefuls like Colourburst. Live shows were the place to be seen and the Free Butt became every Brighton band's spiritual home. That it happened to be situated right at the bottom of the street where Gary and I were now living was just one of many reasons why the various members of Colourburst could be found there most evenings during that glorious summer.

TOP TEN GREAT LOCAL BANDS FROM THE FREE BUTT IN 1995/6

1. Eeyore
2. Fizzywig (featuring John from The Others on bass guitar and big hair)
3. Luminous
4. The Spines
5. Tampasm (briefly signed to a major label)
6. The Pedestrians (featuring actor Paddy Considine behind the drums)
7. Elephant
8. Buggy
9. The Surfin' Lungs (the only band from this list still playing in 2013. Good you, boys!)
10. Action Painting!

Not forgetting; Fludd, Euphoria, The Madding Crowd, The Fly Kicking Badgers, Spit Baby, Beat Hotel, Channel D (sorry Ian Mackenzie, no you do NOT make the Top 10!), BBMF's, Special Patrol, Foil.

Melody Maker journalist Everett True was often to be found lurking in the shadows of the Free Butt. Disappointingly, he viewed Colourburst with some suspicion, although like many others he did seem quite taken with the bevy of young ladies who regularly came to watch us play...

IT'S A SHAME ABOUT RAY

Jennie had been living in Brighton since her exodus from Maidenhead in the early 1980's. During that time, she had played lots of gigs in bands such as 'Little Green Honda's', 'Jesus Couldn't Drum' and 'Fischer-Z'.

Up until the time we met, my girlfriend had never actually fronted her own band. This was all about to change as 'Ray' made its debut live performance in that scorching summer of 1995, where none other than Captain Sensible looked on with interest as we rattled through a bunch of Jennie's pop creations. We also played a rocking version of *It's Not Over Yet* that predated the bloody Klaxons by at least ten years.

At the time, the good Captain (whose real name is Ray, incidentally) was living with ex-Dolly Mixture guitarist Rachel Bor. They had a place in nearby Hassocks, not to mention three very hyperactive children. Jennie and Rachel had been friends for years and it wasn't long before we were all out at Sensible towers. Cool - I had always loved *Glad It's All Over* and told the Captain in a slurring voice after more than a few glasses of potent homebrew.

Shortly after this introduction, Ray (the band) was selected for an industry competition at the Newport Centre in Wales. Jennie's songs, and in particular those well placed harmonies, had quickly garnered us a little attention. Of course, there was no way she could hope to sing all the parts at the same time, so we asked Rachel to join the group. But even with our nuts gripped in a vice, there would be no way that Gary and I were ever going to be able to contribute backing vocals to this particular band.

171

And so it was that three sugar-rushing children ran about our house breaking things whilst we tried to teach their harassed mum how to play Ray's clutch of pop nuggets. And, once again we were ready to play live inside of a few short/fraught rehearsals. Travelling to Newport in the beaten up old Colourburst van, Ray made it through the heats of a glorified Battle of the Bands but were eventually beaten in the final by a sour-faced duo that promptly fell off the face of the earth after picking up the 'coveted' award.

TOP TIP FIFTEEN:

NEVER EVER ENTER A BATTLE OF THE BANDS COMPETITION.
It's humiliating.

LAST CHRISTMAS

Gary, James and I continued to perspire our way round the various shit-holes of East Sussex at every given opportunity. Colourburst recorded new material with some of its Chuffey Aid, and as a 'thank you' to our loyal followers, lovingly released a fan club only (!) version of Wham's *Last Christmas* in December 1995. Of course, our version had a rather large rocket shoved up its seasonal bottom. Unexpectedly, this got us played on local radio so we decided to film a cheap video in our front room with local promo-wizard Steve Brewer. This was later aired twice on late night ITV over the Christmas period. I'm sure George Michael would have approved if he had seen or heard it. Thankfully, Sony missed a stonewall opportunity to sue us for everything we had. For those interested parties, Steve recently stuck this video up on You Tube.

Despite Colourburst merchandise selling steadily at local shows, we were, of course already well in the hole to our android manager. It was becoming all too easy spending someone else's money.

Colourburst (Mk III) 1995
(Simon Parker, James Portinari, Gary Capelin
- photo Jennie Cruse)

THE GIRL FELL OUT OF THE RADIO

Colourburst geared up for another release on JLF records. And Chuffey seemed happy to pump his hard earned cash into the band in return for the chance of some real life interaction with females that he didn't have to pay for by the hour. So we were all winners, really.

The Girl Fell Out of the Radio/Twelve o'clock Forever is an infinitely superior single to Throw Me a Rope, which I have quietly tried to disown over the years. Or snap in half. This latest Colourburst 7" dealt with the pressing issue of dating girls from other planets (as first touched upon by Ash on their classic Girl From Mars), while the B-side referred to the secret meeting place Jennie and I had, directly underneath a broken clock face which always broadcast the same time.

It's twelve o'clock forever, here in my heart
You were so familiar right from the start

(Twelve o'clock Forever. Simon Parker/Colourburst 1996)

Elegantly manufactured on a limited run of five hundred purple 7" singles, Girl/Radio became our second

173

release in February 1996. Once again, we found that we didn't possess enough financial resources to consider press or promotion teams, (even Chuffey balked at this suggestion), so the record was left to trickle out at local gigs and through Brighton's Virgin Megastore.

TOP-TIP SIXTEEN;

WHEN SELF-RELEASING A RECORD, ALWAYS BUILD THE COST OF SOME BASIC PR INTO THE INITIAL OUTLAY

And when she smiled, her eyes lit up like Christmas lights

(*The Girl Fell Out Of The Radio*. Simon Parker/Colourburst. 1996).

GOING BLANK AGAIN

As we 'reinvested' larger amounts of his money, it was only right that we let our manager take more of an active role in the band. With this in mind, Chuffey's first job was to send copies of the new single to label scouts. Although we had been advised never to send vinyl to A&R departments (on account of the fact that everybody had long ago upgraded to tapes and CD's), His Royal Chuffey-ness insisted on distributing our purple circles to a large number of record companies, details cribbed from the Musicians Yearbook (1994).

I suspected that after a couple of weeks the novelty would wear off and the man would simply relinquish this soul-destroying task back to the band. But, unexpectedly, news began filtering through that Chuffey was chalking up quite a success rate. A number of meetings had been added to our manager's diary as A&R teams unanimously gave our single the big thumbs up. I decided that at least one band member should tag along to keep an eye and ear on proceedings. No prizes for guessing which of us volunteered...

Come the day itself I had to brave black ice, motorway snowdrifts and Chuffey's quite outrageous driving misdemeanours as we slid towards various offices in the heart of London town. Within ten seconds of arriving at our first port of call, it became horribly apparent that no one knew anything about these 'meetings'. Indeed, we failed to get past security at some places and were left in reception for what felt like an eternity at others. When the helpful expressions turned perceptibly darker, we would leave packages with the receptionist before slithering back out into the arctic tundra.

When I politely questioned our manager as to what exactly was going on, Chuffey protested his innocence and bemoaned the fact that he was ruining a perfectly good linen suit by traipsing about like a door-to-door salesman. Not quite the answer I had been expecting. This excruciating day ended with just one face-to-face meeting with those very hospitable people at China records whom, as luck would have it, were the label busy putting out records by the bloody Levellers at the time. A junior scout ushered us over to his desk and gave Colourburst approximately thirty-five thoughtful seconds before telling us that it wasn't 'quite what he was looking for'. Somehow, Chuffey re-interpreted this as 'China want to sign you', and drove me off to the nearest posh restaurant to celebrate. I was cold, tired and hungry. So I went along with the charade and made sure to order a dessert as well.

At this point, I began questioning the wisdom of letting our manager keep a hold of the reins. A few weeks later, when we quietly turned down a support slot with the recently reformed Then Jerico, our befuddled benefactor became apocalyptic with rage. Colourburst were forced to endure days of sullen phone calls for turning down what Chuffey saw as another shot at the big time. Now, even though Jimmy and I would have secretly loved to watch Mark Shaw belting out *Big Area* from the side of the stage, we knew full well that Colourburst would have been heading in completely the wrong direction should we get on the 80s nostalgia circuit! On another desperate occasion we drove over a hundred miles to play at a

Chuffey-arranged Horn Of Plenty show in St. Albans. It was here that the bar staff looked at us blankly as we innocently enquired where the soundman and other bands were. It wasn't long before we were driving back from Hertfordshire to Brighton with murder on our minds.

TOP 10 VERY INTERESTING COVER VERSIONS

1. China Drum - Wuthering Heights
2. Sparklehorse - Wish You Were Here
3. William Shatner - Common People
4. Dinosaur Jr. - Just Like Heaven
5. The Posies - I Am The Cosmos
6. Thistle - Love Not Dead
7. This Mortal Coil - You And Your Sister
8. Paul Anka - Smells Like Teen Spirit
9. R.E.M - Ghostrider
10. The Wedding Present - U.F.O.

SUPPORT SLOTS

When an unsigned band reaches a certain level of notoriety around its hometown, local music promoters will come crawling out of the woodwork and magically start to offer a support slot with a touring act. Occasionally, this will be because of the local group's growing musical worth, but more often than not it will have rather a lot to do with the fact that the artist in question will pull in a good crowd to help the promoter pay for his headliners. Bands spend much of their working lives searching out such supports, but the grim reality of performing at 7.45pm on a desolate Wednesday evening to a smattering of bewildered mates (not forgetting the person looking after the headliner's merchandise table) means that fame and fortune will still be light-years removed, even if you do happen to find your band playing on the very same stage as The Sultans of Ping or Joyrider.

Colourburst had been drawing big crowds locally for quite a while by this point, and Brighton promoters were offering us all sorts of weird and wonderful supports. Some of the better acts that we opened for were 60 ft. Dolls, Catatonia and Perfume. On each occasion, a large group of our most faithful friends and fans would dutifully pay three times what they were used to, just to witness us squashed into a cosy corner of the Brighton Concorde stage. It's strange, isn't it? Touring bands habitually treat local acts like the lowest form of life - despite the fact that they too were, not so long ago, in the very same situation. Furthermore, not one of the groups that we supported ever saw the faintest glimpse of our spirited performances, so Colourburst remained resolutely unloved by the music business at large. Still, we always made the best of a bad deal and usually managed to steal beer and/or pee in the sink of the headlining bands dressing room. Take that, Northern Uproar.

After one such doomed but otherwise enjoyable affair, Colourburst and its blathering manager were out in a nightclub celebrating with assorted friends. As we congregated at the crowded bar, Chuffey violently convulsed and dropped to the floor in a big, grey heap. I thought he had suffered a bloody heart attack and we carefully moved him up onto a nearby seat. A couple of the more-concerned females then sat with him for the rest of the evening and watched nervously as he proceeded to wade through another couple of bottles of overpriced plonk. From my vantage point on the other side of the club, Chuffey looked the picture of health as he engaged unsuspecting young beauties in deep and meaningless conversation...

GOODBYE

Eventually, the joke became distinctly unfunny and we summoned Chuffey to an important band meeting. Uncannily, just minutes before we were due to confront our misfiring benefactor, Gary developed a migraine and declined to attend these summit talks. Worryingly, Gary's inability to deal with us not getting signed was leading him into a stoned fug of lethargy. The

Goth Prince of Bad Air was fast retreating into a marijuana shell.

Jim and I set off alone and nervously sank a few pints whilst we awaited the arrival of our unpredictable manager. Chuffey finally turned up over an hour late, and as sullen-faced as George Bush trying to explain his way out of weapons of mass destruction. By this time I was already more than a little bit tipsy. You can guess what's coming, right? Poor Jim was caught in the crossfire of dysfunctional android babble and a pissed-off bass-playing gob-shite. Chuffey took offence at my accusations of mismanagement and started bashing his alien claw on the table. He then retorted with accusations that the band was only using him for his money. I dug back with questions about those bogus meetings in London. The floodgates well and truly opened, with the meeting swiftly descending into a volley of petty insults from both sides. Jim did his best to remain balanced and impartial, but when I offered the particularly non-Shakespearian quote of 'if I wanted to call you a cunt I'd just do it to your face', our (ex) financier got up and stormed out of our bank accounts for good.

With little or no return on his investment, Chuffey must have quickly tired of watching his money disappear down the drain. But his involvement hadn't been purely about money as the guy enjoyed the benefits of a decent social life for the first time in years. Hell, it sure beat sitting at home and 'knocking one out' to a Garbage CD, didn't it?

For a while, our ex-manager's spectral presence hung heavy in the air. I half expected to receive a large and intimidating bill for services rendered. But, not unlike various other ex-associates, Chuffey would go on to become just another mythical creature that may not have existed at all.

That was until one particularly drunken Saturday evening, when Jim staggered into a late night take-away to be greeted by the surreal and blurry sight of Chuffey busily flipping burgers and obeying incoherent food orders from messed up clubbers. Oh no. Surely we hadn't reduced the man to such a desperate financial state, had we?

Fear not, dear reader for the ever-entrepreneurial businessman had simply decided to branch out and invest in the glamorous world of fast food. At which point Jim was engaged in a short mechanical conversation before disappearing back out into the street with an undercooked lump of meat and some reconstituted potato chunks.

I didn't fit here, I didn't fit there
All the holes for my pegs were square

(*Inside the Outside*. Simon Parker/Colourburst. 1996).

From time to time, I still find the odd Colourburst single for sale on the Internet. In fact, there's one of those purple vinyl editions of *The Girl Fell Out Of The Radio* knocking about on-line in Sweden if anyone's interested. But beware: it retails for a bit more than your everyday Britpop era 7" does. God bless the Swedes. Colourburst are now officially collectable. Love it!

▶ chapter eleven

WOWEE ZOWEE
COLOURBURST [MK. IV] 1996-7.

Not unlike a disappointing ball of gum, Britpop quickly lost its flavour. So I looked back across the ocean and connected with a growing wave of brilliant American lo-fi bands.

MY TOP TEN LO-FI BANDS CIRCA 1996

1. The Flaming Lips
2. Sparklehorse
3. Guided By Voices
4. Pavement
5. The Breeders
6. Sebadoh
7. Sonic Youth
8. Neutral Milk Hotel
9. Sammy
10. Papas Fritas

This change in taste marked the start of a slightly new direction for Colourburst. We had tried most of the options open to a three-piece and I longed to play guitar again. Besides, I figured that looking for a new bass player and becoming a quartet would help shake everything up a bit. Gary seemed to be losing the will to live...

A TREEBOUND STORY

Jim and I remained upbeat about life in Colourburst, but our drummer showed little interest in rehearsing the latest clutch of songs. Instead, he devoted all of his spare time to the cultivation of a hash plant that grew visibly taller every time you looked at it. Alas, when it came time to harvest and sample the wares of this giant beanstalk, the chubby-looking joints tasted like the remnants of a soggy allotment bonfire. Worse still, there was no discernable high.

Undeterred, our drummer smoked his way through the whole bloody thing. Deposited on a threadbare sofa, Gary became lost to a world of rubbish daytime television. I was convinced that he didn't want to be in the band any more, and when I stumbled upon a bundle of newly acquired University prospectuses stashed behind the sofa, I realised that our drummer obviously had more important things on his mind. Just what had happened to that gung-ho spirit which had seen us through so many calamities in the past?

Turn the key once
The getaway car runs out of steam...

(*Planet*. Simon Parker/Colourburst. 1996).

COME ON FEEL THE COLOURBURST

Good old Captain Fate wasn't done with us yet though. The silvery-bearded old bastard thoughtfully tossed Colourburst another of his faulty rubber rings when we took delivery of a new bass player.

By a remarkable slice of coincidence pie, Matthew Cooper and I were distantly related. Anyone here know what second cousins once removed means? No, me neither, but that's what we were (and still are).

I had been semi-aware of Matt's musical existence in Brighton for a while, but it wasn't until he offered his services to Colourburst that I really got to know him. We hit it off instantly, and despite the age difference (Matt was 18 to my 29-and-a-half), he proved to be the adrenalin shot that our band so desperately needed.

Within weeks of his joining in August 1996, we had about ten great new songs ready to go. The only worry was Gary, who showed little interest in contributing. I put it down to that dodgy tree he was smoking his way through and busied myself with other things.

Once again the band image was tweaked. This time it was all about vintage Levi's and black leather jackets. I was very excited about the new songs and this four-piece version of Colourburst sounded like the most accomplished of all our line-ups.

The first live show took place at Worthing's Northbrook College, where both Jim and I were quickly reminded of just how good our band could be when it was firing on (nearly) all cylinders.

I think about it all of the time and I know
I'm bewitched by her butter-melt smile, and it shows, yeah
it glows

(*Hippy Surfer Girl*. Simon Parker/Colourburst. 1996).

Upon our return to the Free Butt venue, all-girl support band Davey paid us the highest compliment imaginable by informing me that we sounded like a heavier version of The Cure. I celebrated this remark by dying my hair black and purchasing a pair of pretend-glasses, in the hope that they would make me look more interesting and front man-like.

Colourburst (Mk IV) 1996
(l-r Simon Parker, James Portinari, Matthew Cooper, Gary Capelin
- photo Jennie Cruse)

We recorded two of our strongest tracks (*Planet* and *Hippy Surfer Girl*) at Brighton's Loophole studio. Top unsigned London venue the Camden Falcon must have liked us too, because they booked Colourburst (Mk. IV) to appear in the autumn of 1996.

Unfortunately, we descended on the venue just as extensive renovations were taking place to transform the dilapidated toilet into the future home of the soon-to-be-influential 'Barfly' organisation. Therefore, on the night of Colourburst's one and only Falcon performance, the venue just so happened to resemble war-torn Dresden. Scarcely able to believe our bad luck, we gamely thrashed out a thirty-minute set amongst bricks and scaffolding to no more than five bemused members of the general public. Everyone skirted the rather large holes in the floors and walls to purchase drinks from members of the bar staff who were all wearing hard hats and reflective clothing just in case the ceiling should fall in.

Back home in Brighton, Gary remained non-committal about the future, even though I tried hard to convince him that 1997 was bound to be our year. I had been predicting much the same scenario since New Year's Eve 1989, so such a declaration was probably about as effective as the Queen's speech. It didn't exactly help matters when we were forced to rent a small flat, thick with the musk of impending doom. Meanwhile Jim, Mattie and I embarked on more new songs as our drummer elected to forego rehearsals completely.

I spent my free time hanging out at Jennie's flat. She had recently changed her band's name from Ray to Fruit Machine, and it would be this group, and not Colourburst, that would grab the attention of the music industry.

Whatever bad luck had befallen me up to this point would be nothing compared to the ill-fated events that lay in store during the next few years. Power struggles, lying, cheating, breakdowns and dodgy recording contracts were all just around the corner.

At your own peril, read on...

Mark Mason & Simon Parker mid-90s (photo – Jennie Cruse)

► **chapter twelve**

13

FRUIT MACHINE (est. 1996)

Things couldn't have started off any better. Captain Sensible paid for us to record a demo and then the National Band Register stuck the strongest track, *Sickly Blue*, on an industry-circulated sampler. This quickly prompted various A&R departments to call Jennie about any forthcoming London shows. Armed only with her bright yellow cassettes and a small list of promotion companies operating in the Central London area, she and Rachel set off in search of some gigs to capitalize on the attention.

In the tiny Barfly offices, then situated just off of Oxford Circus, Rachel and Jen mistakenly walked into the domain of a young, entrepreneurial manager called Zack Hoffman. He just so happened to be sharing the rent with the Barfly team, and after a quick listen to the demo, and intrigued by the notion that our band was fronted by two girls, Fruit Machine was instructed to return to London for a more in-depth discussion.

When the girls relayed this news to us, Gary and I marvelled at the luck of such a chance encounter. We couldn't remember the last time anybody had shown any interest in one of our musical ventures. It was at this moment that I sensed my first seed of doubt concerning future commitment to the Colourburst cause.

THE MAN WHO WOULD BE DAVID GEFFEN

Once back in that busy London office Zack began by savaging the A&R fraternity, so I warmed to the guy immediately. This was the first time I had ever been in a room where everybody had a mobile phone. Well, everybody apart from our band, of course. Although still

185

barely out of his teens, Zack harboured serious ambitions about building his own David Geffen-like Empire. And as if to prove this, a well-thumbed copy of said music mogul's biography sat proudly on his desk.

Zack quickly hit his stride and imparted scurrilous tales dredged from the very bowels of the business. Recently, he had lost a promising band to another management company just weeks before they signed a six-figure recording contract. Indeed, Zack insisted that he had patiently nurtured this struggling group for well over a year without demanding any form of contractual agreement or payment. This mystery band was launched shortly after our first meeting and did go on to become one of the UKs biggest rock groups of the late-nineties. And they are still going to this day. Gallingly for Zack, he lost control on the eve of a major record deal and never received a penny for his troubles. I was never completely sure how much of this story to believe (Zack even claimed to have given the band their name), but boy, did he bear a grudge!

The five members of Fruit Machine listened on in silence, realising that they had just unwittingly opened the door to a whole new world of shady dealings. We were tickling the sordid underbelly of the beast. Welcome to the real business of music.

IN A NUTSHELL

With hindsight, I must have been shockingly naive to reach my twenty ninth year on Planet Earth and still not fully comprehend how things worked. It was only from the confines of those busy Barfly offices that I finally started to put two and two together. The number one rule for fast tracking any unsigned artist in this day and age must be to secure the attentions of an established manager or music lawyer and let their careers do all the talking for you.

SECRETS OF THE BEEHIVE

The record industry lives in constant fear of
change and harbours a pathological distrust of anyone
that doesn't come from an established company. This
means that a rookie band manager will be forced to work
ten times harder to get his or her foot in the corporate
door, regardless of how great the artist they represent
might actually be. But record company lines of
communication will always be open to those with proven
track records, no matter how brief their previous successes
might have been.

There was, and still is, a trick to fast-tracking new
bands into the attentions of the music business. This
revolves around the fabricating of a story to give the
impression that a small circle of tastemakers has already
deified the new artist to an un-named record label. Of
course, the better connected your management happens
to be, the more this story will be believed and then further
leaked. Nowadays such grass roots hype will also involve a
lot of movement on an artist's social media sites. Record
companies want to see a lot of Facebook 'likes' and You
Tube hits before they are even remotely interested in
talking to an artist. That's right kids; you have to do all the
hard work yourselves. And then sign everything over to 'the
man'.

Actually, becoming superficially popular on the
net isn't as difficult as it sounds, for there are online boffins
who can fabricate your popularity in return for just a few
measly quid. Hiring a PR team, with a proven track record,
is also a very good idea, but watch out as that will cost.

187

Maybe send some name producers an introductory email. They wouldn't readily admit it, but they need an injection of new band blood just as much as the next person. And it's all just a couple of clicks away...

Fruit Machine 1996
(l-r Simon Parker, Rachel Bor, Jennie Cruse, Gary Capelin, James Portinari –
photo unknown)

ELEVATE ME LATER

Incredibly, within just a few short weeks of Zack entering the picture at Fruit Machine HQ, we would become one of these momentarily feted acts.

But, annoyingly, right from the get-go Zack had a knack of making us all feel like country bumpkins that had come to the big city in search of a fortune. Who knows, maybe that's what we were, but it wasn't a pleasant thing to be reminded of on a daily basis. Still, the advantages of working with such a well-connected individual were just too great for Fruit Machine to turn down at this point in their late-starter careers. Ah, we're back to that old chestnut; date of birth...

Despite his sharp business acumen and strong sense of industry savvy, on that first meeting Zack Hoffman never once thought to ask our ages. I am absolutely convinced that if he had been made aware that four members of our band were nearly thirty years old, and worse still, Rachel was a thirty-five year old mother of three, we would never have been given a second thought by either Zack or the music business at large.

So, on subsequent encounters we studiously avoided the issue of age and let our new best friend do all the talking. By successfully manipulating this situation we managed to hide the rather large skeleton that was busy clanking around in our closet.

THE SHOWCASE SCENARIO

Zack's first plan was to set up a showcase slot with the mighty Sony Records. I laughed when we were told that the show was going to take place at the refurbished Camden Falcon, for this came just a few weeks after Colourburst's adventure on the former building site. Irony is a total bastard, is it not?

Afternoon showcase performances tend to take place behind closed doors, often in the ghost world of natural daylight where the strangeness of playing to three or four important people is compounded by an eerie feeling of having to perform in a venue bereft of audience, atmosphere and lighting. Consequently, this type of gig can be very hard to impress at, especially if those invited parties spark up a conversation mid-way through a song, or worse still, start giving various members the evil eye. Maybe I was just being paranoid...

Fruit Machine had progressed from rehearsing once the Rachel's kids were stashed, to playing before coveted private audiences with the most powerful record companies in the land. To be honest, we were just not ready for such close scrutiny. At the first showcase we regretfully stood around like morons after Rachel broke a string during the second song. When we finally reconvened it was impossible to recover the lost momentum and I played out the rest of the set feeling as if we had already failed, even though Zack did his bit by clapping loudly after every song. Our second session for V2

189

Records, and, like the first, staged at the empty Falcon venue, fared marginally better, when, at the end of our twenty five minute musical interview, V2 offered us some free studio time. We had just pulled off something akin to a 'one-all draw' with the label, as studio time is a convenient stalling tactic employed by A&R scouts who haven't quite yet made up their minds about an artist currently under the microscope.

It was head spinning to see how things could change so quickly. Within days of securing a decent manager, we were playing to all the right people. But the music business is a spoiled brat who will steal your toys and smile as it smashes them to pieces. You have to keep your wits about you for careers are defined or broken by strangers making snap decisions.

Fruit Machine had been thrown in at the deep end and weren't able to up their game enough to warrant a lightning-fast signing. London was competitive and incestuous. I got the impression that everybody was just waiting for us to screw things up. And not wanting to disappoint them, this is exactly what we did.

Jennie had arranged a London gig just prior to Zack becoming our manager. We foolishly decided to honour this arrangement, even though Zack did his best to dissuade us. Thanks to the industry grapevine, word spread quickly that Fruit Machine was about to play in a run-down pub on the back streets of Camden. Suddenly the world and his wife were on the guest list. After all those years of not being able to attract a single industry person to one of my band's shows, now I was faced with pages of bloody names. The game was changing but we were slow to comprehend.

Come show time everything decided to break, including the sound system and Jen's microphone. She sounded like Norman Collier gone indie. The show was a complete disaster and the A&R world was quick to disappear, like rats from the sinking ship.

Eventually I found our manager sitting outside on the fire exit with his head in his hands. To be fair it wasn't just the shoddy equipment that ruined things. The band played in a nervous rush that instantly cast us as small town losers frozen in the headlights. Well, the one or two spotlights that had been working. Jim had looked distracted and ill at ease while the rest of us clanged like oafish Morris dancers.

What now? Was it over so soon?

ON MY RADIO

Luckily, Gary Crowley started playing *Sickly Blue* on his Capitol Radio demo clash. This song went on to win the phone-in vote for five straight weeks and was lofted high into his 'demo hall of fame' with other luminaries such as Suede and Dodgy. This repaired some of the damage and helped to keep us on the radar up in London.

Smash the stones against your window, tear the sheets to break your fall
Climb the walls that carry on for miles

(*Sickly Blue*. Jennie Cruse/Fruit Machine. 1996).

Not so easily defeated, Zack dug in and booked another date for December 1996. But this time he left nothing to chance and hired Skunk Anansie's sound engineer and an image stylist. The five members of Fruit Machine were unceremoniously thrust into posh threads with price tags hidden in the pockets. My black velvet suit alone was worth £700. And we were heading off to Camden for the night. We'd never get out alive! I pinched myself to make sure this was all really happening and that I hadn't just dozed off after mistakenly partaking in another of Gary's bifta's.

Encouragingly, Zack's expert handling of the situation meant that Fruit Machine's final London gig of 1996 would become a must-see engagement for A&R scouts everywhere. The Dublin Castle was packed to the rafters with label types as our manager loudly introduced us to representatives from a selection of the main players - which back then was a lot of record companies. With a head full of names, and trying hard not to spill lager on my posh new clothes which all had to go back to the rep thirty minutes after the show, I knew this was going to be a career-defining moment. Nerves duly jangled like a set of jailer's keys. My time had finally arrived. Again.

And so it was, and totally against the odds, Fruit Machine came off the substitutes' bench to play an absolute blinder that night. Jennie's partially see-through dress certainly helped to secure the attentions of the industry for the full duration of our set, but we all played with a confidence derived from well-drilled rehearsals and a genius behind the sound desk. Not to mention some nice new threads. For once, everything went off without a hitch. Nobody broke any strings and Jen looked every inch the pop chanteuse. Within twenty five minutes, we had managed to redress the balance and left the stage to a huge cheer.

Zack quickly took up residence at the busy bar, where he basked in the reflected glory of his band doing good things onstage for a change. Out of the corner of my eye, I could see interested parties engaging him in quick conversations whenever they thought the other labels weren't looking.

TOP-TIP NINETEEN:

WHEN ENTERTAINING AN A&R CROWD, MAKE SURE THE SET IS SHORT AND BOOKENDED WITH YOUR STRONGEST TRACKS.

For the briefest of moments, I thought I had finally arrived. We had just played a great gig in front of the music business. I was just about to turn thirty and this really felt like the last roll of the dice. But, once again fate was about to administer me an eye-watering wedgie.

It swiftly came to light that Fruit Machine's transition was far from complete. Despite the fact that several labels did seem very interested in securing the services of our band, not one of them appeared to be willing to enter into negotiations just a few days shy of the Christmas holidays. The industry is governed by an unwritten rule that it can never sign cheques during the Yuletide season.

Alas, it transpired that Zack had created his industry buzz at the worst possible moment of the financial year. December sees the corporate mind fixating over getting off with the secretary at the Christmas party and then hoping she'll forget all about it during that generous four-week holiday that follows. Coupled with those looming profit and loss reports, perhaps we should have guessed that the company chequebook was going to be locked away until further notice. But from the look on his face, this was obviously news to Zack...

We returned to Brighton feeling hollow inside. Now we would have to go back and do it all over again in the New Year. There could be no resting on laurels. You can go from 'hot' to 'not' virtually overnight in this business. I mean, can anyone recall what happened to Menswear or Gay Dad?

▶ chapter thirteen

THE RISE AND FALL

Jim announced his departure from Fruit Machine in January of 1997. I was pretty shocked by this and tried reasoning with my friend that this might be our very last chance of making it. Spring chickens we weren't. Alas, Jim's mind was clearly made up and I had to get used to the fact that he wasn't going to be around as much anymore.

To the people who knew us, our guitarist's departure seemed totally amicable. Jim had left the fold due to 'musical differences'. But in reality, there were darker forces at play. Rachel was going through an emotional crisis and had made advances towards him. Things became awkward and he decided it was better to leave. At the time I knew little of this, although it was clear for all to see that Rachel and Captain weren't getting on terribly well.

ONE STEP BEYOND

There began a frustrating period of frantic missed phone calls, blown out rehearsals and unsuitable human beings. Luckily, just as things started to look a little desperate, an unlikely figure reappeared on the scene.

Ex-Violet Trader Greg Saunders telephoned out of the blue and we swiftly offered him the gig of replacing Jim, even though he wasn't a guitarist. Hmmm, that's a little lop-sided, right? But Greg had changed a great deal since those time-frittering days in The Violet Trade, and four years on, his accomplished keyboard skills and impressive collection of associated gadgetry presented us with the opportunity to re-think our strategy. It was at this point that Fruit Machine started contemporising with the introduction of sequencers, samplers and an old black box with knobs on just like the one Roxy Music's Brian Eno had messed around with on The Old Grey Whistle Test.

Underneath his outwardly confident demeanour, Zack was starting to show worrying signs of being out of his depth when dealing with record companies. V2 had requested a budget for the proposed demo time and our mentor had mistakenly demanded a hefty sum to bankroll the session, instead of doing things as cheaply as possible. Whenever money came into the equation Zack always thought that scamming unfeasible amounts of cash was the wisest course of action. That might have been the case back in the 70s, but things had changed since David Geffen's biography.

V2 understandably got cold feet and pulled out of the session. Obviously we were disappointed but before we could take Zack to task our resourceful hook-up merchant introduced us to Steve Lovell, a much-respected producer whose name happened to appear on a good deal of my record collection. In the past, Steve had worked with the likes of Blur, Julian Cope, A Flock of Seagulls and A House. More importantly, he was also a massive fan of Brian Wilson and had identified the talent behind Jennie's vocal harmonies.

Fruit Machine met with the affable scouser in February of 1997 and quickly discovered that we shared the same musical references and warped sense of humour. Steve agreed to record our demo if we agreed to let him produce our first album. This felt like a very good idea, so we all shook hands and forgot about Zack's clanger with V2.

You daydream of the night before the morning you had yesterday...
Butterflies around your heart

(*Ariel*. Jennie Cruse/Fruit Machine. 1996).

ONE STEP BEYOND

To put it mildly, I had become more than a little bit concerned about Gary's sanity. Rejuvenated yet oddly edgy, Gaz refused to practise, but picked holes in other people's performances. Over the past few months, his playing had suffered some sort of nervous breakdown, and we all struggled to follow his wonky fills and uneven tempos. Gary's total lack of interest in anything other than getting stoned was ruining his ability to think straight and hammer out a decent beat. Oh shit.

I didn't see it at first, but Rachel had now started coming onto me. I've always been a clueless bugger when it comes to the come-ons, so I didn't heed the warning signs. But Jennie certainly did and relationships within the band became very tense indeed. Oh shit. (Part two).

It was a delicate situation, and by rights we should have kicked Rachel out of the band. But Jen and I chose to play down the problem, as we knew our troubled guitarist was going through a hard time in her own love life. Besides, if we had rid ourselves of another guitarist at this point we would have probably lost all interest from Steve Lovell. Unknowingly, Rachel's reprieve would repeatedly come back to haunt Jen and I over the next couple of years.

GREY DAY

With all this simmering away below the surface, Steve arranged studio time to record some songs. In February of 1997, Fruit Machine decamped to the Playground rehearsal rooms in Camden Town, where sixteen years previously, The Cure had staged a playback of their-then-just completed *Faith* album. It was reassuring to know that our paths were still criss-crossing at regular intervals, even though I was still without a record deal. But when Fruit Machine embarked on an intensive pre-production session with Steve Lovell and his partner Pete

Jones, it felt as if my days of being in an unsigned band were finally coming to an end.

Pete had recently worked on Morrissey's *Your Arsenal* album, and over the years had also engineered many other big names, including the legendary Dusty Springfield who was another of Jennie's most cherished singers. The signs were all good. Well, they were so long as I didn't have to engage Rachel in any eye contact in the rehearsal room.

'Pre-production' is industry jargon for sprucing up the songs a bit. It is also one of the key areas where the producer gets to extol his wisdom and help guide an act to greater heights. This was Fruit Machine's first time under the production microscope, and we were all excited at the prospect of working with the duo

Or were we?

Over the course of a gruelling six-hour session, our producers ruthlessly dissected the songs that Fruit Machine intended to record the following day. We were all issued directions to change parts or make them less busy. Gary really struggled with his and the hours started to crawl by. Steve and Pete seemed to hone in on the drum parts and this only added to Gaz's confused state of mind. Realising that our drummer was rapidly losing the plot, the decision was taken to end the session earlier than arranged. We were scheduled to begin recording at Matrix Studios the following morning and were instructed to get an early night. Yeah, right. At this juncture, we all left for various destinations around London.

It was hard to sleep that night as I was desperately excited about working in the same room where Blur and The Boo Radley's had recently completed some of their best works.

EMBARRASSMENT

Fruit Machine and its' production team re-grouped at a horribly early hour the next day, *well* before lunchtime, and descended upon Matrix Studios in the heart of London. After a quick look around the facilities, we picked up where we had left off and started rehearsing the songs again. Gradually, every member of the band was quietly asked to leave their respective corners of the live room until only Gary remained, harassed, harangued and totally deconstructed by Steve and Pete's desire to get a good performance. As the rest of us sat around in the studio's lounge area idly watching music videos on the television, poor old Gary was smashing away at his battle-scarred kit.

Ages later, Gaz emerged looking somehow smaller than I ever remembered him. He wearily informed us how Steve and Pete had been experiencing some technical difficulties with the recording equipment and that his parts weren't yet committed to tape. So this is why bands take two bloody years recording an album, I marvelled, before going back to another game of pool with new boy Greg.

Soon after this Jennie and I were both summoned to the control room and calmly informed that the session was being cancelled due to the fact Gary couldn't drum to the standard required.

Errr...pardon?

What was supposed to have been the proudest day of our musical lives had just turned into one of the worst. Wondering whether Jeremy Beadle was about to jump out from behind the mixing desk to reveal this all as a big joke, I desperately enquired if there might be a way of using drum machines to finish what was already started. Steve and Pete intoned they could never work in such a manner and that Fruit Machine needed to re-think its game plan if it was going to stand even the remotest chance out there in the unsigned cattle market.

Steve asked if we really wanted to take that big step up to the next level. Both men seemed adamant that Fruit Machine would face the exact same scenario with any producer we chose to work with in the future. And this meant it was very likely that we were going to see out the rest of our days playing to an ever diminishing audience on the unsigned circuit, hopelessly trapped on a slowly turning wheel of failure.

It wasn't just Gaz who came under fire: I was also under scrutiny. Jesus! Why hadn't anybody warned me that recording with producers could be so career threatening? Luckily, I had somehow steadied my performance nerves just enough to avoid being in the same boat as my beleaguered partner.

Despite such negativity, both producers liked our songs enough to want to reconvene the session should we be successful in recruiting a new drummer. Steve even went so far as to say he would help us audition possible candidates. Jen and I returned to the studio's lounge area and found it hard to look at Gary. Seconds later, he disappeared into the control room to be told of the decision to abort the session.

Zack chose to show up at this moment, totally unaware of what was transpiring and laden with crisps and chocolate bars, the staple diet of a band in the studio, after drugs and booze, of course. He listened slack-jawed as we relayed the morning's activities, and when Gary returned looking as though his world had just suddenly ended, our manager took his own private audience with the production duo. He quickly returned as deflated and thoughtful as the rest of us. Disappearing out into the studio's reception area, Zack quietly whispered into his mobile phone while the rest of Fruit Machine sat around in a daze.

Muttering an awkward goodbye, our drummer explained that he would be back in the morning to help load out our equipment. I could tell that Gary thought we were going to put this episode down to experience and simply start looking for another producer. The gravity of the situation appeared to be lost on my friend who had just spectacularly blown it after so many years of waiting in the wings.

That evening, we called an emergency band meeting. Greg chose not to attend because he knew we were going to have to make a tough decision regarding our drummer's immediate future. This left only Jennie, Rachel and me. Uncomfortable as it was after the events that had recently transpired between the three of us, we talked through that whole wretched evening, endlessly debating a long list of possible scenarios, and every time we did so, it made a little more sense to let Gary go. Whichever way we looked at it, it felt as if our drummer was holding the rest of us back. What had started as little more than a side project between musical friends had quietly developed into a gateway to a record deal. Yet it now felt as if the party was taking place on the other side of the motorway, and to get there we were going to have to dodge the lorries. For the three oldest members of Fruit Machine, time on Planet Pop was in desperately short supply. We simply couldn't afford to slither all the way back down to square one again.

Drumming is perhaps the hardest art to master if you are not a born natural. I knew that I was going to have to work hard at improving on the bass, although, in time the old adage 'less is more' would certainly help me win the confidence of producers. But Gary had always refused to take this route. I knew from long experience that he was a manic thumper, in his element when performing to a rowdy live audience. The subtle nuances of playing with restraint were simply not his style. Suddenly my long-suffering mate had become the weakest link in our musical chain.

Gary and I had reached the end of the line after eight long years together. In that time we had been through quite a lot. From those very first evenings of fighting off unsavoury underwear in a cramped Chichester bedroom, right up to the moment where we got to perform for two top producers in a swish London studio: it had been quite a ride. Up until the last few months, I would never have contemplated booting Gaz out of any band that I was in, but his recent actions had left him virtually unrecognisable from the Gothic accomplice who had stuck by me through so many past misadventures.

Understandably, Gary was crushed when Jennie and I sat him down to tell him of our decision to look for another drummer. In truth, he looked utterly betrayed as we explained the reasons behind our actions. Fruit Machine drove back to Brighton in total silence. As luck would have it, Colourburst were booked to support These Animal Men at the Richmond pub that very evening. Wishing we could cancel, but not wanting to upset fellow members Mattie and Jim, Gaz and I elected to play the show rather than let our band mates down. Backstage, we kept a good distance from each other and once onstage, I remember it feeling distinctly odd whenever our voices 'touched' during vocal harmonies.

After this joyless show, Mattie paired off with Gary whilst Jim and I had a heart to heart at the bar. At the end of the evening, Gary and I still returned home together to our shared flat, where there would be no possible way of escaping each other for the foreseeable future. We were trapped.

And all of this happened on St. Valentine's Day 1997. No really. It did.

COLOURBURST AND WHAT CAME NEXT

Somehow, Gary and I managed to keep things civil, but our friendship was well and truly decimated by his sacking from Fruit Machine. Colourburst (Mk. IV) bid farewell to the world following one final evening where we recorded live demos of all of the songs that would have made up our first album, should we have stayed together.

Mattie and Jim went on to form a punk-pop group called 'Magnetta' in 1998. Jimmy continued to drink for England and sometime later, unofficially changed his surname from Portinari to Lager. It was Mr Lager who formed The Others in 2002, and they signed to Alan Magee's 'Poptones' imprint in 2004. The band then released four singles and became well known for playing guerrilla style gigs in bizarre locations such as the London underground and in the foyer of BBC's Broadcasting

House. On February 12th 2005, The Others starred on the front cover of the NME. I felt immensely proud that one of my best friends had finally made it to that seemingly mythical level where records and touring became a reality. Alas, all too soon the band's fairy tale romance with the music press fell apart and The Others were dropped when their debut album struggled to make an impression on the charts. Ever resilient, the band signed to Lime Records and released a second album in late 2006. Not to be discouraged, The Others continue to play live and release new material to this day.

Jim and I still go out drinking, but usually only when neither of us has anything planned for the following morning. We're now those sad old blokes that lurk in the corners of quiet pubs, reminiscing about such hugely important things as The Cure and A-ha.

Gary left for London in 1997. I always felt guilty about his departure from Fruit Machine, although in my heart I knew it had been the right decision. But as far as I was concerned, being in a band wasn't much fun anymore.

▶ chapter fourteen

SLOW EMOTION REPLAY

FRUIT MACHINE 1997-1999

Gary's departure cast a long shadow over proceedings. When it became apparent that this was to be no easy transition for our band, we awkwardly settled for employing a session drummer to sit in on a couple of important engagements. Although this felt rather odd, it did help to keep us at least partially notorious to producers and record labels alike.

IF YOU DON'T WANT ME TO DESTROY YOU

Zack started to lose the plot. You know things are going seriously awry when A&R scouts call you at home imploring you to ditch the arrogant knob-end currently doing a wonderful job of screwing up your musical prospects.

TOP-TIP TWENTY:

NEVER SIGN ANYTHING WITH ANYBODY UNTIL YOU HAVE WORKED TOGETHER FOR A TRIAL PERIOD OF AT LEAST SIX MONTHS.

As the weeks wore on, Zack became a bit of an embarrassment. He would drink heavily at gigs and then make derogatory remarks to the very people he should have been schmoozing. Once again Fruit Machine found itself with a tough call to make, and it was left to me to deliver the bombshell via a phone call from a call box in Croydon. Mobile phones were still not a part of regular life.

And don't ask me why I felt the bloody need to travel to Croydon to make the call. Idiot.

Zack seemed to take the news quite well and I put down the receiver and stared at the phone in disbelief. That had gone better than I thought. The phone rang again. It was Zack, threatening me with all sorts of legal unpleasantness. And when I got home the calls from his big-shot lawyer started. If we didn't re-think immediately, Fruit Machine would be destined for instant obscurity. It wasn't pretty. Actually, it was quite scary. But we stuck to our guns and disappeared into musical hiding until things calmed down a bit.

A week later we received a bill for the aborted Matrix session even though Zack had ended up giving the time to another of his acts. So that was why he had been whispering into his mobile phone on the day Gary was given the bad news by Steve and Pete. This resulted in Fruit Machine having to sell off a good deal of its equipment to help foot the bill. God, I even had to sell my Music Man Stingray bass. I was gutted. It certainly wasn't getting any easier, was it? Fruit Machine was beginning to implode.

ON AND ON

Over scattered moments between March and June of 1997, Steve and Pete found a few afternoons to audition a handful of eligible drummers. The standard was very high and the band would have gladly recruited any one of the talented players we sparred with, but Steve was adamant we needed a very special person. So we kept on looking, and a few months later we found him.

Our 'special' drummer happened to be a six-foot five-inch Welsh beanpole who resembled a particularly startled looking giraffe. But boy, was he a great player. Even I could very nearly dance to his grooves.

On the day of this audition, Nick Hopkin joined us under a purple bruise of heavy clouds and awaited his first meeting with band and production team. All the while, indie, weirdoes Salad sat around in the Camden rehearsal studio looking for all the world as if they had just been dropped, which, come to think of it, they quite possibly had.

Everyone stared as Nick walked in through the door. He really was the tallest, skinniest guy any of us had ever met. It was a miracle he could lift his drumsticks, let alone career around the kit. We played a few songs before Steve and Pete subjected Nick to a bout of intimate managerial grilling.

Sample question:

POPCORP: "So, Nick, would you be prepared to leave your flat and move to Brighton if you got the job?"

NICK: "Mate, have you ever been to Wolverhampton?"

And with that, he was in. We celebrated by running around in the tropical storm that tore through the skies at the exact moment of Nick's appointment. It was like something out of a Hammer Horror movie. Steve and Pete stood laughing at us from a nearby pub doorway. It felt great to be in a fully functioning band again, but maybe we should have paid more attention to those dark clouds as I suspect they were a portent to the future. But at the time I just danced around in the deluge and celebrated his appointment.

Nick and his Italian girlfriend Mani relocated to Brighton a few weeks later, where for a short while they would join Jennie and me in our cramped top floor flat.

CLOSER

Under Steve and Pete's strict tutorage, Fruit Machine then spent the next few months writing and rehearsing. Both producers were busy working for other clients, so we bided our time by sketching out ideas in Captain's home studio whenever the old bugger was away.

Greg was still living in London and started to drift away from the band. He would soon join ace-faces Magic Alex , featuring pre 'Life on Mars' actor John Simm on guitar, no less.

In October of 1997, Fruit Machine finally embarked upon that much delayed recording session with Steve

Lovell and Pete Jones. Rachel hinted that she was thinking of making a play for the unsuspecting Pete. Luckily he was married, although we weren't sure if this would necessarily stop her from having a go anyway.

Bloodied by a turbulent year, I was excited to find myself at Pink Floyd's Britannia Row studios in North London, where Robert Smith and Steve Severin had recorded The Glove's *Blue Sunshine* album back in 1983. During our stay I searched for giant inflatable pigs and stray bricks from *The Wall*, but the only relics (excuse the Floyd pun) that I managed to unearth were a couple of non-descript electric organs which may or may not have performed on certain Pink Floyd recordings over the years. Somehow, I managed to break one of them and quickly sidled away to the other side of the studio before anybody could notice.

Over the course of one all-night session, we recorded the basic backing tracks to eight of our songs. Steve and Pete were great to work with and kept the mood upbeat. There was no repeat of the former pre-production disasters. Drums, bass and guitars were all finished by 6am. Vocals and overdubs were added a week later at a tiny recording studio in West London's Ladbroke Grove. This multi-tasking one-bedroom flat, where Marc Bolan and Joe Strummer had both spent part of their early careers, would soon become Fruit Machine's London HQ after Steve and Pete talked an acquaintance into renting the property to them for an agreeable sum.

FRUIT MACHINE IN SHOCK SIGNING RUMOUR...

Fruit Machine's producers gave the Britannia Row recordings to a number of music business associates. First to respond was Arista's Martin Heath, who was so taken that he offered to release a single without even meeting us. Once again, I found myself being reminded of how ridiculously easy everything could be when furnished with the right contacts.

Driving on a fast day with you
The hills of Monte Carlo in bloom
Wake me up and tell me it's true...

(*Monte Carlo*. Simon Parker/Jennie Cruse/Fruit Machine. 1997).

IT'S OK - FRUIT MACHINE NOT SIGNED

Alas, this particular piece of good news lasted but a few days. Martin was unexpectedly, and, I hasten to add, temporarily, suspended from his position at Arista Records. All hopes of imminent pop stardom instantly came crashing down like a decommissioned Sputnik.

Martin Heath eventually left Arista to establish his own Lizard King label. They signed that rather successful act The Killers.

PLAN B

Buoyed by this positive start, Steve and Pete offered Fruit Machine a production deal. The guys waxed lyrical that a partnership of this nature was guaranteed to bring success, and for our part, we were more than happy to entertain such an idea, especially after finally letting our producers in on that dirty little secret concerning our real ages.

Production deals are often viewed with much suspicion in the music industry, generally because they don't leave much room for labels to wield their own power over proceedings. Unaware of the nature of a production deal at the time, Fruit Machine reasoned that installing their musical collaborators to the rank of business partners was nothing short of a genius move. After our experiences with the unpredictable Zack, we all felt considerably safer in the hands of our new mentors. So Fruit Machine agreed to sign should the funds become available for the duo to launch their own company.

Pete successfully approached his bank for a not-insubstantial loan of £20k and Pop Corp. was born soon after. Within a few days we were all staring at a multi-paged legal document, utterly bamboozled by that came after the second paragraph of heftily worded clauses and sub-paragraphs.

At this point, Fruit Machine employed the services of a music business lawyer to help explain the terms of the contract, and also to iron out anything that we didn't agree with. Steve and Pete informed us that the deal was extremely fair and we assured them we would sign it quickly. Our legal team was based just off Oxford Circus so we were going to be able to combine legalities and shopping in the same trip. Perfect...

MEANWHILE, BACK AT THE RANCH

While the legal deal was being hammered out, we honed our live show, which had become a source of some concern to our new partners. Fruit Machine was never the most confident live act, as Jennie was a shy front person and Rachel a very static performer. Of course, on the other side of the stage it probably didn't help matters that I was completely the opposite and forever busting those jerky moves.

Utilising the latest technology available, well, one of Captain Sensible's cast-off DAT players, we started to rehearse with a backing tape laden with keyboards, effects and vocal harmonies. Suddenly, we sounded like a cyber-sensation from Planet Pop. Back there on the drum kit, Nick had to get used to wearing headphones with a click track because if anyone should happen to venture away from the beat (now, why are you all looking at me?) our mask would slip and the song would start limping as we wandered out of time.

Interestingly, our DAT player turned out to possess a temperamental streak and would often skip tracks without any prior word of warning. At this point both band and machine would end up playing completely different songs at the same time. It kept us on our toes, to say the very least.

But Fruit Machine diligently persevered with their new-fangled set-up, largely because everyone said we sounded much better when it was all working properly.

LAW - WHAT IS IT GOOD FOR?

Bad news. Our lawyer deemed the contract untenable. Over the course of thirty long (and costly) minutes, we were casually informed of a whole world of hypothetical gobbledygook that went straight over our heads. At the end of a brain-twisting conversation, Jennie, Rachel, Nick and I were told it was in Fruit Machine's best interests to demand a bigger percentage of absolutely everything the contract had to offer.

And with this, we awkwardly instructed our legal team to do just that, despite feeling very uneasy about going against Pop Corp's wishes. These guys were our friends. In fact, they had even agreed to foot our legal bill in a show of good will. Effectively, we were now about to spend a considerable part of Pete's bank loan on legal wrangling. Band and production team forged ahead, uneasy in the knowledge that money was leaking through a puncture in their second-hand Zeppelin.

RISE

Around this time FM were introduced to the Directors of Rise Management. Back in the late 90s, these guys were a well-respected team based on the Harrow Road. The company's other clients included Brit-pop hopefuls Rialto and Republica, the latter fronted by Saffron Sprackling who would later go on to duet with Robert Smith on The Cure's *Just Say Yes* single. See? It just keeps on happening. We were signed to Rise for management and they wasted no time in distributing the Britannia Row demos.

BRING ON THE DANCING HORSES

The first person to get in touch was one of the team behind a meteorically successful 1990s boy band. No, I'm not about to name him or them. I just don't have the money. But he was a big fish at the time and Rise had done a great job ensnaring him.

By 1998, Spice World and Girl Power had replaced Brit Pop at the top of our charts, leaving indie bands to drown in a brave new world of teeth, tits and gym fetishists. The likes of Oasis, Blur and Pulp were all still hugely popular acts, but Brit Pop had eaten itself and quickly tarnished anyone still within spitting distance.

Against this oncoming pop juggernaut, even bands like The Cure struggled to keep up in the UK. With the release of *Wild Mood Swings,* English music journalists unjustifiably slaughtered the album. By the way, it hadn't escaped my attentions that Robert Smith had just included a song called *Return* for this record. Remember that long-lost Onion Johnny classic? Of course you do. Who knows, maybe big Rob was a fan after all?

Either that or great minds really were thinking alike...

Back in the story 'Mr. X' as he shall be known henceforth, had just laid down some pretty severe ground rules for allowing us to pursue him. From this point onwards, Rise was strictly forbidden from sending demos to any other label. In return, we got no assurances, just a flimsy half promise that he might turn up at a future gig. And like the desperate fools that we all were, this is exactly what we agreed to. For three long months Rise would book us countless London shows and Mr X would occasionally turn up and talk in a very loud voice. I could hear him from the stage. It was deeply off-putting.

One afternoon he dropped by the Ladbroke Grove headquarters of Pop Corp. for a cup of tea and a private audience with the band. He immediately accused me of liberating David Byrne's stage persona. He then spent the next hour talking about his former glories, conveniently forgetting to mention if he actually liked our songs or not. Eventually, after much deliberation he called Rise and said that he didn't think it would work and we were back to square one. Again.

Pop Corp. was very disappointed with this outcome and promptly sacked Rise without even bothering to consult the band members first. Becoming frustrated with the amount of time things were taking, Steve and Pete decided to steer their ship alone. Meanwhile, an expensive game of contractual tennis was still raging above our heads. Money left the Pop Corp. bank account faster than Elvis had ever exited the building. By refusing to sign the agreement we were now effectively flushing Pete's bank loan straight down the legal lavatory. So just what were we supposed to do? I know, let's all go out to a gig and get very, very drunk...

A NIGHT OUT WITH GRANDADDY

Jen's ex-boyfriend was playing bass for a Brighton band called 'Tidy'. We went to watch them at the King's Cross Water Rats, sharing the bill with a little-known bunch called 'Grandaddy'. Within minutes of these beardy wonders taking to the stage, I was experiencing another of those 'eureka' moments peculiar to my musical life. Pitched somewhere between ELO and Pavement, Grandaddy swiftly became my favourite new band while single-handedly redefining how I thought about music. Loud guitars and symphonic lo-fi keyboard squiggles, sir? Why, yes please! Someone leaned over and told me that the group had just signed to V2 records and I cursed the memory of Zack Hoffman and his dealings with the label's publishing arm.

I loved every note that evening and drifted off into a musical daze... but when I came round I found myself back at Steve's West London flat, watching in horror as Rachel administered a suggestive massage to a pair of hairy producer feet.

Welcome back matey.

Yep, that's right. Rachel and Steve became an item. It wasn't that we didn't want her to find happiness; it's just that she always seemed to be doing it at the band's expense. Such is life.

Thus ended our days of confiding any Fruit Machine-related business with either our guitarist or our producer. But, on the bright side, witnessing Grandaddy for the first time had been a very special moment in my life. For the next ten years I would avidly follow the career of this truly amazing band.

TWO TRIBES

Eventually we signed the Production agreement, but it was more out of guilt than desire. We knew that if we weren't careful, Pete's entire bank loan was going to disappear in legal costs. This was exactly what the lawyer wanted. Since then I have spoken with a lot of artists who have endured similar scenarios. Is it possible that the biggest crooks in the music business are actually the ones entrusted with the law?

At this point, Fruit Machine became divided into two distinct camps with Nick, Jennie and I on one side and Pop Corp. and Rachel on the other. Life was awkward and everything ended in a 3-3 draw.

THE ROBBIE WILLIAMS B-SIDE INCIDENT

Through Steve's connections to top producer Guy Chambers, Pop Corp. was offered the chance to work on the B-side to Robbie Williams *Millennium* single. At the same time, Guy and Robbie were also looking for an Italian-speaking girl to ad-lib over one of the single's bonus tracks. And this was how Fruit Machine's drummer's girlfriend went to number 1 long before we even made a record. We didn't even get to support Mr Williams, although Jennie and I did frequent a terrible live show at Hammersmith Hippodrome just before *Angels* came along and saved his career...

IN THE MEANTIME

Talking of live shows, Fruit Machine got to support bands such as The Chills, Linoleum, Speedy and The Clint

Boon Experience (word up, Clint). We also got to open for the legendary Shack, who had been a particular favourite of mine since those balmy school days of 1982, when they dressed like something out of an Enid Blyton novel and were still known as The Pale Fountains.

MY TOP TEN SHACK, MICHAEL HEAD & PALE FOUNTAINS SONGS

1. Pale Fountains - Jeans Not Happening
2. Shack - Neighbours
3. Michael Head & the Strands - Something Like Me
4. Shack - Undecided
5. Pale Fountains - These are the Things
6. Shack - Cup of Tea
7. Pale Fountains - Start a War
8. Pale Fountains - Reach
9. Shack - High Rise Low Life
10. Pale Fountains - Just a Girl

Alas, when I finally got to meet lead singer Michael Head backstage at Brighton's Pressure Point venue, I made a bit of a tit of myself due to a misunderstanding caused by his thick Scouse accent. Embarrassed and mortified, I then spent the rest of the evening trying to hide from this living legend. But the gig was unforgettable and Shack turned in a journeyman's set, even playing songs from the legendarily lost *Water Pistol* record. Michael even watched some of our performance from the side of the stage and later on gave us a musical thumbs up, despite continuing to issue me funny sideways glances for the full duration of the evening.

There's a strong argument for never meeting your heroes, isn't there? Fruit Machine continued to record in Ladbroke Grove and pretended that everything was great. But quite clearly this wasn't the case.

► chapter fifteen

IN THE STUDIO (pt.2: 1998/99)

Occasionally, having little money frustrates me, but generally I think I handle it pretty well. One thing I know for sure is that I have never been as poor as I was after Fruit Machine plighted their troth to Pop Corp. At this time, Jen and I were living on white rice and beans whilst watching our overdrafts sink ever deeper. In such moments of angst I would often berate Steve and Pete by telling them that it didn't feel as if we were actually signed to anything. There had been no advances or even a cursory amount to upgrade our woeful array of amps and instruments. I mean, I didn't expect much, but *anything* would have been an improvement. So, when we were installed in one of Brighton's most expensive recording studios it came as something of a shock.

Clarion had at one time been a church, but was converted into a state of the art recording facility back in the good old demonic 80s. Even Duran Duran and The Cure had been there. And I can vouch for this as I found an old Goth Kings reel-to-reel tape on my first good rummage through the studio's darkened back rooms.

By this point, Pop Corp. were struggling financially thanks in no small part to those hefty legal bills, but had managed to wangle some much-needed studio time from an acquaintance working at the studio. In the event, Fruit Machine wouldn't actually have to pay anything back until the album was officially released on a major record label. This was literally a godsend for our ailing producers and work began at the end of 1998.

We started by recording a song called *Electric*, which everyone agreed was a great first single. Upbeat and dynamic, and more than a little bit like prime-time Blondie, it may not have mirrored how we were feeling as

214

a unit, but it was an excellent choice of song. A cool indie label called Global Warming home to Magoo, Cousteau and Bellatrix, also thought so, as they offered to release it as a 7" single.

> *You're so electric, when you're projected*
> *On the silver screen I selected...*

(Electric. Jennie Cruse/Fruit Machine. 1998).

Disappointingly, things didn't quite go to plan in the studio and we ended up spending four weeks, half of the time allocated for the whole album, recording and over-dubbing the single. Everything sounded dull and uninspired. It wasn't long before Pop Corp. was agreeing terms on three further months of scarily expensive studio time.

The problems lay with the fact we were all trying too hard to put on a brave face and pretend we were friends. The division within the ranks made it a draining experience for everyone involved. Pete and I argued constantly and Jennie rarely shared the same room as Rachel. Nick's drumming sounded tired and laboured whilst Steve was coming down with an illness that would lay him low for months. Consequently we were all finding it hard to commit the required magic to tape. When we tried to record as a band, huge cracks in our performances were revealed.

As a result, all four members of Fruit Machine ended up working on their parts in isolation. This gave us a wooden, lifeless platform to build on, or at least it did to my ears. At the time I was listening to The Flaming Lips *Soft Bulletin* and Mercury Rev's *Deserter's Songs* and wanted to bring something fresh to our album. But Fruit Machine had nothing to do with this particular strain of progressive lo-fi so I was quickly banished from the sessions, outside of playing bass and occasional guitar parts. Weeks of painfully expensive studio time crawled past yet I knew very little about how our record was progressing.

As the studio bill grew, Pop Corp. had to turn down the single offer from Global Warming. With it went the chance of my first record with a proper barcode. Everything hinged on Steve and Pete being able to sell our album onto a major record company, once it was finally finished, that is.

Respected American publication Billboard ran a small piece on Fruit Machine and instantly created a noticeable stateside buzz. Pete was inundated with calls from U.S. scouts and eventually had to stop working on the record just so that he could fend off the advances and send monitor mixes of *Electric* overseas. Once again, this slowed progress down and yet another month at Clarion was deemed necessary.

Due to Billboard's 'Continental Drift' feature, U.K. interest was re-ignited and we found ourselves playing at The Water Rats in Kings Cross (Ah! Such bittersweet memories of that recent Grandaddy show!) with a guest list as long as the M25. It's a strange thing to come out of studio isolation and suddenly have to deal with the A&R world again. But encouragingly, the band sounded all the better for its recent recording schedule and Steve and Pete seemed confident of financial offers to help get the album finished.

DARKLANDS

It was amazing to see what one piece of favourable press could do. Suddenly Fruit Machine were creating ripples again, although most of the names on our industry guest list had seen us at least once before.

TOP TIP TWENTY-ONE:

MAKE FRIENDS WITH A MUSIC JOURNALIST.

As we parked up outside the Water Rats, we remarked on how gloomy this part of London looked on an otherwise reasonably pleasant winter's afternoon. The promoter joined us in the street and explained that there had just been a freak power cut that was currently affecting most of the Gray's Inn Road area.

So we sat in a darkened venue lighting candles, awaiting normal service to be resumed. It was reminiscent of a World War Two blackout. As our stage time drew ever closer, I became convinced that a supernatural force was messing with our hopes of impressing the music industry. Years later I learned there was a Magic Circle club situated directly above the venue. This might explain a few things.

Suddenly, electric lights spluttered into life up and down the street. For a few seconds we had been saved. Inexplicably, The Water Rats remained without power, whilst all around nearby office buildings resumed with their work-a-way days.

Ever since that gloriously naïve fiasco of performing at the Arun Leisure Centre, it felt as if my life had been slowly building towards a moment of recognition. But due to a freak power failure in Central London I was no longer going to be granted the chance to perform in front of the biggest A&R crowd of my entire career.

Looking out through the early evening murk, I watched in disbelief as the first industry hopefuls were turned away. Steve and Pete adopted a brave face and tried to hold court with a small army of key label contacts, but within thirty minutes the street was devoid of man bags and mobile phones as the A&R world simply elected to move on and look for the next big thing in other, illuminated areas of London town.

If the power had returned in time, there was every chance Fruit Machine might have played a great show that night. Whether we could have convinced a record company to sign us on the strength of one such performance is debatable given the way things worked back then, but at least we would have known. Fruit Machine and Pop Corp. were now officially fully paid-up residents of limbo land.

I knew in my heart that we had missed our moment. I think we all did, actually. But we tried to pretend everything was alright. The gig was re-scheduled and eventually took place a couple of weeks later but only a handful of the A&R crowd turned up and we played a distinctly average show.

Irony laughed in my face every time I mentioned that our first single was called *Electric*. Hah bloody hah...

My, how the paint on the picture starts to run
My life of Sundays has never begun

(*Life of Sundays*. Simon Parker/Fruit Machine. 1998).

'WHEN I WOKE UP I WAS LYING ON THE FLOOR, I'D PISSED MY PANTS AND IT WAS NO FUN ANYMORE'

(Borrowed from Magnus Carlsson's *Robin*)

Regretfully, our inter-band problems had worn away at us to such an extent that we left the studio with an exhausted album, cobbled together from hundreds of takes. We had also spent another twenty thousand. Worse still, the record wasn't finished and Jennie had to record most of her vocals back at Ladbroke Grove.

The last day in the studio was memorable because Rachel informed us that she was leaving the band to devote more time to her children. She still considered herself to be a part of the recording 'team', but her days as a gigging member of Fruit Machine were finally coming to an end.

Oddly, this news didn't make the remaining members feel much better. The whole thing was broken. Jennie went off to London and started work on the lead vocals, whilst Pop Corp. ran an advert for a guitarist in NME stating that we were a 'signed' band. Beware! Not true! We auditioned several likely candidates before Steve surprised us all by electing a shy 'Silverchair' loving 19 year-old as Rachel's unlikely successor. No, me neither.

Luke Morris hadn't been the band's personal first choice but his tender years would certainly help bring the average age down a bit. Dave Balfe, ex-Teardrop Explodes keyboard player and one-time head of Food

Records, had recently confided to Steve that he would never sign a band aged over twenty three. At this point I was precisely thirty two years old. So I kept my mouth well and truly shut and never told Luke my real age. How on earth had I come to be almost a generation older than our youngest member?

On the day Luke arrived in Brighton from Edinburgh, he unexpectedly turned up with his sullen girlfriend. Bad news. Lizzie Crabbe would quickly become the bane of our lives. But for the time being there was no time to waste and the pair were deposited in the back room of our flat. To put it simply, Fruit Machine rehearsed whenever Lizzie didn't need Luke for shopping expeditions.

One day I heard a commotion in the street and looked out to see Lizzie banging her head against a lamp post. Luke was sitting on the kerb watching her. Apparently she was used to getting her own way all of the time, so when Pop Corp. arranged a weeks' worth of warm-up shows in Nice, she completely lost the plot. Funds were tight and our producers understandably couldn't justify taking the love interest along. Hell, they would have left *me* behind given half a chance. Luke had no option but to raid the piggy bank and buy his dreadful belle a ticket of her own.

And Lizzie wasn't the only unexpected guest. Just days before our flight, Rachel was re-installed as well. Out of the blue, she and Steve had broken off their relationship and it was decided that Rachel should oversee Luke's transition into fully-fledged band member. Honestly, things had become so ridiculous that I couldn't fight it anymore.

We set off to France with a distraught mother of three and two bickering teenage delinquents in tow. Happy bloody families it was not.

(NOT SO) NICE IN NICE

We landed in the South of France to be bundled into the back of a small windowless van, much like condemned prisoners on their way to the gallows. Our apartment was next to the venue, high above the city centre of picturesque Nice. We were shown into dark and mouldy rooms, pungent with seed and seediness. I quickly came to know just how the Beatles must have felt on arrival in early 1960s Hamburg.

Disappointingly, the bar was a small, over-priced English pub. The stage had roughly the same dimensions as a postage stamp. We spent a hilarious first evening trying to avoid bumping into each other while playing the gig. It was like performing on a tube train during rush hour. Luke sat it out and glowered at the pissed-up audience from the side of the stage whilst Lizzie bemoaned the fact that she hadn't been able to locate a McDonalds yet. She then ran off into the night and that was the last we saw of the dysfunctional couple until the early hours of the following morning.

Over the next few evenings, we entertained a different nationality at every performance but were always met with the same apathetic response. Luke was still refusing to play, so it was lucky that Rachel had tagged along after all. Jen and I visited street markets and went halves on the odd baguette, but we were so broke our only other food and drink was what the venue bequeathed to us.

Following a stern word from Pop Corp. on the telephone, Luke was suddenly ready to play on the final evening of our stay. On each of our previous thirteen performances we had been told to turn it down until we might as well have unplugged altogether. It was a humiliating and depressing experience for all involved. So, on the very last song of that final set we decided to get our own back. As the last tune started skidding towards its inevitable conclusion, we simply turned everything up as loud as we possibly could. Nick beat the shit out of his kit whilst Jen screamed into her microphone. A maelstrom of noise spewed onto a busload of unsuspecting Japanese tourists who all ran screaming from the venue with blood dripping from their ears. Well, it wasn't quite like that, but they certainly covered their ears and made for the hills.

We immediately slunk off back to our stinky hovel and proceeded to guzzle the best part of our duty free.

We left Nice with bad hangovers and even worse memories of a beautiful city.

DISINTEGRATION

Fruit Machine's contract with Pop Corp. was at an end. Or, at least that's what we thought. However, owing to our overseas sojourn Jennie, Nick and I had just missed a golden opportunity to walk away from the deal. Somehow, nobody had thought to inform us that to activate the termination clause, we would need to inform our partners in writing within thirty days of the contract's original expiration date. Now, we hadn't been anywhere near a lawyer's office since spending most of Pete's bank loan, but you would have thought someone from the firm would have contacted us, wouldn't you, seeing as we made them so much money and all? But, as the deal had been left to naturally run its course, Fruit Machine had missed the one and only chance to walk away, and so, our services were legally retained for another twelve months for the sum of one pound. I'm not joking. I kept that coin for years.

Soon after, Steve and Rachel started seeing each other again and this time she did leave the band forever. Things were going from bad to worse with Luke and Lizzie and relationships became frayed, frazzled and under considerably more strain than Robert Smith trying to fit into a pair of Russell Brand's jeans.

We played some University dates with our new teenage prodigy. On one particularly morose occasion in Bath, we struck up a fleeting conversation with a bunch of black-hearted Northerners who also appeared to be suffering rather too much for their art at the hands of the unfeeling music industry. After trading various hard luck stories for a few minutes in the early evening drizzle, both acts disappeared into their respective venues to entertain sparse audiences.

That band was called Elbow.

C-DRIFT

Back at Ladbroke Grove, we started work on one of Jennie's more recent songs. This was to be an important change of direction for the band as the new track, *C-Drift*, hinted at unexplored territories, far away from the traditional pop that we had created for our overdue album. Equal parts Bjork experimentalism and laid back Brian Wilson masterpiece, Jen's latest creation made me feel excited about music again.

Believe me, this was no small thing back in 1999.

Make sure you keep your wristwatch wound
Make every single second count

(*C-Drift*. Jennie Cruse/Fruit Machine. 1999).

YOU NEVER WASH UP AFTER YOURSELF

While Jennie was away singing in London, it became painfully clear that Luke and Lizzie had absolutely no intentions of finding work or paying any rent. It was like I had become the surrogate parent to a pair of lazy teenage freeloaders. They ate all of my food and ran up huge phone bills whilst pleading with their real parents back in Scotland to send them wads of cash for skateboards and Lizzie's addiction to Cola. When that stopped working Luke stiffly asked to be put on a weekly wage. I tried not to laugh and told him to take it up with Pop Corp.

Eventually we fell out over something as gloriously rock and roll as the washing up. Following a huge row in the kitchen, the scheming couple slithered off in the early hours of the following morning while the just-returned Jennie and I lay in bed praying that the pair wouldn't change their minds and stick around. Luckily, Luke and Lizzie stayed true to their half-arsed plan, which involved dragging all of their gear down onto the street and then hopping from leg to leg in the rain and wondering exactly what to do next. Eventually, they begged to come back in and use the phone and a few hours later a very pissed off family relative turned up and drove the troublesome pair out of our lives forever.

It was finally over. We were no longer in a band. The twentieth century was just a few weeks from finishing and Fruit Machine was technically dead. By killing the group we could live again.

EVERYTHING BEAUTIFUL IS FAR AWAY

With just five weeks of the century remaining, a hastily arranged crisis talk was arranged with Pop Corp. for Monday 22 November 1999. Scarily, this date was just six days short of one whole year since work had begun on that ill-fated album.

Jennie and I had already decided to take a break from music, in the hope that we could rediscover some of our zest for life. Nick was experiencing recurring abdominal pains and needed a long rest. He was so thin his bones were literally poking through his skin. Yet despite such turmoil, in private we suspected Pop Corp. would simply re-instate Rachel and plod on into the next calamity.

Within minutes of the producers arriving for our meeting, it was clear that anything but this was going to happen. Pete looked bug-eyed crazy, launching immediately into a long rant about how he could no longer ward off a long line of impatient creditors who were now banging on the doors of their Ladbroke Grove office. As a band we all felt bad about this. Pete was a good guy and didn't deserve such financial hassle. By a stroke of remarkably good timing though, Lovell and Jones had just been approached to oversee the second Longpigs album. This would go a long way to ensuring that both producers didn't end up losing their houses when debts were finally called in.

And so the production company idea was left in its final resting place on that scrap heap of good ideas gone very badly wrong. Steve Lovell barely uttered a word all evening. I realized that this must be goodbye.

Pete Jones retired from the world of production not long after working on that second Longpigs album. I'm not entirely sure if he and Steve even finished the record, but I do know that this was the end of the road for their partnership. He quit production to become a music business lawyer. There's logic in that, isn't there? I haven't seen or heard from him since the day of our final meeting and I'm sad that we fell out so badly. Towards the end of our relationship I tried to turn things around, but somehow my every action just seemed to further annoy Pete. But, I'm sure whatever he did next will have been a success.

Steve Lovell also quit music production before moving in with Rachel and her three children. These days the couple run an Eco-paints business in Sussex. I bumped into them in 2012 and spent twenty minutes catching up. It was good to see them and things were friendly. But I foolishly lost the business card Steve gave me so we've not been for that pint yet.

I miss those long, late night music discussions with Steve and hope that one day maybe we can do it again. When people quit music, most choose to wash their hands of the whole sorry business. I hope Steve hasn't done that. Without him it would have taken me years to discover the Beach Boys *Sunflower* and Babybird's *Fatherhood*. Despite everything that transpired during our hexed liaison with Pop Corp., Fruit Machine enjoyed a lot of opportunities that very few other unsigned artists are ever afforded. Thank you, Steve and Pete.

But just what were we going to do now?

LADIES AND GENTLEMEN, WE ARE FLOATING IN SPACE.

I awoke on Tuesday 23rd November 1999, feeling ten years younger. For the first time in living memory I had absolutely no musical commitments whatsoever. And you know what? That was fine. With only a little over a month until the new millennium, it seemed like a very good time to welcome in the 21st Century and just see what came with it, man.

So, if someone had informed me that by Monday 6th December 1999, Jennie, Nick and I would be rattling through another industry showcase, I think I would have run away screaming.

But, this is exactly what happened. Despite flimsy self-made assurances that Fruit Machine would now withdraw until further notice, by early December the three remaining members would be ghost walking back into London for one final shot at the title. Here, ensconced at Camden's Dublin Castle yet again, we would entertain a German record label manager who had flown in especially to watch us breeze through just six numbers.

But before we get into all of that, I feel a little distraction is in order. By now, our journey towards the muddy heart of the music industry must surely be weighing heavy on your shoulders, because it most certainly was on mine. So cast your mind back and see if you can recall this little lot.

TOP 20 UNDERRATED 1990s SINGLES

1. Wheat - Don't I Hold You?
2. Scarfo - A Year from Monday
3. AC Acoustics - Stunt Girl
4. Sebadoh - Skull
5. Kent - If You Were Here
6. The Jeremy Days - Sylvia Suddenly
7. Gene - Where Are They Now?
8. Scarce - Glamorising Cigarettes
9. The Posies - Solar Sister
10. The Snapdragons - The Eternal in a Moment
11. Sammy - Encyclopedite
12. The Would Be's - My Radio Sounds Different in the Dark
13. Violent Femmes - American Music
14. Dinosaur Jr. - Take a Run at the Sun
15. Urusei Yatsura - Hello Tiger
16. Neutral Milk Hotel - Holland, 1945

17. Rialto - Monday Morning, 5:19
18. Tiger - Race
19. Gorky's Zygotic Mynci - If Fingers Were Xylophones
20. PWEI - Def Con 1

Lest we forget...
Paris Angels - Perfume, The Slingbacks - No Way Down, Power Of Dreams - One Hundred Ways to Kill a Love, Eat - Shame, That Petrol Emotion - Sensitize, Nilon Bombers - Cracked, Archive - You Make Me Feel, Shack - Al's Vacation, The Cocteau Twins - Iceblink Luck, Cud - Sticks And Stones, Gin Blossoms - Hey Jealousy, Deus - Hotel Lounge, Gavin Friday - Angel, Olivia Tremor Control - Jumping Fences, Flowered Up - It's On, Nick Heyward - Rollerblade, Ash - Girl From Mars, Idlewild - Actually, It's Darkness, The Breeders - Divine Hammer, Velo Deluxe - Ballad of Lobster Boy, Crashland - New Perfume, Passion Fruit and Holy Bread - Crush, Salad - Drink The Elixir, Orange - Judy over the Rainbow, The Rockingbirds - Gradually Learning, Sterling - Lucy is Fine, Boo Radleys - Does This Hurt?, Velocette - Bitter Scene, Spacemaid - Baby C'mon, Venus Beads - Shackled, Molly Half Head - Barny, Evil Superstars - It's a Sad, Sad Planet, Buffalo Tom - Sodajerk, Archers Of Loaf - Harnessed In Slums

Guilty Pleasures;
Fish - A Gentlemen's Excuse Me
Belinda Carlisle - California

TOP 10 1990s ALBUMS NOW DUE FOR RE-EVALUATION

1. Suede - Dog Man Star
2. Talk Talk - Laughing Stock
3. Julian Cope - Jehovakill
4. Cornelius - Fantasma
5. The Lemonheads - It's a Shame about Ray
6. Dinosaur Jr. - Hand it over
7. The Boo Radleys - Giant Steps
8. American Music Club - San Francisco

9. Guided By Voices - Alien Lanes
10. Immaculate Fools - Another Man's World

(Anything and everything released by The Trashcan Sinatra's)

TOP 20 UNDERRATED 1990s ALBUMS

1. Sparklehorse - Good Morning Spider
2. Denim - Back in Denim
3. Trash Can Sinatra's - A Happy Pocket
4. The Auteurs - New Wave
5. The Posies - Amazing Disgrace
6. Shack – Water Pistol
7. Nick Heyward - The Apple Bed
8. Wilco - Summerteeth
9. Flaming Lips - Clouds Taste Metallic
10. Band of Holy Joy - Positively Spooked
11. Throwing Muses - The Real Ramona
12. Weezer - Pinkerton
13. Guided by Voices - Do the Collapse
14. Immaculate Fools - Another Man's World
15. Michael Head and the Strands - Introducing the Magical World of...
16. A House - I am the Greatest
17. Super Furry Animals - Radiator
18. Grandaddy - Under the Western Freeway
19. Divine Comedy - Liberation
20. Idlewild -100 Broken Windows

Not Forgetting...
All albums released by The Lemonheads, Teenage Fanclub, XTC, Babybird, Edwyn Collins and The Cure (yes, even *Wild Mood Swings*).

Guilty Pleasures;
Del Amitri - Waking Hours,
A-ha - East of the Sun, West of the Moon

TOP TEN UNDERRATED 90s BANDS

1. Ride
2. Wannadies
3. Catherine Wheel
4. Salad
5. Cable
6. My Life Story
7. Neutral Milk Hotel
8. The Posies
9. The Longpigs
10. Sammy

▶ chapter fifteen and a half

THE EDWYN COLLINS APPRECIATION CLUB

I can pinpoint the date at which I became a fan of Edwyn Collins to mid-December of 1982. *I Can't Help Myself* had just underperformed in the charts so I was able to rescue a copy from the bargain bins. And what a single it turned out to be; a fearless attempt to fuse Motown and jangling Scottish Pop with suitably stupendous results.

Of course, I had been reading about the band all year, as 1982 was a busy period for Orange Juice. *I Can't Help Myself* was actually their fourth single in eleven months since moving from the uber-hip Postcard records. Once the music stork had deposited them on the doorstep of terminally un-groovy Polydor, Edwyn and his cohorts had struggled to make an easy transition from indie cool to major sales, but each successive 7" release had climbed a few places higher than the previous one. Surely something had to give?

At school, I would recognise other Orange Juice fans by the fashioning of an Edwyn-inspired floppy fringe. My drama buddy Stuart Worden was one prime example of this. It was a good day when *Rip It Up* snuck into the Top 10. There was probably never a more life-affirming sight than watching Edwyn chuckling his way through a couple of performances of Top of the Pops in early 1983.

I followed the band's career with interest, loving the singles, but in truth, only liking the albums from which they were culled. It was a sad day when they officially split not long after the release of the temperamental *Third Album*.

By the time Edwyn kick-started his solo career, the charts were full of Stock, Aitken and Waterman productions. Make no mistake: the 80s didn't become officially crap until PWL started releasing Rick Astley records.

Evenings spent in London's New Cross Venue were the scenes of some of the more memorable Edwyn Collins live performances, not long after he delivered the first of his solo albums. These shows were reassuringly chaotic and it was good to see that so many Edwyn fans still existed, even though hairstyles had mutated from floppy fringe to rockabilly quiff, and in my case at least, an exploding hedgerow from the planet Zarg.

The *Hope and Despair* (1989) album is another long-lost classic, now ripe for re-discovery. Rendered truly indispensable thanks to some of the man's finest song writing outside of Orange Juice (*Wheels of Love, Coffee Table Song* and *50 Shades of Blue*), press reception was strangely muted and the record sold modestly (as did 1990s follow up *Hellbent on Compromise*). In fact, things didn't seem to be going too well for Edwyn, and this was most definitely the case at 1991's Reading Festival.

Back when it was still the done thing for lower billed festival artists to over-run their allotted time slots, Reading '91's big-top headliner took to the stage nearly an hour later than advertised. Experiencing major technical problems from the off, Edwyn and associates gamely battled their musical gremlins in front of a tent full of politely drunk worshippers, Mark Mason and me included, but of course).

Obviously continuing to play past a strict curfew, a Neanderthal security guard suddenly blundered onstage and forcibly tried to remove Edwyn from the microphone. This resulted in a bit of a tussle with both parties throwing punches. Of course, all of this transpired in full view of an open mouthed audience. The show immediately ground to a halt and the house lights were hastily switched on. Gig well and truly over. Dismiss, there is nothing to see here. But our angry mob wanted Edwyn back at any cost, and when we didn't get him we just started smashing the bloody tent to bits.

It was here that my newfound friends and I enjoyed that once in a lifetime thrill of becoming half-arsed festival anarchists. I ran about intermittently tugging at anything that might help bring about the downfall of Western civilisation. Of course, it was only minutes until security reinforcements and their leg-chewing Alsatians turned up, and for me at least, this was where I stopped being naughty and returned to my tent like the good little poll-tax paying citizen I really was.

If memory serves correctly, Edwyn Collins was profusely apologised to via the music press and then asked to perform again the following year, where this time his set went off without a hitch.

During the early 90s things would calm down a little and Edwyn found time to build his own recording studio at West Heath Yard in London NW6. Nothing more was released until the *Expressly Edwyn* EP at the tail end of 1994. Lead track *A Girl Like You* became a massive worldwide hit when it was re-released a few months later. At this point, everything exploded.

Back in demand and more popular than ever, the *Gorgeous George* album became an early Britpop classic, and the follow-up, *I'm Not Following You*, spawned the memorable *The Magic Piper Of Love*, used to good effect in 'Austin Power's The Spy Who Shagged Me'.

Around this time, coincidence saw Fruit Machine's producers hire the very same valve compressors and antique effect units that had recently graced various Edwyn recordings. His next project hit even closer to home as the mini TV series 'West Heath Yard' oddly mirrored the A&R hell Fruit Machine were experiencing at that precise moment. 'West Heath Yard' was a bunch of black comedy shorts first shown late at night on Channel Four, with our hero cast as the ludicrously bewigged 'Denny Lorimer', a dismally failed and jaded producer/manager figure, seen guiding his own musical protégés ('Expo 70') around the industry's various pitfalls in the late 90s. This was a caustic Edwyn sideswipe, aimed at the advancing corporate music business executive. It deserves searching out if you can find it. To the best of my knowledge it has never been officially released on any format since its once and only showing back in the day.

2002 saw the release of the marvellous *Doctor Syntax*, which slid into the racks while almost nobody was looking. This severely underrated album boasts a fine selection of Northern Soul grooves and acidic pop vignettes such as *Mine Is At*, *Never Felt Like This* and the quite remarkable *The Beatles*. But *Doctor Syntax* would struggle for recognition in a musical bakery that had unwisely elected to cut all the crusts off of its pop stars. Alas, it would take the shocking news that Edwyn had suffered a double cerebral haemorrhage to return him to the music press in 2005.

Amazingly, by 2006 Edwyn's miraculous rehabilitation was already starting to take shape. With the help of his teenage son, the singer could be found posting regular bulletins on My-Space throughout that year. When my own band finally opened an account with one of Rupert Murdock's playthings, Edwyn was the first person I decided to contact. A couple of days later I was stunned to receive a reply from the great man himself. This was another privileged moment in my musical career.

In 2007, Edwyn signed to Heavenly Records and released the miraculous *Home Again*. Containing several Collins classics, such as *You'll Never Know (My Love)* and *Then I Cried*, the great man was then the subject of a BBC4 documentary detailing his heroic attempts to return to the stage. In the autumn of 2007, Jennie and I sat just three rows from the front whilst our protagonist, ably assisted by a fine cast of musical friends including Aztec Camera's Roddy Frame, ex-Ruts drummer Dave Ruffy and Andrew Hackett of The Rockingbirds, took to the stage at the London Arts Theatre and belted out a catalogue of timeless Edwyn classics such as *Blue Boy*, *What Presence?* and *Rip It Up*. It was a hell of an evening.

More recently there has been the heart-rending 'Falling and Laughing - The Restoration of Edwyn Collins' written by his fearless wife Grace, a book which details the family's harrowing ordeal in full. Since then there have been two more fine albums *Losing Sleep* (2010) and

Understated (2013) and a great Orange Juice box set entitled Coals *to Newcastle*.

People, charge your glasses, please. Let's hear it for Edwyn Collins, the thinking man's King of Pop.

▶ chapter sixteen

LAST DANCE
STANDING AT THE ABYSS WITH MY WALKMAN ON

I'm pretty sure you will have worked out for yourself that by November 1999, everyone connected to Fruit Machine wasn't enjoying it anymore. The only thing that kept us together was the continual lure of something better appearing on the horizon. I stood at the threshold of a brave new century, realising that I had somehow wasted the entire 1990s in pursuit of an ever-darkening nightmare. Worse still, I had absolutely nothing to show for my artistic endeavours and little option but to carry on in the same hopeless manner. I was so far in that I could see no possible way out.

While friends back in the real world enjoyed salary rises, luxury consumer durables and an ascent of the property ladder, Jennie and I were still struggling to find the necessary £10 a week to cover our food bills. Children with paper rounds had more disposable income than we did.

To any right-minded individual, this should be where the story ends. My head fizzled like a long-wave radio signal, yet somehow I knew music wasn't completely done with me yet. This unexpected offer of some fresh overseas record company interest would drag our band back into the bedroom for one last butt-fucking.

It's funny, because what follows should have been easy to recall, if for no other reason than it happened more recently than everything else I have transcribed here for you thus far. But rather like memories of a past life, all details of post-Fruit Machine activity come cloaked in a fuzzy little question mark of disbelief. It was as if I hadn't really been there at all.

HOW TO GET SIGNED SEVEN DAYS AFTER FORMING A BAND
(November 1999).

Pop Corp. had sent countless Fruit Machine demo recordings to established overseas record labels. One of these labels suddenly became very serious in its attempts to sign us.

Edel Records of Hamburg, Germany, was a thriving European independent organisation, at that time actively looking to expand into the British pop market. Sometime prior to our break-up with Pop Corp., Edel had been talking with Pete who had even thought to book us a London date after the labels A&R manager Martin Schumacher agreed to fly over and watch us perform. So far, so tentative.

Of course, a week before the gig was due to take place Fruit Machine was without both production team and guitarist, so I had despondently called the promoter at the Dublin Castle and cancelled our slot. Somehow I couldn't bring myself to phone Edel and tell them it was all over for our band. This turned out to be a remarkable stroke of good fortune, as the very next morning I received a call from Joe Harlin of Ice 9, offering his services as a replacement guitarist. I'd seen Ice 9 play on several occasions and already knew that Joe was just what we were looking for. My only reservation was that he was nineteen to my thirty two, but he swore blind this made absolutely no difference. After a quick heart to heart with Jennie and Nick, we decided that it would be rather churlish not to take this opportunity to play in front of the single biggest independent record company in Northern Europe, and steeled ourselves for yet another assault upon the music industry. I hastily re-instated the band to the Dublin Castle showcase and watched the craziness start up all over again.

Incidentally, the other members of Ice 9 all went on to better things like Brakes and The Pipettes. It was quite a band.

TOP 10 THINGS WE DID THAT WEEK

1. Changed the band name to 'Alumina' at our first meeting with Joe.
2. Re-jigged this to the more alluring 'Lumina' a few hours later.
3. Triple-checked with Edel Germany to make sure they were still intending to fly over.
4. All went out and bought some new clothes from H&M.
5. Talked a friend into taking some decent quality pictures of our new line up.
6. Convinced Will Moore to let us play a warm-up show at the Free Butt on Saturday 4th December 1999.
7. Further convinced Will to let us rehearse under the shop where he was working.
8. Taught Joe Harlin six of our songs.
9. Promoted the hell out of both shows to all of our friends.
10. Arrived in London and quickly made sure there hadn't been a power cut before we unloaded the van.

On Monday 6th December 1999, Lumina took to the Dublin Castle stage and delivered half a dozen perfectly formed pop moments to an excitable record company executive who showed his appreciation by punching the air every time we got to the chorus. Joe's clipped approach to the guitar made us sound relevant for the first time in ages and we played with a confident swagger. Not quite as cocky as those Gallagher brothers, but there was definitely an element of 'fuck you, we've seen it all before'.

Following the gig, Martin Schumacher took us out for pizza and offered to sign the band on the spot. It was funny because this was the way I had always pictured it happening. You know, book a show, invite an A&R man and then get signed on the strength of the music. Finally, we had done just that.

Poor Martin was blissfully unaware that little more than a week before this momentous occasion we had been a spent force with neither a guitarist nor the will to carry on. Lumina had been offered a record deal just seven days after forming. I like to think that this may be some kind of record. The curse of Fruit Machine had been officially laid to rest.

Hadn't it?

On December 31st 1999, I found myself merrily snorting cocaine off of a toilet seat. Well, it was the end of a century. A few days later, Jennie spoke to the manager of Moloko who hooked us up with a heavyweight mentor of our own.

It was all systems go. Now, where had I heard that before?

THE INVISBLE MAN

To a number of people, Clive Marshall was a music business legend. Alas, I'm not able to disclose the man's true identity for fear of costly reprisals, but I will say that back in the early 1970s, Mr M had founded a respected and commercially successful independent record label. In return, a number of weird and wonderful artists had gone on to sell a lot of even weirder sounding albums. But punk saw to it that song lengths were shortened and trouser widths tightened. Around this time Clive's label began a long, slow descent that would eventually see it sink completely during the 1980's.

Yet everyone we spoke to regarded the man as a force of nature, although this didn't stop us from thinking we had just bumped into a used car-salesman the first time we met him at a pub near Victoria station, but Clive swiftly won us over with some slick talking and a jacket lined with stolen watches... comedy drum roll, if you please.

So as Clive picked up the slack with Edel, we set to work on a cluster of new material with Joe Harlin in the basement of Will's Mexican artefact shop on Sydney Street.

237

Global Warming re-approached Jennie and me with a view to signing Lumina for the UK, if we first agreed to let them release the aborted Fruit Machine album sessions from Clarion. Tempting as this was at the time; we politely declined to sanction such a Pandora's Box of bad vibes and hexed recordings. Clive bragged that this would only be the start of rekindled record company interest in the band and then advised us to steer clear of independent labels for fear of selling ourselves short.

Global Warming went on to release a clutch of critically acclaimed singles and albums by artists such as Drugstore, Bellatrix and Seafruit. Meanwhile, Lumina nervously awaited the offers to start rolling in...

I HAVE ALWAYS BEEN HERE BEFORE

It soon became apparent that Clive was a master of hollow guff. Our new manager sounded completely out of touch with the industry and relied on interest first generated by Jennie and myself. He would disappear for weeks on end and rarely return our calls. Over in Germany, Martin Schumaker was finding it difficult to convince his bosses to sign a band based in the U.K. Things slowed down and we became re-acquainted with that familiar feeling of dread.

Perhaps not unexpectedly, Joe Harlin experienced a change of heart and decided that what he really wanted to do was join the teenage brothers Tom and Alex White in an early incarnation of The Electric Soft Parade. The age-gap had indeed proved too great to straddle, and sadly our guitarist left after spending less than five months in the fold.

Joe would go on to play for a number of groups over the next few years, amongst them the excellent Actress Hands. Eventually, he gave up the guitar for a life as a sound engineer and travelled the world with The Magic Numbers and British Sea Power. Then, following yet another change of direction, he relinquished his position behind the mixing desk to return to University, where he studied computer technology. Good luck to you Joe. Without you we would never have been signed.

In the spring of 2000, the remaining members of Lumina were left with little choice but to seek out another guitarist before Edel (or Clive) got wind of any ruffled feathers. Through the vagaries of the Brighton grapevine (cheers 'Mola Ram', soon to be 'The Mutts') we stumbled upon another available musician, co-incidentally christened 'Joe'. Well that would make introductions easier, wouldn't it? Lumina swiftly enlisted Joe Hunt before anybody realized there had been a staffing problem over at 'head office'. Indeed, such were his actions that to this day I swear that Clive never realized our band had been forced into a line-up change and that he was now talking to a completely different Joe.

ROUND AND ROUND

Getting old is weird, isn't it? One moment you're laughing at all those old codgers still out there playing in bands, and then you find you've somehow become one too. By the dawn of the new millennium, I had finally stopped believing in the NME. I can still remember how frightening it felt when I first realised this simple yet chilling truth. Where now with my musical knapsack? Cliff Richardville? Perhaps a long walk in the valley of Clannad? Who's that in the distance welcoming me with open arms? Why hello, Ms Celine Dion. How wonderful you sound...

Over in mainland Europe, the perpetually optimistic Mr Schumacher was still dreaming up ways to get us signed. Edel re-launched their U.K. publishing arm and Lumina became one of its first targets, along with Brian Harvey, ex of East 17 (we always kept such good company!) Thanks to Martin's long conversations with company M.D. Phil Hope, the swish Camden office did take a shine to us. Of course, we knew that proceedings would slow to a death-crawl once our manager became

239

involved, so we busied ourselves with teaching Joe Hunt as many of our songs as we could remember. We had amassed quite a back catalogue by this point, with around twenty top-grade tunes stuffed into our pop satchel.

The Bat phone rang again. Another of our Pop Corp. assisted demos was causing consternation over in Los Angeles, California. Precinct 27 Records called me at home and begged that Lumina not talk to another American label until they had secured a hefty $70 000 to sign us with. Company boss Carl Crosby was a fast-talking Mormon with an incurably sweet tooth for English pop. Apparently, we were the band he had been searching for all his life. Carl called virtually every day for the next couple of weeks with other huge compliments. After a while, I had to remind him that we were English and didn't react very well to praise.

Shortly after this, another American label started leaving messages on the answerphone. Unbelievable really, but all part of the continuing madness. In the event, I had several long discussions with Art Hermann, the heart, soul and ears of Zip Records, San Francisco. He couldn't match $70k, but I detected a passion for music that went far beyond the every day. Of course, Clive dismissed both labels at first, but on hearing that a figure of $ 70 000 was being bandied about, he quickly forgot his mantra of 'major labels only' and got on the phone to Precinct 27.

Despite such pin-balling behaviour, things were kind of moving in the right direction. Although we knew Clive was paying very little attention to Lumina, he was occasionally negotiating deals on our behalf. We contemplated parting company but suspected this would upset the relationship with both Precinct 27 and Edel Publishing. Besides, without a manager to fight our corner, who would negotiate on our behalves? We certainly didn't fancy handing things over to a lawyer again. Some of us had already seen the damage this could do, thank you very much. So Clive lived to fight another battle, and pocket twenty percent of everything, should we sign any agreements. Not bad for someone who couldn't even reel off three of our song titles without a painfully long struggle...

The only way to block out the relentless grind was to burrow away in our new rehearsal room which was elegantly situated in an old converted lavatory, and stay true to the music.

Come to think of it, this wasn't the first time that an American party had been interested in one of my bands.

HANGING ON THE TELEPHONE

Back in good old punky 1994, and not long after John Smith had first stepped in to replace the kidnapped Steve Tett, a certain Mr Kim Fowley had called me at home to express an interest in signing Colourburst. Actually, Kim had already spent a good part of the morning badgering Jim's rather confused mum after mistaking her for our manager. We had put Jim's home number on the cassette and Mr F was obviously of the opinion he was introducing himself to our conduit. Hurriedly dispatched in my direction, I dismally failed to decipher just what the hell this fast-talking stranger was wittering on about.

Unbeknown to the seemingly interested Mr Fowley, Colourburst (Mk.II) had recently superseded Colourburst (Mk.I). Musically speaking, this meant no more Radiohead-friendly posturing on our part, as by this time we were delicately infused with the spirit of Buzzcock abandon. But it was our previous line-up's demo that seemed to be causing all the fuss after improbably reaching Kim's hotel room on Los Angeles' Sunset Strip.

For a few minutes I tried to get a word in and explain how we had 'moved on', but my words just seemed to fall on deaf ears. It was very possible that I was conversing with a psychopath. Those of you who have seen 'The Mayor of Sunset Strip' will doubtless know what I am talking about, for Kim features prominently throughout. For the benefit of everyone else, talking with this man was exactly like facing up to Sir Ben Kingsley's Don Logan character in 'Sexy Beast': dark, scary and totally impenetrable, although I'm not sure if Kim treats toilets in the same way as our Don.

Back in the story, Mr Fowley continued with his intense rant and asked if we would be prepared to move to America to find fame and fortune, confiding that he had been living in a hotel for longer than he could remember. At this point I thought I might be talking to a homeless old acid casualty, but hung on in there just in case it was Gary winding me up with a crank call from the phone box at the bottom of our street. We continued to talk at glorious crossed purposes about just who or what Colourburst really was, until finally, when Kim started banging on about 'how the only decent female recording artists are the ones that go out into the desert and let their pussies stink ...' I made my excuses and said we'd be in touch.

Back in that gloriously innocent moment of 1994, I had absolutely no idea that Kim was a self-styled visionary who, since the 1950s had been skilfully masterminding a wayward but maverick career. No sir. I also wasn't particularly aware of 'The Runaways' or of those various song writing pseudonyms the guy had used to write smash hit singles. Fast-forward to 2013, and I can indeed see just why Kim is regarded in such high esteem but back then he was nothing more than a yakking hindrance as I tried to concentrate on another classic episode of 'Ironside'.

Kim, thanks for calling. I think I get it now. Even the bit about lady gardens.

GHOSTS

Clive Marshall found himself in LA on urgent business for a bunch of hairy metal pensioners who had just reformed to cash in on a slew of re-releases. Whilst there, our manager visited the offices of Precinct 27 and came back with thumbs firmly aloft.

Now all we needed was the contract.

Sweet dreams torn at the seams,
fall at your feet, never complete

(*Ghosts*. Jennie Cruse/Lumina. 2000).

But the band was at breaking point. The three long-term members were emotionally all played out and living under the constant fear that another catastrophe was just about to rugby tackle them to the ground. Our lives were not our own, and much like musical zombies, we drifted from one interested party to the next, forever cautious of reading too much into any given scenario. Nick's health had deteriorated to such an extent that he was now under the guidance of a liver specialist. Even more worrying was the fact that both he and Jennie were blacking out at regular unscripted intervals. We were running on an empty tank.

COME TO MILTON KEYNES

After more weeks of promised finance and big ideas, and sensing that a goodwill gesture was needed, Carl Crosby flew over to the UK to meet Lumina. We found ourselves booked into the impressive Linford Manor residential studio, where PJ Harvey had just finished recording *Stories from the City, Stories from the Sea*. More recently, Feeder had just started work on their *Echo Park* album, and as we drove into the stately grounds in a beaten up old hire van, I smiled at the irony and felt good to be keeping such good company.

Only, we weren't keeping any company at all really, because this happened to be the weekend of Glastonbury Festival, so the manor house was largely deserted. The only people around were a couple of junior engineers who cast us odd glances as they unloaded our dilapidated equipment into their state of the art studio. Actually, the producer took one look at our gear and promptly told us to plug straight into Feeder's top of the range amplifiers. Well, hello swanky bass rig!

This was an important day for Lumina. The fact that Clive Marshall had even bothered to show up proved

243

this to me. We began with an informal meet and greet in the studio's stunning grounds before squaring up for an impromptu game of football on a six-a-side pitch (final score: Lumina 10 Americans 8). Following this, the studio chef cooked us all a hot meal, although Joe Hunt refused to eat anything other than cocoa pops for the full duration of our stay. 'Funny guy' I pondered, before getting stuck into precisely two portions of everything.

In the afternoon, we sat around listening to a bunch of CD's that we had been instructed to bring along to show our own influences.

LUMINA'S TOP FIVE MUSICAL INFLUENCES (SUMMER 2000)

1. Bjork - Joga
2. Blur - Death of a Party
3. Brian Wilson - 'Til I Die
4. Smashing Pumpkins - 1979
5. The Cardigans - My Favourite Game (or was it Flaming Lips Race for the Prize?).

We then spent a relaxing couple of hours drinking Earl Grey tea from posh crockery in the mansion's antique dining room. Nobody actually went anywhere near the recording studio until much later that evening. Of course, the song Carl really wanted us to record was the only one we hadn't really shown Joe how to play, but he manfully bluffed his way through and made up parts on the spot.

By three in the morning, we were ready to call it a night, but Carl re-appeared from one of the manor's many rooms and asked if we wouldn't mind first running through a quick take of our entire repertoire whilst the tape was still rolling. We dutifully complied with his wishes, recording live to tape as we went. Those months of practising in an old toilet paid dividends on this evening, as the band sounded confident and tight. Enjoying the studio environment Jen sang her heart out until, at 6am, we crawled off to bed be-fuddled but elated to have given such a good account of ourselves. To me, this justified our bands persistence. Out of the ashes we had once again given birth to a tiny phoenix.

The four members of Lumina left the following morning before Feeder could return and accuse us of mucking about with their amplifiers. The journey home was punctuated with lengthy conversations about whether or not we had done enough to convince Carl to sign us.

WAITING FOR THE GREAT LEAP FORWARDS

Lumina eventually signed both of their contracts on 16th October 2000, some ten fraught months after that hastily arranged Dublin Castle show. There were no executives from either label present, just Clive Marshall and a stack of papers. We celebrated with fizzy wine and Jaffa cakes. At the end of the briefest of discussions, our manager disappeared before any of us could inquire 'Twenty percent for what exactly?'

A week later, Edel's publishing advance arrived in the post and I noticed that the Company Director had somehow forgotten to sign the cheque. At the second attempt, we split a modest £12.5k between the four band members and its errant manager. At thirty three years young, I had finally earned my first income from music publishing. Jennie and I went out and celebrated by buying some new clothes from TK Maxx, but I'm afraid that was about it for tales of wanton opulence.

Precinct 27's advance was, of course, worth $70,000 upon completion of signing. With this, we intended to decamp to America and start working on our first album. As the label was friendly with Billy Corgan from Smashing Pumpkins, his name had already been mentioned as possible executive producer whilst Carl was busy in talks with a studio in Salt Lake City, Utah.

So there you have it. I did get signed in the end. Didn't I tell you that I would? To all intents and purposes I was now going to get paid for writing songs courtesy of the Edel Publishing deal and then release these tracks in the USA via the Precinct 27 agreement. Ok, so I was still technically unable to release anything in the UK and

245

Europe, but, once again, Clive reassured us that it would only be a matter of time before somebody came on board and offered Lumina a deal for the rest of the world. But he wasn't exactly doing a great deal about it...

At thirty three years old I was already a musical pensioner compared to those post Britpop bucks like Muse and Travis. There was nothing I could do except lie about my age. I remembered the stink caused by Guy Chadwick from House of Love signing his record contract at thirty two. God, what was the world going to say about Lumina? Jennie was thirty five so we were both going to have to keep a big old lid on that thorny topic of our real dates of birth.

How strange. I thought it would be different once I had been signed. But rather than feeling as if I was part of something, I actually felt more alone and totally cut off. It was like being a member of an exclusive gang, but without directions to the clubhouse. The most memorable thing about being signed was watching Jennie carry her advance round in a bum bag fastened to her waist, rather than deposit it in a bank.

The Edel advance didn't last very long (well, you try splitting twelve grand between five people and see how far it gets you), and Lumina anticipated the arrival of the rather more substantial amount from Precinct 27. Carl called about twice a week and kept apologising for the delay in wiring the money over, but he did assure us that the funds would be in our accounts within two weeks of returning the contract.

Four months later this advance had still not arrived in the U.K. and Clive Marshall had taken the opportunity to disappear into thin air. Jen and I stopped phoning Carl Crosby when we realized he was blatantly lying to us. The money was always *just about* to be sent. After some good old fashioned detective work on our part, we found out that Precinct 27 was actually using those Linford Manor recordings to try and secure some much needed start-up capital to launch their label. There was no record company, just the shell of an idea.

And one very unhappy band.

Bass:

How low can you go?

Lumina 1999
(l-r Nick Hopkins, Joe Hunt, Jennie Cruse, Simon Parker – photo unknown)

► chapter seventeen

WHERE DOES IT GO FROM HERE - IS IT DOWN TO THE LAKE I FEAR?

Like a coin clinging precariously to the edge of a penny falls machine, the long-suffering Nick Hopkin finally hurled himself out into the void on March 2nd, 2001. Following a tearful three-hour telephone conversation, our drummer broke down in tears and revealed just how mentally and physically ill being in a band was making him. Nick thought that by turning his back on the music industry he would be free to elevate his mind and body from the pit of despair it had fallen into since joining. There was nothing we could do or say. After all, Jennie and I completely understood how he felt simply because we had been thinking much the same thing for ages now.

Sadly, following his departure from the band things didn't go to plan for Nick and his life continued to slide out of control. He split from his Italian girlfriend and then fell into long episodes of serious mental depression. Following years of breakdowns and prescription drugs, Nick Hopkin was eventually diagnosed with a bipolar disorder that made him a virtual prisoner in his own home for long periods of time. When Nick moved out of Brighton and holed up in Hassocks, Jennie and I rarely saw him, but ex-Fruit Machine alumni Steve and Rachel came to his aid at various stages of his difficult return from the darkness.

Happily, there is a silver lining to this gloomy tale, as Nick's new girlfriend gave birth to a baby daughter in 2007. Nick and family relocated to Wales, where the second tallest drummer in pop now builds and sells bespoke drum kits for a living.

I KNOW IT'S OVER

It was at this point that Lumina really ground to a halt. Nick's unexpected departure sent us all into freefall, and unsurprisingly, Joe Hunt also chose to quit music after becoming totally disillusioned with the reality of being in a 'signed' band. These days he's back in his hometown of Felixstowe, writing and recording whenever he feels so inclined.

It's a sad state of affairs that finds the four core members of Lumina estranged from one another. We haven't all been in the same room since late February of 2001. As a band we never fell out but the memories of our troubled times together means we've never felt the urge to meet up and relive them.

So now I'm doing this for us.

HERE'S WHERE THE STORY ENDS

Suddenly, my time in music was at an end. I felt old, damaged and worn-out. Jennie and I knew that we didn't have the energy or motivation to create another line-up from scratch. I had run into my very last brick wall.

In the months that followed, Jen would decide to carry on alone as Lumina, in the faint hope that Precinct 27 might eventually find investment and honour its contractual agreement. Clive Marshall occasionally reared his ugly little head and feigned interest. On one occasion my girlfriend even got as far as Heathrow Airport with a suitcase, where, of course, that golden ticket to the USA failed to materialize just minutes before the flight was due to take off.

As a musician I had become superfluous to requirements. When Jen carried on without me, I felt pangs of sadness and betrayal, but I also knew that it was for the best. My girlfriend no longer needed a traditional band bashing around behind her, as technology and a decent producer could far out-strip anything we might bring to the table. Bjork? Stina Nordenstam? You get the picture. Jen and I had remained a couple but, thanks to our involvement music, our relationship had taken a lot of body blows.

So what the hell was I going to do now?

STARING INTO THE ABYSS WITH MY WALKMAN ON (again)

After chasing record deals for most of my adult life, I wasn't really equipped to make an emergency career change. In reality, the technological revolution had completely passed me by, so at this point there were legions of ten year olds more competent than myself when sat in front of a computer. I didn't exactly have a lot of options.

Against the odds I started writing prolifically again. Gone were those soul-sapping pressures and disappointments. Gone too was the need to write songs that I thought other people wanted to hear. Now I could do whatever the hell I wanted and only have myself to blame for the results. Over the years, being in a band had changed me for the worse. I had to find a way back to enjoying the art of making music again.

After all, it was still the number one love of my life.

Time is running out on me, nine lives drift into the sea...

(*Volcanoes*. Simon Parker/Villareal.2001).

TOP TEN ARTISTS THAT KEPT ME GOING IN 2001

1. Sparklehorse
2. Grandaddy
3. Teenage Fanclub
4. The Wannadies
5. Super Furry Animals
6. The Trash Can Sinatras
7. The Cardigans
8. Flaming Lips
9. Guided By Voices
10. Wheat

THAT JOKE ISN'T FUNNY ANYMORE

Jennie parted company from Clive Marshall not long after the Heathrow incident, and has rarely heard from the little goblin since. He's still out there though, talking his way into decent appointments in return for huge sums of cash. Clive's most recent position sees him cast as a C.E.O. for a large business consortium. I smiled. I really did.

TOP-TIP TWENTY-TWO:

STAY POSITIVE. YOU'RE GOING TO NEED A SENSE OF HUMOUR TO SEE THIS THING THROUGH, OK?

BACK ON THE CHAIN GANG

A short while after Clive's departure, Edel Publishing was sold lock, stock and barrel to Warner Chappell, who swallowed up the labels entire back catalogue during 2002. This technically meant that Jennie and I were now officially signed to one of the biggest publishing houses on the planet. Well, how about that then?

Jen elected to co-write with other Warner artists and went on to score a couple of notable successes, including a song on the film 'Everything' which starred Ray Winstone. Chart-wise, Jennie's *Got Your Number* was a Top Ten smash in Ireland and she even had a hit single in Taiwan via the artist called 'Sun'.

Meanwhile, I devoted creative energies to my next band, figuring out that my songs were just a little too wonky to expect anyone else to have a go at singing them.

▶ chapter eighteen

IN DREAMS

VILLAREAL (2002-PRESENT DAY)

Dreams are magnificent beasts, aren't they? I love pondering the significance of being repeatedly chased across a railway line by a grinning dwarf with very large hands. This was both the most memorable and unpleasant of my recurring childhood dreams, but it bears re-telling. In the nightmare I was at the beach with my parents and sister on a beautiful summer's day. Suddenly, the skies would darken and I could hear the electronic beeping of a level crossing in the distance. My family and I would all run towards a set of descending railway gates as the blackest skies imaginable descended upon us. An evil dwarf with massive hands would appear from out of nowhere and chase us across the tracks. All the while I could sense this thing drawing ever closer as those oversized digits groped at me from behind. Now, just what the fuck is that all about? And why am I still thinking about it in my forties?

Fear not, dear reader. Rather than lumber my next band with another dreadful name, 'Beach Bastard' doesn't really work, does it?, I simply used something more palatable from another vivid apparition. This vision was only ever dreamed the once, back in 1997 to be precise, whilst Zack Hoffman was still hell-bent on messing up the career of Fruit Machine.

Following a head full of whisky one evening I had stumbled off to bed and fallen into a weird fretful sleep. In the ensuing dream I found myself walking round a dusty and deserted town, complete with comedy tumbleweeds and rusted cars that were slowly decaying in diner parking lots. I presumed that I was in America, somewhere Deep South and remote. It was a hot and airless day and not a single soul stirred upon the streets. All the buildings were boarded up and empty. It felt post-apocalyptic, otherworldly and sepia toned. Walking very slowly in the intense heat, I stumbled upon a road sign lying in a ditch at the side of the road. On it was but a single word word: 'Villareal'. I awoke immediately and made a mental note that should I ever be in need of a new band name, this was most certainly going to be it. I also made a note to stop drinking large quantities of whisky before bedtime.

So, five years later in 2002 I honoured this agreement with my subconscious and set to work on a bunch of demos with second cousin (once removed) Mattie Cooper. My philosophy was very different to those label-chasing days of yore. This time things had to be fun and I would choose to avoid those unseemly elements of the music business that had previously made the whole process of being in a band so bloody desperate and miserable. It all seemed very easy in theory.

Villareal 2002
(l-r Beau Barnard, Matthew Cooper, Jennie Cruse, Simon Parker
– photo unknown)

Due to Warner Chappell owning the Edel copyrights, Villareal was contractually obliged to submit any finished song for publishing purposes. Sadly, it soon became clear that if I didn't play the game and subject the band to that well-worn circus of pointless London gigs and dehumanizing A&R torture, there was little Warner Chappell could offer us outside of a monthly list of people I didn't particularly want to write songs with.

So I came up with a plan and made an appointment to have a meeting with the A&R junior who was fresh out of college and green as the grassy knoll. Coincidentally, on the day of my visit Teenage Fanclub were also in the house and very possibly ending their own relationship with the company. I took this as a good sign, but was far too star-struck to say even the meekest 'Hello' to Messrs Blake, Love and McGuinley. Once the Scottish tunesmiths had vacated the office, I came to an agreement with my harassed adversary that I would never ask for anything if I could just simply sit it out and re-acquire all of the Villareal copyrights when they expired in 2004/5. Now, thanks to the Edel buy-out, Mr Junior A&R had just inherited a lot of unwanted writers, so this must have sounded like a good deal and in time I was indeed able to terminate my publishing adventure. How strange that I should end up pleading to be set free after spending so long trying to get the industry to take notice of me in any shape or form.

I returned to Brighton and set about financing my own album. Mattie left shortly after this to join Coin-op, and they quickly signed to Fierce Panda before releasing one mini-album of material. During this time, I built a new line up of Villareal that included ex-Ice 9 drummer Jon Barnett and bass player Beau Barnard. Interestingly, these two would eventually go on to play in The Upper Room, who were signed to Sony and had two top forty singles in 2006.

Always the bridesmaid...

WE ARE THE CHAMPIONS

And so, ever since 2002 Villareal has been my outlet for releasing the songs that I write. To date we have released four albums and I am proud of each. The line-up is best described as 'floating', with me being the only full-time member. I have worked with a lot of brilliant people, amongst them Phil Vinall, the legendarily eccentric producer who many years previous had been the engineer on XTC's *Black Sea* record. As I'm sure you'll have guessed, the fact that there is now a link between XTC and my own band warms this battered heart. I also got to work with the amazing Phil Bodger who produced the first Housemartins record. I bloody love that album.

Villareal has supported Mew, Okkervil River, Electric Soft Parade and also performed at several festivals including The Wedding Presents annual 'At The Edge Of The Sea'.

> *Night falls down on a station town,*
> *and the truth has been delayed...*

(*What Do You Do For Encores?* Simon Parker/Villareal. 2004).

Without the aid of either a proper record label or management, Villareal has been able to achieve a number of minor triumphs, even though these are generally regarded as being too small to be noticed by the majority of the record-buying public. But thanks to the Internet, Villareal's music keeps reaching distant corners of this lonely planet. I cannot ask for anymore.

In November of 2013 we released the *Unravelling* album. Atmospheric, downbeat and eerie it channels just a little bit of Talk Talk and David Sylvian. I'm older now and more reflective. So I need the music to react in a similar way. Working in conjunction with a lot of talented players, *Unravelling* is the collection of songs that I am most proud of.

I recently calculated that at a conservative estimate, I have been involved with approximately eighteen albums worth of material since those innocent beginnings with Violet Trade. These moments are all snapshots of a life spent on the outskirts of the music business.

I'm out there somewhere, so find me.

Villareal 2013

▶ chapter nineteen

LOVE WILL TEAR US APART

Though we had just about made it through the rigors of the music industry, there was one eventuality that Jennie and I could never outrun, and that was growing ever older and all the associated heartache that comes attached. Almost imperceptibly, our relationship had been falling apart for a very long time. I think neither of us had ever really planned for failure even though we were continually staring it straight in the face.

Being in a group with your other half is not so easy. For proof of this, just look at all those other musical divorcees that have tried and failed. Abba, Fleetwood Mac and Blondie. I'm not sure what happened to those two from T'Pau? But even if your band does go on to sell millions, couples still end up in hurtling towards romantic destruction. From the days of working with Pop Corp. onwards, Jennie and I had been made to pretend that we weren't an item. Over time, this act became draining. If I'm honest, when in public I like nothing more than to hold hands with my girlfriend. A moment lost in each other's gaze is priceless. I am a romantic. But once we started down this road, everything slowly drained out of our relationship leaving just the bare bones. And it was all because of the band.

Following our time in music together Jennie and I began to drift further apart as the years rolled on. By 2010, there were large cracks appearing in the walls of our relationship. We had discussed the idea of having children but I worried about being able to support them properly. Jen's health suffered due to bouts of chronic insomnia and I'd often find myself sleeping in a different room. This became more frequent and although we were still living together we would operate at different times of the day. I found myself getting stressed out about the most stupid things and we would inevitably argue. Finally, when Jennie was made redundant from the Virgin/Zavvi group in early 2009, she took the opportunity to go travelling with a girlfriend. They flew out to New Zealand on February 28 2010 and from this point our days were numbered despite the fact we both pretended not to hear the relentless clanging of alarm bells.

I flew out to New Zealand in November 2010 to spend time with Jennie who was now travelling on her own. To all intents and purposes things looked much the same and we had a great time, but something felt very different. Time apart had driven a wedge between us. We were no longer lovers. We were just very good friends clinging onto the past, even though that was where all the troubles lived. I came back after a few weeks and from that moment went into some sort of denial, living on my own like some sort of lovelorn ghost. When Jennie extended her stay for the umpteenth time in 2012 we finally agreed that splitting up was the only way forward. All of the things that had once been on the horizon were now a long way behind us, and suddenly I was not in a relationship for the first time in over twenty years.

Time holds out a hand, which snaps like a branch
We are unravelling

(*Last of the Pale Winter Sun.* Simon Parker/Villareal 2013)

When I look at the lyrics for Villareal's fourth album *Unravelling*, it's clear they unwittingly document our break up, even though the majority of them were written about eighteen months prior to us separating. It was as if my subconscious had already dealt with the situation and was getting ready to tell the rest of my brain about it.

And I guess that's the magic of song writing.

► chapter twenty

GOING BACK TO MY ROOTS

HOMETOWN UNICORN

After denouncing my hometown for much of this story, I'm happy to impart that Chichester and I have started to get reacquainted. Age brings a certain softening and forgiveness. Or maybe we just start to focus on the good things. Whatever the truth, I now regularly find myself returning to that picturesque cathedral hamlet only to stumble upon some long-forgotten memory that will momentarily find me splitting an ear-wide smile. After all, we are all ridiculous teenagers at heart, right?

Chichester will always be full of such vivid recollections for me, and sometimes I half expect to bump into the younger version of myself racing through the streets on his way to a gig or rehearsal. But life moves on and nowadays I'm just another human shape impatiently frequenting coffee shops and ATM's.

When I was younger, I was utterly convinced that music would save me from having to work particularly hard for a living. It's somewhat ironic that I then spent over twenty years as its poorly paid slave, but I'm thinking the riches I predicted are spiritual and not financial, right?

Chichester, I love you. There, I've said it at last.

TOP FIVE XTC SONG TITLES CONSIDERED FOR 'ROAD TO NOWHERE'

1. Drums and Wires
2. The Disappointed
3. Making Plans for Simon
4. Are You Receiving Me?
5. I am the Audience

RETURN TO DOMINO

One of the childhood places that I missed the most was Domino Records in Portsmouth. After moving to Brighton in the early 90s, I had little need to visit Domino as my new hometown had a stack of its own top-notch record shops. But a while ago I decided it was time to pay my respects to the shop that had first set me off on my vinyl conquest. Back when boys fashioned curly perms and you dared not laugh at them for fear of losing copious amounts of blood or teeth, or both, I had braved the Pompey casuals to discover my very own record shop heaven. And now I felt the time was just right for a pilgrimage. It was like something out of a Nick Hornby novel.

The cross-coast train pulled into Portsmouth just before midday, and I strolled through the tranquil Victoria Park on a roundabout way to the town centre. I was now no more than a stone's throw from the Guildhall where, long ago during my earliest days of going to gigs, I had encountered The Cure, Prefab Sprout, Pixies, The Housemartins and Then Jericho. Passing the war memorial, I recalled the time that Kate Smith and I had bunked off of studies to go and buy marked-down Rolling Stones and Talk Talk records instead, and of those dim and distant afternoons when the hapless Robbie Wheeler would be viewed suspiciously by track-suited Rottweiler's hovering in condensation-saturated cafés.

In fact, my mind pictured everything existing just the way it had done when Bergarac was still solving his first season of cases. But, of course, back in the real world Portsmouth no longer looks anything remotely like this. Cutting through the new identikit shopping mall I stepped out onto Charlotte Street to be greeted by... a flat expanse of overpriced car park.

The Tricorn Centre has been bulldozed out of existence in the name of progress. Every trace of that concrete monster has been wiped off the face of the earth, all except for one small section of wall that now serves as a reminder to those of a certain age and record-buying persuasion.

Somewhat taken aback, I took a few minutes to privately recall some dusty memories spent at the racks in Domino. Sure, a lot of the bigger names live on, but what of Philip Japp and Floy Joy? Private Lives and Fiat Lux? The Jack Rubies and Bob? My musical life flashed before my eyes. So many great songs have yet to be discovered. In this brave new computer age it's fair to say that many of the artists I've name-checked throughout this story will never even exist in a compatible digital format. Therefore it is up to sad, obsessed people like me to remind, re-alert or re-post about these banished artists in the spirit of keeping their names alive.

Our Price, Virgin, Woolworths and most of the HMV chain: all gone and never coming back. Record shops are a thing of the past. Music sits near the bottom of the shopping list as the corporations get us all to invest in overpaid sporting heroes, mobile phones and modern gadgets. Footballers are the new Rock gods. We should never have debunked the myth of the pop star. By dressing it all down at the beginning of this century, bands like Coldplay effectively helped destroy the magic fed to us in regular doses by an earlier version of their very breed. I don't know about you, but I preferred it when bands looked like they came from other planets. Now legions of teenagers aspire to bone-headed deities and show it by copying their spitting techniques. Music comes for free to generations who have absolutely no concept of paying for it. Worse still, record collections don't really exist anymore. For me, music is memories. I can pull out any record or CD from my collection and be immediately transported back to a vivid moment in time. These flashbacks are magically triggered by the simple selection of something from my own stash. You just don't get the same level of interaction with an MP3. Surely, people are missing out on something? Or is it just my personal mid-life meltdown talking here?

After pacing round that freshly laid car park for longer than is generally acceptable in CCTV-assisted modern life, I slid off and steeled myself with a pint. The face of music is changing and you either adapt or die. I'm just glad that I grew up when I did and was able to experience the excitement of chasing great music.

TOP 10 THINGS I WISH I COULD BUY FROM DOMINO BUT CAN'T

1. Talk Talk - Live at Hammersmith Odeon 1986 (DVD)
2. The Chesterfields - Kettle (CD)
3. Jonathon Richman - Jonathon Sings (CD)
4. The The - Infected (DVD)
5. Cardiacs - All That Glitters is a Mare's Nest (DVD)
6. The Keys - The Keys Album (Vinyl or CD)
7. NME - Carry On Disarming Compilation (DVD)
8. Private Lives - Prejudice & Pride (CD)
9. The first three Trashcan Sinatra's albums on re-mastered CD's
10. XTC - Greatest Hits DVD (as mentioned earlier but worth pointing out again to anyone at Virgin Records)

▶ chapter twenty-one

PARK LIFE

TOP-TIP TWENTY-THREE:

NEVER USE A CURLY LEAD.
(COURTESY OF THE LEGENDARY STEVE PARTER)

When I was a kid, a few of us used to play hide and seek at the local park. But as we approached our mid-teens, Rob, Andy and I decided that we were finally past such folly. Part of the human condition is that we spend too much of our youth wanting to be older and then too much of our middle age looking back to more innocent times. However, in the summer of 1984, my friends and I did partake in one final impromptu evening of childish games with various other hormonal question marks that were rattling about on the cusp of their own awkward teenage feelings. It's worth remembering that before the Internet and X-Box gaming, children used to spend a good deal of time interacting with each other outside in the elements.

On this particular evening, the sky was already burning red as we randomly crept through the undergrowth and chose our hiding places. A group of about ten of us played long into the dusk and for long periods nobody could locate my whereabouts. Silent and stealth-like, I breezed through the woods avoiding capture at every turn. This was an epic performance on my behalf and it felt as if I was cloaked in a gown of invisibility. As darkness enveloped the twilight I vividly remember looking up at the undulating sky and realizing we would never play as freely again. And I was right, for soon afterwards we would all become pre-occupied with drinking and chasing after inappropriate partners.

Yet I often find myself wondering if something strange happened that evening. Maybe there is a part of me still out there wandering around in the fading light of Oaklands Park, waiting to be found.

HE'S ON THE BEACH

And now the sun is setting over Brighton beach. You and I have finally arrived back in the here and now. Of course, everyone else has made their excuses and long since departed, all with other places to be. In a short while the darkness will descend. And then I'll disappear as well, leaving only the music I have made as proof that I was ever here at all. It's out there somewhere. So find it.

This tale is at an end. There is no more news to impart. I've awkwardly stuck the pieces of my life back together again despite the fact that some of the bits are almost certainly in the wrong place and others don't seem to fit at all. For better or for worse, it's true to say that I never cared about anything as much as music.

And I really have no idea why this happened. But I'm glad it did.

▶▶ afterword

Since leaving the music industry I've been lucky enough to earn a living working in music promotion while also enjoying the odd spot of teaching work at a Brighton music college. For the past twelve years I have been running a successful live music night for new acts called 'Cable Club'. For me, there is still nothing better than the thrill of discovering great artists. In the event, I gave The Cribs, Kasabian and Sixty Five Days of Static their first Brighton shows and even got to work with Babybird's Stephen Jones, another of my long-time musical heroes. And this makes me very happy.

As this book is largely about the underdog, I feel it only fitting to include a short list of some of the amazing local artists I have worked with since Cable Club first opened its doors.

MY SHORT LIST OF GREAT ARTISTS WHO PLAYED CABLE CLUB (2002-2014)

Turncoat, Sparrow, Bat For Lashes, 4 or 5 Magicians, Little Trophy, Desperate Journalist, Garden Heart, White Star Liners, We Spies, Bird Eats Baby, Two Jackals, The Sleepwalks, Telegraphs, Boy Patient, Young Soul Rebels, The Educated Animals, The Recoil, Paul Steel, Winteria, The Mojo Fins, Enid Blitz, Lovepark, Paper Playground, The Sarah Michelles, The Customers, Actress Hands, The Messaround, Neenor, The Half Sisters, Written In Waters, Little Fears, The Valentines, Jennifer Left, Lionbark, Republic Of Heaven and Digo.
(With apologies to the countless bands I have not mentioned.)

Of all the acts I have promoted I even got to manage my favourite through two record deals. Turncoat came to me as a rough diamond and together we refined, polished and turned them into something very special. Timing and luck may not always have been with us but there are two 7" singles to remind me of what we achieved. Good on you boys. And thank you Nigel Coxon for your faith and friendship.

In 2009 I started Numbskull HQ records, primarily to release the Turncoat album but I ended up putting out others by Sparrow, White Star Liners and my very own side project Lightning Dept. This spin-off band deal in short, sharp songs that usually last no longer than two minutes and fifteen seconds in duration. This is the perfect length of a pop song. The first Lightning Dept. album, *Things Keep Blowing Up*, was a lot of fun to make (fifteen songs in just three days!) and there will be a second.

But perhaps my proudest achievement outside of writing **Road to Nowhere** and releasing the four Villareal albums, has been contributing to the 'Spirit of Talk Talk' project. This book details the band's history and also offers a striking pictorial appreciation of the artist James Marsh, the man behind all of the groups beautiful artwork. Including contributions from a number of infinitely more successful musicians than I (take a bow Guy Garvey from Elbow, Richard Reed Parry from Arcade Fire and Kevin Drew from Broken Social Scene), nevertheless my own thoughts on the *Spirit of Eden* album are there for all to see on page 103. Equally amazing is the fact that James Marsh has now designed sleeves for both Villareal and Lightning Dept.

I count myself very lucky to have a bunch of great friends, and I still regularly meet up with ex-Violet Trade manager Mark Mason who is now married to the lovely Jade. As mentioned earlier, teen music confidant Stuart Worden is now the Principal of the Brit School in Croydon and we still regularly introduce each other to brilliant music. We've also got tickets for both Lloyd Cole and Neutral Milk Hotel in 2014. Jimmy Portinari still regularly performs with The Others and we share that same unswerving adoration for The Cure. I've even patched things up with Gary Capelin, ex drummer of Colourburst and Fruit Machine. Time is indeed a great healer.

Recently Villareal got to support Mark Eitzel from American Music Club. Mark has been a very important person in my musical development since circa 1990 and it was good to share some decent malt whiskey with the man after our show. While playing bass for White Star Liners we were unexpectedly selected to support Grandaddy on two dates of the bands 2012 reunion tour. Performing to around two thousand people a night, if I had been able to locate a spare couple of fingers I would have pinched myself. But instead I simply marvelled at the beautiful irony of finally being able to share a stage with such an amazing band so late in my musical life.

See, good things do sometimes come to those who wait...

TOP ELEVEN GROWN UP THINGS I DO IN MY FORTIES

- Not settling for the cheapest bottle of wine (or investing in Thunderbird to 'save time')
- Reading something more substantial than the gig listings
- Explaining to bands that they maybe shouldn't drink so much before performing
- Occasionally deploying the soft drinks option for myself during daylight hours
- Wearing the colour brown if the mood takes me
- Asking myself 'Is this shirt too young for me?' while still in the fitting room
- Generally avoiding drugs and nicotine
- Checking the backs of food packaging for fat and calorie content
- Trying harder to keep the place tidy
- Swimming
- No longer feeling so obliged to number my charts from one to ten

more lists of great music

TOP TWENTY UNDERRATED SINGLES 2000-13

1. The Walkmen - The Rat
2. Mew - She Came Home for Christmas
3. Johnny Boy - You are the Generation that Bought More Shoes and you Get What You Deserve
4. The Radio Dept. - Where Damage Isn't Already Done
5. M.Craft - Sweets
6. Preston School of Industry - Falling Away
7. Fans of Kate - A Pattern
8. Electric Cinema - Heat Exchange
9. Spoon - Everything Hits at Once
10. Beezewax - When You Stood Up
11. My Luminaries - The Outsider Steps Inside
12. Straw - Sailing Off the Edge of the World
13. Magnet - The Day We Left Town
14. New Rhodes - I Wish I Was You
15. Kashmir - Rocket Brothers
16. Beirut - Elephant Gun
17. Mark Eitzel - I Love You But You're Dead
18. Sparklehorse - Don't Take My Sunshine Away
19. Turncoat - Wasted On You
20. The Cure - The End of the World

Oh so nearly:
Gerling - The Deer in You, Shack - Cup of Tea, The Spinto Band - Oh Mandy, The New Pornographers - Myriad Harbour, Edwyn Collins - You'll Never Know (My Love), Serena Maneesh - Sapphyre Eyes, Madness - NW5

TOP TWENTY UNDERRATED ALBUMS 2000-12

1. Spoon - Ga Ga Ga Ga Ga
2. Wheat - Per Second, Per Second, Per Second, Every Second
3. M.Craft - Silver and Fire
4. Destroyer - Kaputt
5. Stephen Jones - Almost Cured of Sadness
6. Edwyn Collins - Doctor Syntax
7. Trash Can Sinatras - Weightlifting
8. The Clientele - God Bless the Clientele
9. The Zillions - Play Zig Zag Zillionaire
10. Redjetson - General New Catalogue
11. The Cardigans - Super Extra Gravity
12. The Sleepy Jackson - Lovers
13. American Music Club - Love Songs for Patriots
14. Sparrow - Playtime
15. Avalanches - Since I Met You
16. Turncoat - An Adventure in Skill and Chance
17. A-ha - Analogue
18. White Star Liners - The Years That Slid
19. Tim Burgess - I Believe
20. Villareal - Unravelling

They also served;
The Stills - Logic Will Break Your Heart, Stina Nordenstam - This Is, Babybird - In Between My Ears There Is Nothing But Music, The Pernice Brothers - Live a Little, Darren Hanlon - Early Days, Spoon - Transference, Desert Hearts - Let's Get Worse, Lloyd Cole - Antidepressant, Semifinalists - Semifinalists, Superchunk - Here's To Shutting Up

TOP TWENTY GREAT TRACKS FROM THIS NEW DECADE

1. Spoon - Out Go the Lights
2. Twinshadow - Tyrant Destroyed
3. Vampire Weekend - Diane Young
4. Atlas Sound with Noah Lennox - Walkabout

5. Deerhunter - Memory Boy
6. Tim Burgess - White
7. Lightships - Two Lines
8. Lonesound - The Great Outdoors
9. Sparrow - Move
10. Panda Bear - Surfer's Hymn
11. Crystal Castles with Robert Smith - Not in Love
12. Pure X - Easy
13. Paul Buchanan - Mid Air
14. The Pains of Being Pure at Heart - Too Tough
15. Broken Social Scene - Texico Bitches
16. Destroyer - Suicide Note for Kara Walker
17. The National - Mr November
18. Earlimart - A Goodbye
19. Guided By Voices - Keep It In Motion
20. Unknown Mortal Orchestra - Ffunny Ffrends

MY TOP TWENTY ALBUMS OF ALL TIME

1. Talk Talk - Spirit of Eden
2. The Trashcan Sinatras - I've Seen Everything
3. The Cure - Disintegration
4. Weezer - Pinkerton
5. David Sylvian - Secrets of the Beehive
6. Spoon - Ga Ga Ga Ga Ga
7. Grandaddy - Under the Western Freeway
8. Sparklehorse - Vivadixiesubmarinetransmissionplot
9. The Pale Fountains - From Across the Kitchen Table
10. Aztec Camera - Highland Hard Rain
11. Teenage Fanclub - Grand Prix
12. E.L.O. - Out of the Blue
13. R.E.M. - Green
14. The Flaming Lips - Clouds Taste Metallic
15. The Blue Nile - A Walk Across the Rooftops
16. ABC - Beauty Stab
17. Destroyer - Kaputt
18. Wilco - Summerteeth
19. Kate Bush - The Dreaming
20. Big Dipper – Craps

► demo-ography

1984

AKE (DEMO)

Thankfully lost/stolen sometime in early 1984. Track listing unknown, but would have definitely contained such titles as 'Faceless', 'Shine', 'Work (a diary of culture)' and other such teenage horrors.

Musicians; Philip Bennett, Simon Parker

1987

OCTOBER FALLEN

Demo album that should have been by the band 'October'

Side One: Call/Hope in the Heart/Empty Days/Happy Sad/Our Father's/The Witching Hour.
Side Two: The Curse/Silver/All our Yesterdays/Blind/Torn in Two.

Musicians; Philip Bennett, Jake Tully, Simon Parker

1988/9

ONION JOHNNY (4 TRACK DEMO)

The Return/Perfect Day/Just a Sound/Black Heart

Musicians: Richard Salmon, Ed Wheatley, Jake Tully, Mark the twitchy drummer, Simon Parker

Guest vocals: Sue Marsh who sang standing on top of a wooden box, hastily erected so that she would be able to reach the microphone.

1990

THE VIOLET TRADE - 'AUTUMN' (DEMO)

New Direction/Nightmare/Ride/Headstrong/Ribbons/ Bucket Bong Ant)

Musicians; Simon Mckay, Greg Saunders,
Gary Capelin, Simon Parker

Guest appearances; Sue Marsh (backing vocals - no box required this time) , Johnnie Windmill and his girlfriend Lisa-Beth who both admirably pretended to be an excitable 'crowd' in the middle section of 'New Direction'.

THE VIOLET TRADE - 'STAR SHINE BRIGHTLY DOWN'

Homemade 'bootleg'compilation.

Included all 5 songs from the 'Autumn' demo, as well as snippets of our favourite artists, and a batch of rare out-takes and live performances of un-released and 'classic' tracks
Namely: Inspire/Disappear with Me/Chase the Wind/Cloud Sandwich/Mad Girl).

Musicians; Simon Mckay, Greg Saunders,
Gary Capelin, Simon Parker

1991

THE VIOLET TRADE - 'GIVE ME THE HAPPY'

Album length demo.

Side One: Light and Shade/Bucket Bong Ant/Peggy
Bottles/Breakdown/Ribbons/King Come Down).
Side Two; Banana/Blackberries/Another Love Song/New
Direction/Fall/Headstrong).

Musicians; Simon Mckay, Greg Saunders,
Gary Capelin, Simon Parker.

Guest musicians; Ed Wheatley (well, it was his six-track
machine, so why shouldn't his voice be mixed louder than
the lead vocals?).
(This demo also featured a deranged individual called
'Stroff' who went all Jimi Hendrix over the song 'King Come
Down').

1992

THE VIOLET TRADE - 'SOLD TO THE MAN WITH NO EARS'

Album length demo.

Side One: Salvation [remix]/Heavenly Side/Twelfth of
Never/Shell Catcher).
Side Two: Aqua Blur/Velocity Street/String/My Single Sock
Collection.

Musicians; Simon Mckay, Greg Saunders,
Gary Capelin, Simon Parker

THE WHISKEY GIRLS - 'DITCHED'

E.P.

Side One: Early Morning/Guessing Game/Just me Being You/State I'm in).
Side Two: My Little Schemes/Falling from Grace/Me and Herbert Lom/Think of this).

Musicians; Sue Marsh, Steve Tett, Shelley Britton, Gary Capelin, Simon Parker

Guest musician; Geoff Mutton and his wonderful mandolin

THE VIOLET TRADE - 'CAMILLE'

Unreleased demo.

This was the nearest VT came to releasing new songs during the latter part of 1992. I only made about six tapes before giving up.
Bad Day/Velvet/Girl Frenzy/Try to see things my way

Musicians: Simon Mckay, Greg Saunders, Gary Capelin, Ted Tedman, Simon Parker

1993

THE WHISKEY GIRLS - 'A ROUNDABOUT FASHION'

E.P.

Happy/Country Love Song/One Hand on the Wheel/Charmed)

Musicians: Sue Marsh, Steve Tett, Shelley Britton, Gary Capelin, Mark Russell, Simon Parker

Guest appearances: Ed Wheatley, Geoff Mutton (real name Keith Sutton).

COLOURBURST - 'NOVA'

E.P.

Minor Character/Everything Falls Apart/Gravitate to Me/Within Without/Time Flies/Halo)

Musicians; Steve Tett, James Portinari, Gary Capelin, Simon Parker

1994

COLOURBURST - 'SINUS'

E.P.

Petrol/Happy/I Wasn't Invited

Musicians: John Smith, James Portinari, Gary Capelin, Simon Parker

LES DISQUES DU POP COR OO5 -
'LOSERS, CHOOSERS AND CREDIT CARD BOOZERS'

E.P.

Features Crawl Limbo, The Dakota Stars And Colourburst 'Petrol').

Musicians: John Smith, James Portinari, Gary Capelin, Simon Parker

COLOURBURST - 'FOOD BOY'

E.P.

Side One: I Can't Sing/Feel/My Guiding Star. Side Two
Repeats 'Sinus' Tracks)

Musicians: John Smith, James Portinari,
Gary Capelin, Simon Parker

COLOURBURST - 'BENDER'

E.P.

Side One: Bender/Petrol.
Side Two; Is It Finally Strong Enough For You?/ Whiplash/I
Wasn't Invited)

Musicians: John Smith, James Portinari,
Gary Capelin, Simon Parker

CRUSH - 'BAD HAIR DAY'

The Poor Relations/Hand Me My Head/Pushed

Musicians; James Portinari, Gary Capelin, Simon Parker

1995

COLOURBURST - 'THROW ME A ROPE'/ BAD HAIR DAY'

7 Inch Single (JLF DAN-01)

Initial copies came with a free demo called 'Party
Games') Tracks on this tape were: Babya/Everybody's Got
Someone Else/It's Twelve O'clock Forever/Columbus.

Musicians: James Portinari, Gary Capelin, Simon Parker

Guest Musicians: Dubious Trombone by an Unknown
Accomplice stolen from a Sixth Form College.

277

COLOURBURST - 'THE APPLE CART'

E.P.

I'm From Nowhere/Usually/Baby A

Musicians: James Portinari, Gary Capelin, Simon Parker

COLOURBURST - 'DEMONICA'

Fan Club Xmas Demo JLF DAN-05

Columbus/Last Christmas

This demo was only available on Tuesday 19th December '95.

Musicians: James Portinari, Gary Capelin, Simon Parker

1996

COLOURBURST - 'THE GIRL FELL OUT OF THE RADIO'/'TWELVE O'CLOCK FOREVER'

(7-inch single JLF DAN-06 CV)

Musicians: James Portinari, Gary Capelin, Simon Parker

COLOURBURST - 'SUGAR HITS'

E.P.

Side One: Dreaming of Aeroplanes/Inside the Outside/Why Are You With Stupid?
Side Two: Babya/In Flames/When the World Ends

Musicians: James Portinari, Gary Capelin, Simon Parker

FRUIT MACHINE - 'ARIEL'

E.P.

All Fall Down/Ariel/How Come You're Such a Hit With The Boys, Jane?

Musicians: Jennie Cruse, Rachel Bor, James Portinari, Gary Capelin, Simon Parker

FRUIT MACHINE - 'SICKLY BLUE'

E.P.

Sickly Blue [Send My Love To Ray]/Away Day/All Fall Down/ Ariel

Musicians: Jennie Cruse, Rachel Bor, James Portinari, Gary Capelin, Simon Parker

COLOURBURST - 'PLANET'

A-A Side Demo

Planet/Hippy Surfer Girl

Musicians: Mattie Cooper, James Portinari, Gary Capelin, Simon Parker

1997

COLOURBURST - 'WAVING AT TRAINS'

Album length live demo.

Side One: Whose Driving?/I Am Your Disco/Planet/Idiot Brother/Columbus/Pushed
Side Two: Insanely Happy Days/Me and Herbert Lom/Hippy Surfer Girl/Usually/Dreaming of Aeroplanes/The Girl Fell Out of the Radio

Given away at the bands final show in April 1997.

Musicians: Mattie Cooper, James Portinari, Gary Capelin, Simon Parker

FRUIT MACHINE

(Industry Demo)

From this point on, all Fruit Machine recordings would be sent out by Pop Corp. During 1997 various songs recorded at Brittania Row in Islington became our 'industry' demo.

Tracks were; Sickly Blue/Ariel/The World Is Upside Down/ Dream/Oxygen/Monte Carlo/Head Explosion/Only the Moon

Musicians: Jennie Cruse, Rachel Bor, Nick Hopkin, Simon Parker

1998

FRUIT MACHINE - 'MONTE CARLO'

E.P.

Monte Carlo/Dream/Ariel

This demo came housed in a special holographic sleeve and was re-issued a number of times with different songs chosen at Pop Corp's discretion.

Musicians: Jennie Cruse, Rachel Bor, Nick Hopkin, Simon Parker

FRUIT MACHINE - 'ELECTRIC'

E.P.

Electric + various tracks

As the album sessions progressed at Clarion Studios, Pop Corp issued a promo of the first single 'Electric' in another holographic cassette sleeve for promotional purposes. Additional tracks again selected by our producers

Musicians: Jennie Cruse, Rachel Bor, Nick Hopkin, Simon Parker

1999

Fruit Machine industry album sampler

Promo CD

Pop Corp continued to send monitor mixes of album tracks as and when they were deemed suitable for public consumption. Of the tracks recorded, Electric, Everybody Needs a Reason, Monte Carlo, Would you do the same?, Oxygen, Smile, Life of Sundays, Dream, The World is Upside Down, Say Goodbye, Sickly Blue and In Colour (non-album track) were all sent to various industry contacts and labels in both the UK and US during 1999).
Note: this was the first time our demos had ever been manufactured on cds.

Musicians: Jennie Cruse, Rachel Bor, Nick Hopkin, Simon Parker

2000

LUMINA - 'STEREO'

Due to having signed to both Edel Publishing (UK) and
Precinct 27 Records (USA), we were advised against
sending out or selling demos. However, we often made
compilations for promo use

Tracks: C-Drift/Landslide/Long Decay/The Boy Who Stole
The World/Mr. Atom/I Can Picture You/Over/Ghosts/My
Inventions/Strange/We Will Shine/Life of Sundays/Chasing
Shadows/Towards the Light

Musicians; Joe Harlin, Joe Hunt, Jennie Cruse, Nick Hopkin,
Simon Parker

2001

FILTH MONKEY - 'CHIMP ROXZ'

Unreleased album

(Hardcore/[I Wanna Ride On] Buddy's Chopper/The Smile
on Your Face/Makeover Monkey/Oddie/Rollin'/Public
Information Film/Namco.80/Monkeys Everywhere/Feint
Episode/Havant/Philosophies on Pop/In My Head It's
Christmas/Funky Bizniz/Mardie/Phil Spector's Mono
Bottom/Rock Sitar).

This is one of two electronic based albums that has never
seen the light of day. While getting bored with the long
gestation of the Fruit Machine saga, Jennie, Nick and I
came up with a bunch of monkey-related tracks that were
put together on an old 8-track machine at home with the
aid of a sequencer and lots of illegal sampling. As it turned
out, I finished this album on the very day that Nick phoned
up and quit the band.

MR LEGGS - 'THE ADVENTURES OF...'

Unreleased album

Introducing Mr Leggs/Brian, Dinner's Ready/Hello Lionel/Lenn's Leggs/Billy Liar/Mr Leggs-Where Are You?/Septic Tanks/Mr Leggs' Dream/Stop Smoking/Simple Simon/D+H: Country Leanings/Say My Name (Mr Leggs)/Dressed In Old Colours/Skipping/Entroducing Mr Leggs)

...And this was the other album, made on my own with more stolen samples and Nicks sequenced loops

VILLAREAL - 'YOU AND ME AND WHAT COMES NEXT?'

E.P.

You're Always Happening to Me/At This Time/King of the Sun/Aimee/Heatwave/Slow Fade/Purple and Blue).

Musicians: Mattie Cooper, Jennie Cruse, Simon Parker

VILLAREAL - 'TIGERS'

E.P.

(All Roads Lead to Villareal/My Head's a Television/Loose Change/Inside Out/There Will Always be a Place in my Heart for You/ Tigers).

Musicians: Mattie Cooper, Jennie Cruse, Simon Parker

VILLAREAL - 'KEEP THE GIRLS APART'

E.P.

Life Could be Easy/The Girl with X-Ray Eyes/Virus/The Girl Who's Everywhere/Sunburnt & Blistering/Volcanoes

Musicians: Mattie Cooper, Jennie Cruse, Simon Parker.

VILLAREAL - 'TRAVELITE'

Compilation of first 3 EP's

You're Always Happening to Me/At This Time/My Head's a Television/Virus/The Girl Who's Everywhere/Purple and Blue/King of the Sun/Life Could be Easy/The Girl with X-Ray Eyes/Inside Out/Tigers/There Will Always be a Place in my Heart for You/Volcanoes

Musicians: Mattie Cooper, Jennie Cruse, Simon Parker

2002

VILLAREAL - 'FAST PEOPLE'

Album length demo

(Another You/Bewitched/What Do You Do For Encores?/Ever End/Seahorses/Sleep Driver/Downers/You Were Served by Kitty/The Honeymooners/The Haunted Dancefloor)

Musicians: Mattie Cooper, Jennie Cruse, Simon Parker

2003

VILLAREAL - 'SKYLINES'

Album length demo

Expect Long Delays/You're Always Happening to
Me/What Do You Do For Encores?/King of the Sun/Silver
Key/Purple and Blue/Wake Up Call/Seahorses/Volcanoes/
Radio/Sisters/Sleep Driver/The Haunted Dancefloor

Some of these songs were re-recordings of earlier demos
but recorded by a different line-up, and then presented to
Warner Chappell as a possible album. They said 'no', of
course.

Musicians: Beau Barnard, Ollie Tunmer, Jennie Cruse,
Mattie Cooper, Simon Parker

VILLAREAL INDUSTRY E.P.

While still with Warner Chappell Publishing, a 3 song demo
was briefly circulated, complete with quite nice cardboard
sleeve and professional on-body printing on the cd.

(Tracks: What Do You Do For Encores? / The Haunted
Dancefloor/Silver Key)

Musicians: Jennie Cruse, Mattie Cooper, Simon Parker.

2004

....Was largely spent recording 'Spook Frequency',
promoting at the Pressure Point and getting Turncoat
ready for the industry.

VILLAREAL - 'SPOOK FREQUENCY'

Album

(What Do You Do For Encores?/Just Like an
Aeroplane/There is Nowhere Left To Go But
Down/Seahorses/Fireboy/Silver Key/Island/Banana

Skins/King of the Sun/The Haunted Dancefloor/Spook
Frequency

Musicians: Alex Hobden, Joss Lindey, Beau Barnard,
Jennie Cruse, Simon Parker

Guest Appearances: Joe Bennett (strings), Rowland
Prytherch (bass, vocals), Chaz Newman (violin), James
Brackpool (programming).

2005

TURNCOAT - 'AT A WINDOW'

7" single on Double Dragon records [DD 023]
Ltd. Edition 500 copies on blue vinyl

At a Window/Absolute Zero

Musicians: Adrian Imms, Chaz Newman, Luke Ellis,
Alex Hobden, Dominic Schofield

2006

VILLAREAL - 'JUST LIKE AN AEROPLANE'

Downloadable single released on Shifty Disco records
(March 2006)

2007

VILLAREAL - 'BLUE SNAKES'

Album

(Waiting for the Day to Start/The 7th/Illuminate
Me/Raincheck on Sunset Street/Hey Day/Dressed for the

End of the World/Linus/We Must Stop Meeting Like
This/Ghost Train/ Sleeping Pills/Hang Dog Smile/Blue Snakes

Musicians: Luke Ellis, Alex Hobden, Simon Parker

Guest Musicians: Jennie Cruse (backing vocals),
Rowland Prytherch (backing vocals), Joe Bennett (strings)

2008

TURNCOAT - 'WASTED ON YOU'

7" single+download on Regal/EMI (REG 149)
Ltd. Edition 500 copies black vinyl

Wasted On You/There Must Be Something

Musicians: Adrian Imms, Chaz Newman,
Luke Ellis, Alex Hobden

VILLAREAL - 'GHOST TRAIN'

Downloadable single released on Shifty Disco records
 (December 2008)

2010

VILLAREAL - 'LIT BY SPARKS'

(Caffeine Slump/Kid Cosmic vs. The Falling Stars/Cindy
65/The Old Days/Panic Button/Girl with X-Ray Eyes/Purple
and Blue/Your Voice/Smoke And Mirrors/Goodbye
Song/Dead Air-Abandon Ship/ Uncredited Track: The Last
Post

Musicians: Sean Mcdonough, Jim Duncan, Ali Gavan,
Simon Parker

Guest Musicians: Jennie Cruse (backing vocals), Luke Ellis (cello), Ben Melmouth (trumpet), Laura Collett (trombone), Ruby Cruse (clarinet), James Harvey (windscreen wipers).

2012

LIGHTNING DEPT - 'THINGS KEEP BLOWING UP'

(Huey Lewis and the News/I Never Knew That You Had Tattoos/Avalanche...Blanche/Whatever You Said, It Worked/Butterfingers/Map of Japan/Corpsing/Melanie Exploded/Goodnight Whalebones/Due to the State of my Handwriting/Am I The Only One Here Not On Drugs?/The Tallest Man In The World/Last of the Great White Hopes/Raccoon/Tiger Fires)

Musicians: Ali Gavan, James Duncan, Simon Parker

2013

VILLAREAL - 'UNRAVELLING'

(Orange Host/New Miracles/Bodies in the Water/Low Cloud Revists/Sirens/Telegraph Hill/Summer is Dreaming/Last of the Pale Winter Sun/Keys to the Back of My Mind/Damaged/Harbouring)

Musicians: Ali Gavan, James Duncan, Simon Parker

Guest Musicians: Sue Marsh (melodica and recorder), Dan Sinclair (cowbell), James Harvey (vocal cut-ups), Kate Brigden (trumpet) Jules Lawrence (sax and musical saw), Craig Sullivan (vocals), Will Wells (trombone), Laurie Carpenter (trumpet)

VILLAREAL - 'FOUR FRAGMENTS'

(Low Cloud Revisits/Orange Host/Huey Lewis and the News/The 7th)

Musicians: Jim Duncan & Simon Parker

'Four Fragments' is an acoustic E.P. of two songs from 'Unravelling' plus a reworking of a Lightning Dept track and earlier Villareal single.Released as a free download Christmas 2013.

Don't forget your free download of various **Road To Nowhere**-related bands at

www.villareal1.bandcamp.com

NUMBSKULL HQ CATALOGUE OF RELEASES

(with thanks to Pepper and Eugenie Arrowsmith)

NS HQ 000…NUMBSKULL HQ MISSION DRIVE (18 Track Sampler)

NS HQ 001…TURNCOAT - 'AN ADVENTURE IN SKILL AND CHANCE' (Album)

NSHQ 002…SPARROW - 'PLAYTIME' (Album)

NSHQ 003…VILLAREAL - 'LIT BY SPARKS' (Album)

NSHQ 004…WHITE STAR LINERS - 'YOU CAN DO IT WE CAN HELP' (EP)

NSHQ 005…LIGHTNING DEPT - 'THINGS KEEP BLOWING UP' (Album)

HSHQ 006…SPARROW - 'THE ROSE GARDEN' (Limited Edition E.P)

NSHQ 007…SPARROW - 'HOWEVER DID THE WOLF GET IN' (Album)

NSHQ 008…SPARROW - 'MOVE' (Limited Edition 7" Vinyl)

NSHQ 009…WHITE STAR LINERS - 'THE YEARS THAT SLID' (Album)

NSHQ 010…VILLAREAL - 'UNRAVELLING' (Album)

PRESS 'EJECT'.

TAKE THE RECORD FROM THE TURNTABLE
AND PUT IT BACK INTO THE SLEEVE.

■